The Cranberry Trail
Misfits, Dreamers & Drifters on the Heartland Road

Kent Cowgill

Kent Cowgill (signature)

Lone Oak Press, Ltd.

THE CRANBERRY TRAIL

MISFITS, DREAMERS & DRIFTERS

ON THE HEARTLAND ROAD

BY

KENT COWGILL

PUBLISHED
BY
LONE OAK PRESS, LTD.
304 11TH AVENUE SOUTHEAST
ROCHESTER, MINNESOTA 55904—7221
507—280—6557

COPYRIGHT © 1995 BY KENT COWGILL
No portion of this publication except for brief
quotations for inclusion in reviews may be used
without written permission of the publisher.
First Edition
ISBN NUMBER 1—883477—09-3
LIBRARY OF CONGRESS CARD CATALOG NUMBER 95—081507

For the ones I've learned from:
   Barbara and Bruce, Paul and David, Jane and Beth.

The ones I played with—Scooter and the Duke.

And for Uncle Barney, the man with the cigar.

So priketh hem nature in hir corages,
Thanne longen folk to goon on pilgrimages.

> Geoffrey Chaucer

I've lived over seventy goddamned years, and there ain't been a one of 'em somebody ain't told me the game of baseball's dyin'. I never believed it, and I still don't believe it—'spite of what all them bustards are doin' to kill it. When baseball dies, this goddamned country's gonna die too.
> Harry Heddes

The Tabelard Honey Bees, 1964
Coach: Harold Heddes
Student Manager: Allison Bathgate

Position	Player	Class
Pitcher	Arden Gilding	Freshman
Catcher	Donald Pierce	Sophomore
First Base	Curtis E. Knight	Senior
Second Base	Robin Miller	Junior
Third Base	Roger Hodges	Junior
Shortstop	Oswald Reeves	Senior
Left Field	Jan Merchant	Senior
Center Field	Aristus Averrois Clark	Freshman
Right Field	Wickliff Lollar	Senior
Reserve	Jeffrey Shoemaker	Freshman

Season Record: 1 Win, 26 Losses.

Chapter 1

It was a Wednesday in the middle of April, and the rain had been drumming for hours on the roof of my apartment when the phone rang. Staring out the window, I shuffled across the room to answer it. Rivulets were sluicing down the furrows of the just-seeded corn field across the road.

"Jeffrey?"

"That's right," I said.

The voice was quiet. Unfamiliar. Everybody I knew called me Jeff, not Jeffrey. I waited for the caller to go on.

"Who is this?" I finally asked.

"Curtis."

He said nothing more, and I still wasn't sure of his identity. The only Curtis I'd ever known had been a senior when I was a freshman in college—a straight arrow from Arizona who'd been the captain of a baseball team I spent a suffering spring on. It was the worst team in the history of college baseball. I hadn't had any contact with him for thirty years.

"Curt Knight from Tabelard?" I blurted. "The Phallus of Phoenix? First baseman the year we finally broke the streak?"

The embarrassed cough was unmistakable across the sands of time.

"*Curt Knight*," I repeated, incredulous. "I'll be damned. Where are you calling from?"

"The Red Rooster. South Fork."

This took even longer to comprehend. The Rooster was an old hotel whose weathered portals were ready for the wrecking ball as far back as the early sixties, when I'd spent my lone year on the Tabelard campus. Unless the place had undergone some monumental renovations, I couldn't imagine it still upright—let alone up to taking in nightly lodgers. I said as much to my old captain. The words served only to nudge him on.

"I suppose one might characterize this whole affair as a kind of 'renovation'," he said.

Again his voice died in a cryptic pause, as if he expected me to divine his meaning. I stood staring blankly out the window. Across the road, a red-tailed hawk plummeted out of the sky into the corn.

"What exactly are you driving at?" I finally asked him. "You didn't call me after all this time to talk about the state of your hotel room. Just what is it that seems to need repair?"

"It's not a what. It's a *who*, actually. Coach Heddes. He's in bad—"

"*Bail*?" I cut him off. "You're talking about renovating *Bail*?"

This time the mumbles of incomprehension pulsed from the other end of the phone line. "Who?" he said.

"*Bail*! Isn't that who you're talking about? Harry Heddes?...*Bail Bond*?"

"Oh yes. I'd forgotten. That is what a number of you used to call him. It's been so long I can't begin to recall the reas—"

"Allie started it. The same way she started all the other nicknames. You remember. She pinned it on him the night his wife had him thrown in jail."

"I certainly recall that—that unfortunate experience," he stammered. "The quarrel with Goodleaf. His hour of incarceration. How worried he was that the Administration would get wind of it.... Would in fact, if they decided to press it, force him to resign."

"*Goodleaf*," I said. "I'd forgotten why we called her 'Goodie'. Jesus, what a name."

Once more the line went silent, and this time I simply waited—watched the hawk lift a limp mouse skyward over the rain-glazed shoots of corn.

"It's about both of them that I'm calling, in point of fact," Curt finally said. "They're having problems again."

"Why doesn't that surprise me?" I retorted, hearing more sarcasm in the response than I'd intended. "I don't know if you've forgotten this too, but Bail used to say they'd been going at it since he tried to cut the wedding cake and nicked the end of her finger. The two of them *always* fought. Remember the time she booted him—"

"This time it's different. I just spoke with her. She's packed up and moved out on him. Gone off to Cranberry Bend."

"Where?"

After thirty years, my memory of Nebraska geography was as misty as the lowering sky over the corn.

"Cranberry Bend.... The little town about sixty miles east of South Fork where Harry always holed up with his cronies? I'm sure you recall it. Don't you remember the road there? Runs right past the old Oregon Trail? You can still see the ruts in—"

"I don't remember it."

In truth I did recall it. I might have spent less than a year on the prairie, but most of its ruts still tracked across my brain.

My informant labored on.

"Getting back to Harry..... A few weeks ago, he bought an old church up in Cranberry—both the church and the parsonage, actually. Bought them without consult...." The stolid voice paused thoughtfully, then resumed. "Well, let's simply say it appears Goodleaf may not have been sufficiently apprised of the transaction.... Not to go into all the issues of contention, suffice it to say that...it hasn't worked out very well."

"Bail bought a *church*?" I blurted. "Did I hear you right? *Church* as in collection plates? Sermons? A suit of clothes without flecks of tobacco and gravy stains on the pants? What the hell...?"

I stopped only because the images had gotten too free-wheeling. If the baseball coach I remembered had a holy trinity, it was stud poker, cigars, and quail shooting. About as close to the sacred as he ever came was "I don't give a good goddam," usually underlined with a few choice epithets he'd hauled north from his native west Texas. Imagining him in a church was akin to learning that the Pope had been funneling funds to Planned Parenthood.

"He had plans," my old captain continued, as if reading my mind.

"*Plans*? Plans to do what? Convert the chapel to a hunting lodge?"

It took awhile before he responded.

"You're remarkable, Jeffrey," he said. "That's precisely what he hoped to do."

This time I was the one coughing into the phone.

"At least, it appears that's what he had in mind as his immediate objective—although it seems he also hoped to turn the parsonage into a bed & breakfast once the duck season closes in the fall. He's fixed on the idea it would supplement his Tabelard pension. As you can imagine, the latter is quite austere."

I watched a bird on the horizon drift nearer...finally become the mottled hawk that hovered again over the soggy field as the voice went on.

"I suppose one might credit him with having...well.... some sort of inspiration—even an *epiphany*, I suppose one might call it. Goodleaf wasn't there. Scarcely anyone else at the auction was bidding. He seems suddenly to have gotten carried away—twitched his hand entirely on impulse. As he tells it, he'd driven over simply because the auction bill listed a dozen goose decoys that had turned up in the parson's study. But when almost no one else bid on the buildings—and the price was so tantalizing—and above his head, in the stained glass window, flocks of waterfowl were settling down on the rivers of Paradise.... Well, in the end he...he seems to have felt some sort of call."

"My God," I murmured, uncertain which of the details demanded the most credulity—Bail Bond Heddes setting foot in a parsonage, or tourists roaming through a western Nebraska winter in search of a B & B.

I turned back to the voice at the far end of the phone line—mentally attached it to the big first-baseman I'd plodded through a season with three decades before:

Curt Knight. I'd heard he'd become a lawman after he graduated—gone back to the desert and left his stony mark on the highway patrol. It wasn't hard to believe. Even after thirty years, he came on in what Allie Bathgate had called *"Sominex Knightly"*—the same old fusion of sober integrity and slightly archaic speech. I imagined him giving a ticket to a speeder. It didn't make me yearn to spend a winter in Yuma anytime soon.

"Let's get down to what Bail used to call the nut cutting," I said, half-trying to needle him. "You still haven't told me why you called."

He cleared his throat, but let the crudity pass unacknowledged. "I want you to come to South Fork," he said.

"What?" I shouted. "You can't be serious. What possible good could I do?"

"It's not you...not *only* you. What I mean to say is—I'm trying to reach as many of the old team as possible. With any luck, we might make a difference. Might get the two of them back on the right track again."

This gave me even more pause. The only track I'd ever seen Harry and his wife on showed every sign of heading straight for divorce court. More unsettling, his "It's not *only* you" conjured up instant, indelible memories of my old teammates.

"Is *Pisser* coming?" I blurted. "Or *Me*?"

Pisser Reeves had been our shortstop, Me Miller our second baseman—a keystone combination who could take your breath away with their glove work on those rare occasions when they weren't winging point-blank double-play tosses at each other's groin. Together, they were the biggest reason that in the spring of '64 our team had surpassed the national record for consecutive losses. Even after three decades, I wasn't coming within a hundred miles of any assemblage where the two of them would be reunited—no matter how much trouble my old coach had gotten himself into. I said so—as emphatically as I could—to Curt.

"Who?" he said perplexedly. "Who is it you're concerned about?"

Somehow I kept forgetting. Not only was the man oblivious to nicknames, most of which Allie had coined during our prolonged death march to and beyond the record, he was a man who had never spoken—from all observable evidence had never *thought*—ill of anyone. I imagined his earnest brow as it must look now, thirty years later—wrinkling confusedly in the Red Rooster's phone booth. He appeared to recall neither our old double-play duo's everyday sobriquets, nor the slash-and-burn contentiousness that had made them stick.

"*Me!*" I repeated. "Rob Miller! And *Pisser!*— You know—Ozzie Reeves!"

"Oh," he said. "Of course. Once again, I'd forgotten. I think you're right, that was what some of you called them.... The two of them were simply Robin and Oswald to me."

I waited for him to go on. To assure me neither one was going to play any part on his renovation roster. But he'd seemingly forgotten the question. In the quiet rhythms of his breath, I could hear the credo he had lived by throughout the single season we'd worn the same dirt-caked uniform: *If you can't say something positive about someone, don't say anything at all.*

"Well?" I finally added.

"Yes?"

"Me and Pisser! Are they *coming*? I mean, fill me in on the ones you've called!"

"I've called you."

"Right," I sighed, watching the rain trickle down my window. "You've called me.... Who else?"

"Well, to be perfectly candid.... No one else.... Not yet."

"You called me *first*?"

It was impossible to figure. I had been the team's benchwarmer—ostensibly a relief pitcher and "utility man" but in fact a punchless pine-rider who saw game action only when the cause was lost. It was true, when you're on a team so bad the opposition calls off its dogs by the third or fourth inning, you can end up with so much playing time there are deluded moments you feel yourself approaching the tainted status of a regular. But it's not an illusion that survives the cold light of the next morning's box score—let alone the settled weight of a third of a century. Why had he started with me—rung my number before any of the others? Before Wick Lollar, our only decent hitter. Or Bookie Clark, who couldn't hit a lick but ran down everything that fell out of the sky in center field. Or our porcine, pussy-chasing catcher, Donnie Pierce.

It simply didn't compute. My mind would have been more boggled only if he'd told me the first person he had tried to contact was our spacy mound ace, Mare Gilding—a wigged-out lefthander who had somehow found his way to the prairie flatlands from his surfer's shanty on a California beach.

It was clearly time to get more specific.

"You haven't called *anybody* else?" I pressed him. "Not Big Stick or Fat Donnie?"

"No."

"Not Jan?"

"No. Jan's.... I'm sorry.... Jan's dead. I didn't realize you hadn't heard it. Forgive me. It was a tragic accident.... He fell out of a tree."

The news momentarily silenced me. Jan Merchant had been our left fielder—a street-smart kid from Brooklyn who thought cowboy country started at the west end of the George Washington Bridge. Dazed, I fumbled on—asked distractedly about one or two of the others. Curt proffered the same benign reassurance that he hadn't attempted to reach them yet.

It wasn't enough. Pouring a cup of coffee, I cleared my throat and tried to steer him back to the pugnacious pair who'd left as big a dent on my synapses as they once had on half the locker-room doors between Omaha and the Wyoming line.

"Pisser and Me," I said. "They aren't coming. Neither one of them. You guarantee it, right?"

"No they're not.... At least, I can't conceive of either of them joining us. Oswald rarely leaves his farm up in North Dakota. The last time he.... I'm sorry. What I mean to say is...it's quite isolated. Only a few miles from the Canadian border. As for Robin...well...to my knowledge, he hasn't set foot in South Fork since 1964."

"Neither have I."

The fact slowed his momentum a little. "Seriously?" he said. "I had assumed, since you live in Iowa, that you must have kept up with Tabelard fairly well."

"I haven't been back since I dropped out," I continued. "That single year was the only one I spent in the place."

What I didn't tell him was that I *had* kept up a little, more or less against my will, through the school's alumni magazine and relentless (and in my case, fruitless) yearly dunnings for money—both of which it persisted in mailing me even though I'd changed jobs and addresses too many times to count. The ferreting skills of the Tabelard solicitors would have shamed the C.I.A.

"It's the '63-'64 team that I'm calling," Curt bore on. "You may find this hard to believe, after all we went through, but we appear to be the crew that means the most to Coach."

"Do we," I said, glancing at the kitchen clock.

"Yes we do.... I'm sure it's because we were the ones who finally succeeded in ending the string of losses." He paused earnestly, then added, "Seventy-six games in a row."

The afterthought was gratuitous. No one who had ever been through even a few innings of it could possibly have forgot.

But my old captain sounded unfazed remembering it, almost nostalgic—a scarred veteran looking back fondly on the years of manning the barricades, even though much of the spilled blood had been his own.

"You played a big role that afternoon," he went on. "The day we finally ended it.... Don't you remember? You scored the winning run."

"Is that why you called me first?"

He didn't answer. And I didn't press him. My role hadn't exactly been the stuff legends are built on. I had been inserted in the game's final inning—a replacement for Fat Donnie Pierce—only because Harry thought I'd be marginally faster than a limping lardbucket who had turned his ankle stumbling over first base in a deluded moment of thinking he could leg it on to second while the ball lay ten feet from the pitcher's rubber. The stricken coach had shouted himself hoarse in the coaching box restraining him, then thumbed me in to pinch-run. I'd barely managed to score the winning tally when a Wick Lollar triple sent me scuttling toward home plate—my right shoe dropped somewhere in my dust-clouded wake. Watching from the dugout, Allie had tagged me "*Shoeoff*" in the wild moments of euphoria that followed my belly-flopping slide under the just-late catcher's tag. The nickname was a brand I carried through the remaining ten games of the season, all of which we lost.

"That run ended the streak," my caller continued conspiratorially. "Coach still talks about it. I don't know if it's struck you yet, but the thirty-first anniversary of that momentous game is this Sunday.... April sixteenth. Thirty-one years to the day."

The quiet voice was a cottony wad of guilt-induction inserted in my left ear. I said nothing. Undeterred, Curt slid it farther in.

"That was your uniform number, if I remember correctly. Thirty-one."

"My number was thirteen," I muttered.

Where seeing silver linings was concerned, Curt had always been constitutionally dyslexic. According to Allie, he'd once bought a used Edsel because he liked the name.

Outside my window, the rain was hammering down so hard the drops flattened like nail heads on the parking lot. Five hundred miles west of me, my former captain pounded on unaware.

"Thirteen. Thirty-one. Whatever. The coats-of-arms we happen to don during our lifetime are immaterial. What counts is the man within. If I can manage to bring a few of us back together, I think it might prove therapeutic for Coach. When I talked to him this morning, he wasn't in very good shape."

I turned reflexively away from the asphalt. Across the road, the hawk crouched wetly on a telephone pole.

"All right," I sighed. "I'll do it...But I hope to God you're right about Me and Pisser. I'm too old for the kind of mileage they put on your soul."

His own sigh was even more pronounced—an exhalation of profound relief, not triumph. It surprised me a little. The stress he'd obviously been feeling as we talked.

"I appreciate it," he said. "I was certain I could count on you. It's the major reason I dialed your number, before any of the others.... That and the fact I was working from the photograph—where you're so prominently displayed."

The photograph. I didn't have to ask him what photograph. It had run in the *Newsfronts* section of *Life* magazine a few days after our streak-shattering victory—shot by a local sportswriter who happened to glance at the scoreboard as he drove past the diamond on his way to a high school track meet. Snapped at the precise moment the game was won, the picture had frozen both Harry and me for posterity—preserved us forever between larger photos of a "rioting mob" of black students protesting segregation in Jacksonville and President Johnson hoisting his pet beagle by the ears. I could still summon every detail in my mind's eye. Against the slightly blurred backdrop of my fist-pumping teammates streaming from the third-base dugout, I stretch dazed and shoeless across home plate—a plump duck under the looming umpire's eagle-winged safe sign. Just behind me, ten feet up the basepath, Harry sprawls belly down in a spread-armed swan dive that mirrors the man-in-blue's beatific blessing. His teeth are still clenched around the stubby butt of a cigar.

"I'll be there Saturday," I said wearily. "But I'm an even worse marriage counselor than I was a hitter. And I can't stay long."

"I understand," he said, "Duty calls."

The voice went silent for a few seconds, then bore dutifully on. "I'm sure you're quite busy. Someone told me a while back that you write for Hallmark.... You must find that rewarding. Brightening people's lives."

"I wouldn't know," I said. "I moved on to other things a long time ago."

"Oh, I'm sorry. But I suppose it's...it's understandable. It must have gotten awfully difficult...coming up with fresh ideas year after year."

He coughed softly in commiseration, clearly concerned that my life hadn't gone as well as it might have. I didn't tell him I had had plenty of ideas, but ran out of rhymes.

"I've gone on to other things," I mumbled. "Worked for the I.R.S. Cooked some books for a construction company. Spent a year or two with a couple of outfits you've probably never heard of.... Nothing to write home about. I get by."

"Oh, I'm sure you do. I'm sure you do. Forgive me, Jeffrey. I didn't intend to pry."

"Don't worry about it.... I'll see you in a couple of days at the Red Rooster. Book me into the pool-side suite."

He either didn't hear the dig—or ignored it in his unshakable eagerness to think the best of me.

"Yes," he said. "I'll arrange everything. Did I mention that you should bring a hammer and a pair of work gloves?"

I hung up, staring out at the hawk in the rain.

Chapter 2

Ten minutes before I left on Saturday morning, I stopped by my neighbor's apartment to ask if he'd feed my cat. He came to the door in his pajamas, rubbing his eyes.

"Where you headed?" he mumbled, yawning.

"I've gotta go back to T & A," I said—falling instinctively into the old shorthand. He'd once told me he'd come to manhood when he was sixteen working on a wheat harvesting crew that had been quartered for three weeks in South Fork. I assumed a combine-jockey who'd spent that much time around the college would be more familiar with the irreverent abbreviation than the ponderous "Tabelard Technological and Artistic Institute."

He was.

"Too bad that old hotel's not still around," he said, winking a bloodshot eye. "What the hell was the name of it—the Rusty Rooster? Best goddam time I ever had in my life—that summer before I graduated from high school. I'm tellin' ya, them little towns out there were somethin' else back then."

Shaking his head, he dropped the bag of cat food in the corner as he shut the door.

No matter what one called it, the little school on the banks of the Platte River was unique. Built in the 1880's by a maverick fundamentalist named D. W. Augustus Tabelard, torched in a prairie fire and rebuilt a decade later, it had gone on to fuse traditional liberal arts education with craft-centered "life skills" to earn a modest national reputation by the time my parents enrolled me there in 1963. In hindsight, I was fairly sure this reputed academic respectability explained the presence of a handful of my culture-shocked freshman classmates. I was even surer that the far more compelling reason lay elsewhere: the campus sat in the middle of nowhere. In Nebraska. Which in the nation's psyche means *bland* and *uneventful* as surely as *Platte* means *flat*.

In sum, the fact that Tabelard was a tiny backwater had only enhanced its appeal to most of our tuition-paying warders. And the end result—that the college coffers were swelling from the largest enrollment in history—could be traced to a pair of equally accidental facts that by the fall of '63 had fallen into the chance alignment of orbiting planets: The only threatening life forms within a hundred miles of the place were rabid jackrabbits and prairie rattlers. And *The Sixties* were about to arrive.

Most of it hadn't come yet—all of it that was about to come—but the echoes had begun to pulse in the ears of edgy mothers and fathers across America like the muffled rumblings of distant thunder: The SDS. Freedom Riders. Kennedy federalizing the National Guard to force integration at Alabama. *The Feminist Mystique.* Two hundred thousand civil rights marchers on Washington. The still faint, yet portentous echoes from Vietnam.

By the summer of '63, the reverberations had lodged in the brains of presciently paranoid parents as deeply as would *Dallas, November 22nd* or *Kitty Genovese* a few months later, and the result was a campus suddenly teeming with teen-age aliens dropped into a sanctuary so parochial the ring of the chapel bell each morning was punctuated by shotgun volleys from local duck hunters a half-mile downstream on the Platte.

Tabelard. The images continued to rise as I drove through the continuing drizzle, down the westbound highway, over the soggy nap of plough-turned cropland that dissolved ahead of me in a vanishing point. I remembered the school as it had been back then—the little riverside campus in the "geographical heart" of the nation. This at least had been the local Chamber of Commerce's proud claim—prominently displayed on flag-painted signs just inside the city limits: *"South Fork. Designated by United States Government Surveyors as the Exact Center of the Original 48 States."* (Speaking for the aliens, as our team bus passed it one night on our way back from yet another ignominious drubbing, Allie had once noted that all the claim meant was the town was equidistant from anyplace you'd ever want to be.)

There was in fact only one fact that had made Tabelard tolerable, at least to those of us who labored under the burden carried by its uniformly inept sports teams, the *Honey Bees*. (The christening had been performed by the college's bee-keeping founder, but the logo's survival was the legacy of our aptly-named president, Peter T. Pinchbeck, who ran the campus with the tight-fisted vigilance of the dowager queen that our beleaguered coach, in his most unguarded moments, swore "that goddam little Pinchpecker" had to be.) This single happy fact was that the school had earned its earthier appellation "Tabelard *T & A*" honestly. Despite—and partly because of—its reputation for cloistered virtue, the college's stone-ribbed chapel spire rose above the randiest hundred acres on the planet. Viewed from a distance, like Chartres, across the region's pancake-flat wheat and corn fields, the place beckoned us back from our occasional forays into the hinterlands like a free keg of cold beer at a softball tournament. Allie had been on campus less than an hour before dubbing its soaring spire *"The Penis of the Plains."*

The often brutal weather only kindled the ardor. On any winter night outside Partlett Hall, the women's dormitory, rows of parked cars pumped exhaust fumes into the frigid prairie air while their window-fogged interiors quivered like rabbit warrens. If the activity appeared slightly less feverish in the spring, it was due only to changes of venue. The couplings now could happen almost anywhere.

Rolling on up the highway, I recalled the strains all of it had put on Harry—whose efforts to keep his team marginally spartan in a world of wallet-secreted Trojans had pushed the hapless coach close to the edge. Half-crazed already by our ever-mounting string of losses, the real and rumored couplings had finally left him with the hollow-eyed countenance of a desert monk.

His problem wasn't the sex. With the possible exception of Hugh Hefner, it would have been hard to find a redblooded American inclined to frown less than Harry on the copulative instincts of his callow charges. His problem was that the sex might be discovered. Uncovered. Sniffed out by Pinchbeck or one of his obsequious minions. And if that ever happened—given the fact that half his team would have topped any informed list of the school's most resolute fornicators—it was his own ass that was going to wind up in the disciplinary sling.

This was so because everybody on campus knew there was only one thing Pinchbeck detested even more than a fleck of lint on his immaculate Brooks Brothers collar. Poverty. Poverty not only for himself (a retired lawyer, he'd made millions on land speculation before finally yielding to the Board of Trustees twice-sweetened offer of the college's top job in 1960) but poverty for the school as well. And behind every one of the hot-blooded, tuition-toting freshmen that by the fall of '63 had begun to swarm the Tabelard campus, Harry saw a Queen Bee driven by his own fears of a doting father and mother poised to hustle their imperiled offspring back to the home hive.

All it would take was negative publicity—a whiff of scandal—the merest hint that the Great Plains weren't as far removed from hipness and hard rock as the school's humming propaganda mills had so unflaggingly implied. And while Harry was no Einstein, he was sharp enough to know that no school's scandal was more scandalous than sex.

The coach couldn't handle it. Or as I once heard him put it to the bus driver after one of our overnight road trips, "Ridin' herd on that bunch of dildos damn near like to give me the trots."

It was a fact everyone on the team soon came to know—and the most depraved exploited with merciless dedication. Already a compulsive clock-watcher—a man cursed to carry an acute awareness of vanishing daylight through a world inhabited by time-oblivious adolescents—the coach had the double burden of knowing that strict enforcement of his eleven o'clock curfew offered his only prospect of keeping us out of our wee-hour escapades.

The challenge was hopeless, and he knew it. Which only made him more dogged in his efforts to succeed. Bail spent so much time patrolling dormitory corridors, in fact, that the R.A.'s started calling him *The Raccoon* in deference to his girdled eye-sockets and shambling, sleep-deprived shuffle. Allie finally memorialized his feckless efforts in a couplet that combined the pronunciation of his last name with what had become his primary coaching duty. *"Harry Heddes. Rhymes with Bed Us,"* she loved to croon.

The job was impossible because the coach couldn't be half a dozen places at once. While our team did harbor a few celibates—our cerebral centerfielder Bookie Clark. Curt Knight. Big Stick Lollar, our devout, gum-footed right fielder—virtually everybody else, including Allie, was in Harry's parlance "horny as a two-peckered goat." And yet in the coach's baggy eyes there was clearly a pecking order—a hierarchy of the most egregious offenders. At the top of which perched our mound ace, Arden ("Mare") Gilding, a pitcher so gifted that on the rare day he decided he wanted to, he might have set down Henry Aaron on strikes.

It says a lot about Mare that rumors of his nocturnal exploits were even more legendary. Most of us assumed he limited his congress to humans, though I doubt if anybody would have bet his life on the fact.

Mare was so proficient, and so mercurial, that Harry finally threw in the towel and simply ignored him. This failure at the top served only to redouble his efforts to nail the player he considered the team's second-worst offender—our two-hundred-fifty-pound catcher, Donnie Pierce.

Donnie, or "Fat Donnie" as he was known throughout the campus, appeared to be everything his cadaverous batterymate wasn't: a slough-footed, slow-witted round man who resembled nothing so much squatting behind home plate as an overfed frog on a lily pad. His face was oval and oily. His eyes were heavy-lidded. He wore a crucifix that jingled softly with each step he took in his (usually futile) pursuit of pop flies. And yet for reasons that baffled the rest of us—reasons that spawned endless locker room jibes and hours of envious dormitory speculation—girls couldn't seem to get enough of him.

That he was the team's biggest ladies' man no one seriously disputed. What provoked us was *why*—whether it came down to a simple advantage of accessibility: the leg up he gained by spending so much time in their company (we all knew that with the possible exception of Mare, no one spent less time in his room than Fat

Donnie)—or whether something else was working that none of us were shrewd enough to recognize.

That he spent so little time in what he called his "cell" was itself a mystery, since to the casual eye Donnie's room was to our cheerless quarters what a room at the Hilton was to Fort Dix. Plush oriental carpeting. Drapes and curtains. An oak bookcase stocked with dozens of volumes whose thick spines had never been cracked. Short of a private bath and maid service, Fat Don lacked nothing that his widower father had sufficient wealth and parental anxiety to provide. It was a suite Pinchbeck would have envied—outfitted by a concerned guardian bent on sublimating at least a few of his heir's most libidinous impulses. There was only one glitch in the paternal logic. None of it worked.

What our coach was up against, in short, was a player who looked at his paneled, book-lined walls the way a lifer gazes at his bars in San Quentin. The one difference was that Donnie could get out. And except for periodic drop-in raids on his room's amply-stocked refrigerator, "*out*" was where the catcher spent virtually all of his time.

Harry tried everything he could think of to catch him—once going so far as to keep an all-night vigil in the back seat of the receiver's new robin's-egg blue Ford Mustang. The sting operation netted the coach two windfalls: a month of hobbling visits to the chiropractor, and rampant locker-room scuttlebutt the next afternoon that Donnie had scored big in the gazebo behind Partlett Hall.

That all such rumors of the backstop's private night games went unconfirmed did little to allay the coach's afflictions, since the one person who could knowledgeably have addressed them—Donnie himself—was habitually as silent on the subject as the ivy growing outside his window. Unable either to catch him in the act—or catch the catcher up in some verbal contradiction that might expose his chronic curfew violations—Harry finally sank, as he had with Mare earlier, into resigned, battle-weary fatigue.

It was the same beagle-eyed sufferance with which he responded to the catcher's equally immutable futility in the batter's box. In a lineup of anemic hitters, Donnie somehow managed, despite hours of practice, to remain one of our most impotent. If anything, Harry's months of sweat-browed mentoring seemed only to make him worse—a fact that roused some of the coach's most memorable profanations. My personal favorite was the steamy afternoon he eulogized yet another of the fat man's flailing, late-inning strikeouts with a pained "Goddammit, Pierce, grip the bat *loose*—the way you do that thing when you're done flippin' it in the morning."

And yet, remarkably, Fat's haplessness with a Louisville Slugger served only to increase his enthusiasm for the game. What we all finally came to understand was that the receiver simply loved to *play*—play anything—pinball and pocket pool included. By the time I left Tabelard, the verb used with reference to Fat Donnie had taken on layers of meaning a linguist would have had trouble trying to decode.

I popped in a Bob Dylan tape and let it hold me there, back in the sixties, as I drove on through the rain toward the old hotel and the indeterminate crew of former teammates who awaited me. I wondered if the catcher would be among them—then cringed at the sudden thought that there might not be a *them*: the realization that Curt might have come up empty in his efforts to strong-arm the others. I pondered forty-eight hours alone with Sominex Knightly. Paint had more fun peeling off a wall.

It wasn't anything you could put your finger on. Insofar as a team that loses seventy-six games in a row can be said to have a leader, Curt Knight won by default—a tireless plodder who never missed an inning and dug out grounders with a doggedness I had no doubt the old lawman still exhibited running down a motorist with a bad headlight. He had never been a good hitter, which usually translates into at least modestly reliable glove work—the kind of tidy vacuum-cleaning around the bag that more often than not the first-baseman in fact did give us. And yet he was also capable, on his off days, of butchering balls so badly Allie once privately dubbed him our "Knight Errant." (That we were a team of nicknames was due largely to Allie's wicked wit, but not entirely. We lived in a world whose defining presences seemed to cry out for nicknames. To us, *everybody* had one—usually more than one. Elvis was "Lids." LBJ was "Lobes." The Senator soon to be his running-mate was "Chuckles" or "Humpalump" or "The Pocket Gopher." The only reason "Knight Errant" didn't stick was Curt's formidable presence in the locker room—which had less to do with his stature as team captain than his three state titles in the Golden Gloves.)

Remembering, I relaxed a little. It was close to incomprehensible he wouldn't have pressured at least two or three of the others into coming. Even over the telephone, it was obvious I was talking to the same relentless battler who would soldier on long after his uniform was tattered and sweat-drenched. Persistence was Curt's middle name.

The question was *who* he had gotten. At that jarring afterthought, I felt my knuckles tighten on the steering wheel. My skin was a fish-belly white by the time I'd run down the row of faces in our dugout and dead-ended at Pisser and Me.

"Me" Miller, our second baseman, was a Pete Rose-style brawler whose already epic stature was solidified the night he'd gotten so drunk in a South Fork tavern he'd crashed headlong into the dead-bolted door of the men's room. That he had done so intentionally—in a more or less successful attempt to get at his refuge-seeking double-play partner, who had called him a pig-headed moron—was only incidentally the explanation behind his indelible nickname. The larger reason was that the ensuing collision with the door's ridged brass nameplate had left its first two letters imprinted for several weeks on his overslung brow. I don't recall who first had guts enough to utter it in his presence, but *"ME"* was a moniker none of us required Allie's inspiration to hang on him. Its monosylabbic bluntness was especially apt given his stubby, bull-necked torso and spiky, bristle-brush red crewcut—both of which punctuated his loose-cannon renown as the team's most ungovernable force.

Me's labors in the classroom were no less legendary. As far as I knew, there wasn't a course paper—of the few papers he ever submitted—that hadn't been flagrantly plagiarized, and his annual struggles to stay eligible for the baseball season merited inclusion in the campus's western folklore archives. The season I played with him, Me had apparently spent most of the summer at a nearby junior college trying to garner enough transferable hours to make up for the previous year's academic shortcomings—a year when a heavy dose of gut courses and divine providence had left him only some ten credits shy of what he needed to stay in school. Miraculously, he pulled it off with room to spare. Over twenty credits to spare, if I remembered exactly. Or at least that's what the ink-smudged transcript that arrived in the registrar's office the last week of August appeared to validate. It was a feat that provoked Harry, our dugout dean of disciplined scholarship, to one of his most profound observations of the season: " If the dumbass had had enough sense to stick around for another three or four periods, he could of had his goddam Ph. D."

"Pisser" Reeves was a different story—as shrewd and calculating as his double-play partner was crude and ham-handed; his taut body as stiletto thin as the second-baseman's was thickly muscled and squat. A sour cynic who had worked on a farm before a run-in with the owner over secretly "borrowed" equipment had pushed him two states south and into a college he never tired of denigrating, Oz patrolled the left side of our infield with the cunning ferocity of a meat-starved jungle cat. He was the only player I ever played with who actually did sharpen his spikes before a game—taking Ty Cobb's militant legend literally. And he was the only one you could be certain to find crouched in the rearmost seat of whatever vehicle or room you were unlucky enough to find yourself occupying with him. (Giving him the benefit of the doubt—which stretched even our captain's superhuman capacities for tolerance—Curt contended that the habit reflected nothing more than the shortstop's constitutional suspiciousness. The rest of us were convinced the reason was a lot more immediate: Pisser had to protect himself against being stabbed in the back.)

At the plate, Oz's one notable talent was an almost preternatural bat control—the ability to put wood on horsehide with such unerring consistency it drove opposing pitchers nuts. As it also did Bail Bond, whose mashed-potato frame slumped lower and lower in the dugout as the reed-thin shortstop proceeded to foul off pitch after pitch. Pisser gave new meaning to the term "punch and judy hitter," conventionally used to describe a player with no power but enough finesse to maintain a respectable batting average through walks and the dink hits that better hitters derisively dismiss as "flares" and "bleeders." In Pisser's case, what punch he showed translated into pop foul flares that usually landed just behind the first-base dugout. And nearly all of his bleeders—aside from the hard hoppers he chopped at Harry's shins whenever the coach dared to man the third-base coaching box—were the opposition fielders he'd carved up on the basepaths with his spikes.

Branded *"Pisser"* because of his petulance and constant whining, Reeves had earned dozens of other nicknames by the time I first found myself trying to steer clear of him—*"Bones," "Blades,"* and *"The Lizard of Oz,"* to name only those that are safe to print. There was locker-room logic behind every one of them. In a year when several of us, following the Beatles, had already begun to let our hair inch down a bit from our fifties buzz cuts, Pisser still clipped his so close to the bone his skull gleamed like the sod-polished blade of a ploughshare. The fact that he also occasionally picked up a few extra dollars doing odd jobs for a local carpenter—when the guy had so many projects he got desperate enough to hire him—reinforced the rationale behind "Blades" or "Blademan." I was never a witness, but those who had seen him work swore that a plane in his hands brought out the same shearing instinct a razor did once he got it anywhere near his thin skin.

Either one of them—Reeves or Miller—had enough talent to have been a potent force on any team where he didn't have to play with the other. Side by side, they were a load even the most patient skipper couldn't have dealt with. And where patience was concerned, it's a safe bet nobody ever mistook Bail Bond Heddes for Connie Mack.

It wasn't that he lacked the artillery. Bail could draw from a verbal arsenal that contained at least as many epithets as Pisser had nicknames or Me had dents in his head. What the bedeviled coach usually called the combative pair was *"dildos"*—abbreviated Heddespeak for *"armadildos,"* the creature he considered the dumbest, ugliest groundgrubber the Lord in his infinite wisdom had seen fit to set down on his native patch of the earth. It was only when Harry got *really* angry (as when Pisser once cost us an almost certain victory by charging the mound and spike-slashing the pitcher in retaliation for an errant changeup he considered a brushback) that Harry resorted to "*Sumbitch*"—a malediction otherwise reserved for the opposition's most black-hearted miscreants. (In the aforementioned instance, the plate umpire had taken one look at Pisser's footwork—a pair of shredded, bloodstained socks that looked as if they had been force-fed through a meat grinder—and immediately declared the game over by forfeit. It was our seventy-first loss in succession—burying Harry so long in his sepulchral hangout, the lobby of the Red Rooster, that when he finally got home his wife had locked the door and gone to bed.)

By that point in the season the coach was already—and ineradicably—"*Bail Bond,*" but for a few days thereafter he also got stuck with "*Backseat,*" since the vigilant night he'd spent in Fat Donnie's Mustang had occurred only a month before this unfortunate interlude which he'd similarly been compelled to while away in the rear of his car.

Pisser was thus "that crazy little Sumbitch" until the coach's displeasure boiled back down to his more habitual slow burn over the shortstop's seemingly incurable dose of what he ruefully referred to as "the red ass." But most of the time, like the rest of us, he was simply "that dildo"—or slightly less often, "that bony little bustard what comes from up around all them icebergs somewhere." (Harry's sense of geography was roughly on a par with his state of enlightenment concerning Goodleaf. Our season's most memorable road trip, to note but one example, dead-ended somewhere on a cattle trail in Wyoming after Harry kept telling the bus driver "Just keep turnin' the damn thing right, and you can't go wrong.")

Foolishly, I once asked the coach about the derivation of "*bustard*"—inquired whether the obscure Australian game bird I'd happened on in my zoology textbook was what he had in mind when he tagged one of us with the term. The look that followed is one I've never forgotten. It was the same one I'd seen on his face the day Mare asked him if he knew how to surf.

Chapter 3

Spooked by the shade of Pisser, I pulled off for gas at a truck-stop cafe, hoping the break from driving might track my overcharged brain toward a more congenial flow of images. As I approached the cash register to pay for the fuel, the fry-cook emerged through the kitchen's swinging door, rubbing his hands on a greasy apron. He took my money, dropped the change on the counter, and grunted an indifferent thanks on his way back to the grill.

I could hear the crackle of a frying burger. Smell the onions. See the ketchup stains on his pants as he disappeared through the door. *"Hotplate,"* I whispered—the sounds and smells accomplishing in five seconds what my mental labors hadn't achieved over fifty miles on the road. Pisser's grim wraith had vanished—dissipated in the sizzle and smoke that followed me back to the gas pumps. What wafted in to replace it, as I eased back onto the highway, was the infinitely more palatable memory of a different teammate. Our third baseman, Roger ("Hotplate") Hodges from Delaware.

The year I'd joined the Bees, Hotplate—or simply "Plate," as we usually called him—had embarked on his junior season, which meant he'd already had two full years of nothing but lopsided losses to get under Harry's skin. I hadn't been around then, but from all accounts Plate had taken full advantage of the opportunities—as even a glancing acquaintance with his unwashed, tobacco-spitting visage and beery breath would have made anyone instantly credit. So impressive was Plate's two-year vita, tales of his Bail-baiting exploits kept us occupied for hours whenever the team bus hit the road.

There were two explanations of his nickname—both of which would have been obvious to anyone spending even a few hours in his odorous company on a game day. The first was his penchant for kicking dirt on home plate every time he struck out. (Since Plate was a free-swinging bad ball hitter who would take a Ruthian swipe at anything thrown within three feet of the strike zone, he whiffed more than anybody else on the team.) Not surprisingly, the practice infuriated umpires—most of whom were portly retirees ill-disposed to look kindly on a player who left the dish so dirty they had to bend and sweep it after every one of his at-bats. And because a rankled umpire isn't exactly the arbiter you'd choose when you're trying to break a four-year losing streak, Hotplate's dextrous footwork became to Harry what another visitation of the boils would have been to Job.

The other reason we called him Hotplate was more literal. He was a hell of a good cook. He was, in fact, given the conditions he had to labor under, a hash-slinger whose best work would have rivaled whatever they could have thrown at him in the Twenty-One Club or Maxim's. This is a claim I don't make idly. For aside from the steamy radiator in his dorm room, a scavenged iron, and a kind of improvised chafing dish he'd somehow managed to manufacture from a couple of hundred-watt light bulbs, the only implement Plate had at his gravy-stained fingertips was the one that had inspired his nickname.

It was enough—as the well-heeled business majors who finally managed to bribe him into their fraternity would happily have attested—for they had discovered Plate's genius the same way the rest of us had: through the smells that drifted over the campus every evening from his third-floor room. Most of us spent hours there. The most gluttonous, by the time Plate moved on to the frat house, had come close to moving in with him. It would have been even money whether Fat Donnie Pierce spent more time out of his "cell" chasing women or hunkering down over one of Plate's batter-dipped chicken-fried steaks.

Unfortunately, Plate's was a talent that didn't come without risk. Since getting caught cooking in your room was grounds for expulsion, the third-baseman's survival depended on Pinchbeck and his flunkies remaining up in their bureaucratic aerie—the six-story Administration complex they loftily referred to as "Terrace Heights." What it came down to, in short, was keeping their uptilted nostrils oblivious to the jock dorm everyone on the plain below affectionately knew as "The Stewhouse." Which depended on all the rest of us keeping our mouths shut. Which we were more than willing to do—as long as Plate kept them stuffed with his food.

There was only a single constricting detail, in fact, that kept Hotplate's room from becoming the de facto campus cafeteria. Unhappily for those with weak stomachs, Plate was to soap and water what toilet training is to a suckling pig.

I wouldn't say Plate was filthy. Not if your nearest frame of reference is a sanitary landfill. What I would say is that appreciating his cuisine required a certain inattention to the methods and conditions of its preparation. Once you got past the congealed egg yolk on his spatula and what appeared to be a fire-resistant fungus on the back of his saucepan, you were home free.

I managed to block out the latter images, as I'd been able to do thirty years earlier, and suddenly realized that in the few miles I had driven since stopping for gas my stomach had begun to rumble ravenously. The sizzle of the frying burger had displaced Curt's supplications just inside my left ear. Or maybe it was one of Hotplate's stews, steaming subliminally—rising like Proust's cookie from the nether reaches of memory's depths.

Ten miles up the highway, a green sign marked an access road into a nondescript town that somehow looked faintly familiar. I followed it down the tree-lined main street to a windowless cafe I suddenly remembered the moment I pulled up at its door.

I remembered the place because it had been the scene, a year or two earlier, of a chance encounter with another of my former teammates—the *only* teammate I had had any contact with in the decades that had passed between my departure from Tabelard and the phone call from Curt. His name was Wick Lollar. He'd been our rightfielder. A Scripture-spouting eccentric from southern Kansas who was the one player we had who could "hit with authority"—to appropriate a sportswriting cliché that fit Wick in ways it's never fit anyone else. On the day I'd run into him, he was sitting at a table with his brother, their backs to me, as I'd unwittingly taken a stool at the counter and ordered a slice of peach pie.

When he'd tapped me on the shoulder five minutes later, I had turned—more than a little startled—and recognized the old slugger immediately. Wick's was not a visage you could easily forget.

"*Big Stick*!" I blurted, the nickname springing reflexively to my lips. "How the hell are you doing?"

For a long moment he'd said nothing—stared at me over the top of his glasses as if he were eyeing a fly circling his soup.

"How the *heck* are you doing?" he finally corrected me, his big hand tightening on my collarbone. I hunched further over the counter—felt the calluses on his palm press like pumice through my thin shirt.

It was the same old Wick. Which is akin to saying the San Andreas Fault is the same old crack in the ground. Generations might pass without seismic activity, but if you suddenly found yourself in the territory, it behooved you to know the pressure points.

One of them had always been, and obviously continued to be, any remark that smacked even faintly of blasphemy. A "hell" or "goddammit" in his company could torch Wick faster than a Zippo lighter on a bale of hay. On this occasion, I considered myself lucky—having kindled nothing more than a mild remonstrance. I silently vowed not to push my luck again.

It had been one of several peculiar, contradictory things about him—this zeal for scourging even the most timorous of blasphemers. Peculiar because the blunt truth was that for all his religious circumspection, Wick had one of the team's saltiest tongues. I don't mean he was a hypocrite. He was in fact as unswerving as a plumb line dropped from the top of Mount Sinai. I mean simply that, where oaths and epithets were concerned, Big Stick made an uncommon distinction between the life of the spirit and the crude but indispensable lexicons of the flesh.

The bifurcation led to some bizarre scenes. On the day a year earlier when I'd felt his long arm reach out to me—peered up into his granite face as his adamantine grip gradually detached itself from my shoulder—I had suddenly begun to laugh so hard I came close to choking on my pie. It was a reflex born of the certain knowledge that if I'd greeted him with a dozen other locutions anybody else in the restaurant would have considered blatantly indecent—a "How the *piss* are you doing?", say, or "How the *balls* are you doing?"—maybe even a "How the *fuck* are you doing, Wick Lollar!"—the words would have provoked little more reaction from the old rightfielder than the barely perceptible twitch of a shaggy eye.

Big Stick was an anomaly. You had to know the man.

Harry had tried, but in the end the task had proved too Herculean. Like Pisser, Wick was a fifth-year senior, but all resemblance between the team's two oldest players began and ended with this single fact that both were considerably longer in the tooth than the rest of us. Pisser had been Pisser forever. (As Allie put it, his first whine undoubtedly accompanied the rude jolt of his conception.) But Big Stick's trip up the mountain had taken so many turns it was doubtful even the college registrar could have begun to chronicle his pilgrimage. The one thing those of us who shared a dugout with him had been told—or thought we'd been told, trying to decipher his disquisitions on the years of spiritual sojourn—was that he had apparently begun as a Catholic; evolved through Lutheran, Baptist, and Pentecostal; only to find himself congregating at last among the "Solomaic Sect of the Brethren," an ardent knot of the sanctified whose archaic language, when Big Stick really got it going, would resonate from outside the foul lines to well beyond the centerfield fence.

Over the years, Stick had spent so much time in the company of the Lord he had come to sound like Him. He was especially given to those "Take off thy shoes, from off thy feet" redundancies that mark Jehovah's curious need of a good editor. If there was a difference, it was that Wick's style tended to be a little earthier. "Rise up off the pine, off your whoreson haunchbones!" was one injunction he favored, usually offered on a hot afternoon when he was convinced one of us had been dogging it. Or, casting a censorious eye at a bare-shouldered couple nuzzling in the first-base bleachers, he'd erupt with "Like dogs to their vomit—the hussy and her consort burning one to another in their lust."

Stick's combination of vocabulary and volume made him the greatest bench jockey I ever heard. No slouch himself, Harry could be reduced to mute, eye-bulging stupefaction when the big clean-up hitter really got on a roll. All it took was the proper provocation—often no more than an opposing hitter, after waving futilely at one of Mare's knuckleballs, taking the Lord's name in vain. Depending on how the game had gone for us up to that point (and it was nearly always badly; you don't lose 76 games in a row carrying too many leads into the ninth inning) the blasphemy could trigger any of the nuclear arsenal of verbal weaponry Stick had under his command.

One incident stands out in particular. By the early sixties, a few of the teams we played had begun to wear the tight-fitting stretch uniforms that are now almost universally in favor, and one afternoon we sat transfixed as Wick reduced a colossally well endowed third-baseman to acutely apparent physical discomfort through repeated allusions to the "wretched swollen member" bulging from his loins. Stick could be equally deadly with "pismires" and "dung," and he bordered on the lethal with "generations of vipers." But his best stuff transcended the formulaic. I once watched in awe as he somehow worked "sackcloth," "sodomite," and "lean kine" into a spiraling sortie on a scrawny shortstop who had muttered a mild "goddammit" after fouling a pitch off his toe.

As an assault weapon, Wick's only rival was Allie Bathgate, whose barbs lacked the rightfielder's mega-tonnage but had a lot more wit.

Allie had arrived at Tabelard when I did, in the fall of '63, and had quickly signed on as the Bees' trainer and student manager. She also sat behind the radio mike on the rare occasion when one of our games was beamed to the locals—an assortment of duties she handled without breaking a sweat. How and where she'd picked up so many talents was a mystery (the rumor around campus, where she'd become an instant celebrity, was that Tabelard was the fifth or sixth institution she had attended). What *was* immediately clear to us—I'll put this delicately, using a word Allie herself especially favored—was that she was *"experienced"* in the ways of men.

I'm not saying she was promiscuous. Or that she wasn't. Allie was so clever none of us knew what in the hell to make of her. Finding yourself a college freshman with her in your dugout was a little like going to Boy Scout camp and discovering that your cabin counselor was Mae West.

I suppose what it came down to was that Allie *talked* a game none of us had ever experienced—one which implied she'd spent most of her twenty-plus years playing in life's equivalent of the major leagues. And, Allie being Allie, she wasn't bashful about sharing what she had learned.

What she was quickest to favor us with were trenchant observations on our play—which slid up and down an aromatic scale of odoriferousness from the merely pungent to the ineffable, garbage-scow rancid. Pinning down the scent was a challenge Allie never backed away from. Unlike Big Stick, who usually managed to keep his heavy artillery pointed toward the opposition dugout, our student manager's scalpel cut closer to home. She was especially inspired behind the microphone. On the day our loss string reached sixty as a result of a (to that point) season-high eleven errors, we became "The Bumble Bees." A week later, when our bats were stillborn and a stubby-armed junkballer held us hitless, "The Mellow Bees" were born. And so on.

Without question, Allie would have found herself shackled to a shower pipe with her mouth taped shut if she hadn't also possessed what were for most of us some distinctly redeeming characteristics.

The first was that she had big tits.

Another was her capacity to outdo even Mare in goat-getting harassment of Bail Bond.

A third was that some of her most pointed sallies were directed at assorted campus fixtures nearly all of us heartily disliked. Pinchbeck was one of her favorite targets. So was Tina Egland, the prim, French-lisping president of the school's most uppity sorority. Tina was the kind of co-ed who made you appreciate Oscar Levant's famous line about Doris Day, "I knew her before she became a virgin"—a snob so affected she kept a poodle in her private room and seemed incapable of speaking a sentence that didn't include the word "*dommage*." Since half the team had tried unsuccessfully to seduce her in the demented hope they'd be the first to crack her by then legendary chastity, we relished the spicy "Tina Tales" Allie regaled us with on road trips—most of which turned on some clever burlesquing of her name. To Allie, Tina was "Prisstina." Or "The Coddled Egland." Or—the one her rejected suitors in the back of the bus most boisterously favored—"Our Lady of Perpetual Pink."

As such examples illustrate, Allie was at her best (or worst, depending on where you were sitting) in her diabolic talent for creating indelible nicknames—a fact nearly all of us painfully discovered at some point during our stumblebum year. I wish I could say we gave as good as we got. God knows we tried our damndest. Weeks of post-practice afternoons turned to dusk as we sat slouched in front of our lockers, wracking our overmatched brains. But in the end, it was no contest. The best we could come up with were a paltry pair with so little sting she only shook her head, cackling with derisive laughter on hearing: "The Balling Allie," and "Allie Cat."

I sat in front of the cafe, thinking of her—was still thinking of her as I stepped through the drizzle, plopped down on a stool at the cafe counter, draped my jacket over a coatrack. The collar of my shirt was slightly damp, and I fingered it absently—triggering the sudden memory of a t-shirt she had sometimes worn thirty years before.

I could see her breathtaking chest. The bright red lettering. The fruitless hours several of us had spent trying to decode its five cryptic monosyllables. They floated as vividly past my mind's eye as the flickering neon sign on the cinder-block wall: *"Freud Should Have Asked Me."*

Sitting there, remembering her, I began to laugh almost as hard as I had laughed perched at the same lunch counter a few months earlier—the day I'd found myself pinned under Big Stick's steely grip. Startled, the waitress bobbed up the aisle toward me, halting warily a few feet away.

"Something wrong, mister?" she barked.

"No," I said. "I was just thinking of a couple of characters I used to spend some time with. One of them lives somewhere around here—at least he used to. Guy named Wick Lollar.... Ever heard of him?"

She reacted as if I'd asked her if she'd ever heard of head lice.

"Big rawboned guy?" she finally answered.

"Right."

"Talks real funny?"

"That's him."

"Runs a Servicemaster outfit with his brother—cleanin' up carpets and such?"

"I wasn't aware of that," I said. "But it doesn't surprise me. He was always a man with an eye for spots and stains."

She stared hard into my face, then asked what I wanted to order—didn't respond until she was halfway to the kitchen. "I don't know him," she said.

Five minutes later she stepped back through the door carrying a microwaved burger and a coffee pot.

"What do you mean, you don't know him?" I asked.

"I mean I don't *know* him. Nobody could know that guy! He's as loony as Richie D. Roll."

I caught the allusion only because the story had appeared off and on in the state's newspapers most of the winter. Roll was a crackpot fireman from Dubuque who thought the archangel Gabriel had visited his room the night before Christmas, leaving a heart-shaped burn in the carpet beside his bed. When his wife had succeeded in having him committed, he'd sued her priest.

"I don't know him very well," I backpedaled. "Wick Lollar, I mean...not Roll. I haven't spent any time with him for thirty years."

"Well you can thank the Lord for that. At least you could if he didn't hear you."

"Atheist, is he?" I said, feigning ignorance, hoping I might prod her to update me on the current state of my old teammate's celestial affairs.

"An *atheist*! Are you bullshitting me? He's got the Lord on his brain like you wouldn't believe. Most of the time, you can't make squat out of all his mumbo-jumbo. I doubt if his own brother understands half of what he says."

"Mumbo-jumbo?" I offered, scratching my head—raising my eyebrows in an even more shameless attempt at pump-priming. I didn't figure Big Stick was likely to show up at Curt's renovation party, but if he did, I wanted to prepare for him as best I could.

"That's what I said. *Mumbo-jumbo*. Some of it's so smutty I get embarrassed just rememberin' it."

"Smutty? Old Wick?.... It's hard to believe."

"Well, you'd better believe it. I mean, what would you call it when a guy starts carrying on about a '*Suck-you bus*'? Or starts buggin' some biker coming out of the john about his leather pants showin' off his 'bull's pizzle.' Or rants and raves about the 'puking and muling' something or others that 'cleave unto' some kind of a weird animal with a clover...a cloving.... Oh hell, forget it. How should I know? Your buddy is—"

"I'm not his buddy," I interrupted, downing the lukewarm coffee and reaching for the check. I'd learned more than I wanted to about my old teammate's obviously continuing evolution up the ladder of spiritual enlightenment. Dropping a five-dollar bill beside my saucer, I rose off the stool.

"Don't get me wrong," the waitress added. "I ain't saying he's a bad sort. He's got a Boy Scout troop. Delivers Meals on Wheels. Does a lot of other stuff I hear he won't let anybody pay him a nickel for. It's just that, you know...the guy's nutso. 'Specially when he gets started talkin' with his brother. '*Another day, another Lollar*.' That's how my boss always puts it after the two of them walk out the door."

I took the hint—set my own stuttering feet in motion across the floor.

"You lookin' for him?" her voice trailed me. "'Cuz if you are, you're not about to find him around here this weekend. He's gone."

My right eyelid started to twitch as she said it. I stopped with my fingers on the door.

"*Gone?*" I croaked.

"Yeah, *gone*. Gone every way you can think of, including driving that old Packard of his out west for some sort of an old school reunion. His brother said he won't be back for three days."

Knight and Lollar. Lollar and Knight. The pair of words tracked across my brain to the grating of my car across the rumble strips as I strayed for a moment onto the shoulder of the highway. A dozen possibilities—countless combinations—and the two I knew for sure would be waiting for me in South Fork were Jeremiah and a desert cop.

It was already one o'clock in the afternoon. I still had several hours of driving ahead of me. The unplowed fields I could barely see through my rain-streaked windshield looked like overturned bowls of shredded wheat on the sodden horizon. And when I did pull in, tail-sore and bone-weary, it would be to a bed in the Red Rooster Hotel.

I considered turning back—lifted my foot off the accelerator—asked myself *why* I had consented to do it.

Why had I?

Was it guilt over my aborted life in academe? Curt's wheedling pressure? The mental image of Wick's dour visage muttering grim imprecations against those who swore fealty only to turn chicken-hearted when the chips were down? None of them fit. Clearly, they had all played a part—had had some effect on me—but just as clearly weren't nearly enough to explain why I'd finally given in.

It was Harry. The allegiance the old bastard could still stir in me. It had to be Bail. There was nothing more.

Or was there?

The question was still working on me, filtered through the memories of Allie, as I passed the *"Nebraska—The Good Life"* sign at the state line a half-hour later. I hadn't found an answer, but I was no longer quite as certain it was for my old coach alone that I'd returned.

Chapter 4

The one thing I *was* sure of was that—whatever my reasons for returning—they were going to seem insanely masochistic if my welcoming committee consisted only of Big Stick and Curt. I had gotten desperate enough to hope that *any* of the others would join me—anybody other than Pisser. Even Me would be a welcome addition. "What the hell, even *Mare* would be," I heard my lips muttering—then realized how far down the road to dementia my apprehensions had led me. "Christ," I murmured, trying to clear my head. Back in the sixties, there were still states where hoping to find yourself within breathing distance of Mare Gilding would have made you eligible for some serious penal time.

I don't mean he was repellent. Far from it. The opposite was true, in fact—Mare had an absolutely mesmerizing presence. I mean only that yielding to the impulse to float along in his quirky orbit opened up possibilities you shuddered to contemplate.

It's not easy to describe him. I can hope to convey the pitcher's stature on a roster replete with eccentrics only in relative terms—as in the poll a few of us once took over whether he or Big Stick was the team's most certifiable wacko. Mare won in a landslide. Allie considered the answer so obvious she declined to vote.

What struck you first was his appearance. His stringy, shoulder-length hair was almost colorless—like his skin—as if the California sun had served to bleach rather than tan him. But there was no hair on his chest. Nor on his small-beaked face—which perched atop a neck so pliant it might have been a tube of jello. When he stood on the mound prior to delivering a pitch—his flaccid body still; his pink, lidless eyes unblinking—the image he called to mind was that of an underfed pigeon peering down from the roof of a barn.

Mare would hold the ball so long it made hitters close to homicidal as they waited—reminding you with every offering he finally deigned to deliver that baseball is a game in which *everything* begins with the pitcher—the center out of which all else flows. (Or in Mare's case, the black hole, since the blank density of his pallid presence could make the mound seem as distant and inaccessible as an imploded star.)

"Th'ow the ball!" Bail would yell forlornly at him from the dugout, the coach's flushed, doughy face going even flusher. "Th'ow the goddam *ball*—that thing what you been holdin' for an hour in your hand!"

When Mare finally did release one of his baffling assortment of knuckleballs, curves, and outrageously doctored greaseballs, the result often turned Harry's face still more crimson, since there were afternoons when even the most woeful hitters hammered the pitcher's unhittable stuff.

This was so because of Mare's utter refusal—or inability—to throw anything but a strike.

If you have only a casual acquaintance with the game of baseball, what I've just said may seem bewildering. After all, isn't the pitcher's *intent* to throw strikes? And aren't those hurlers chronically unable to throw them the harried "wild" bunch who quickly find themselves exiled to the nether reaches of the bullpen's burial ground?

The answer is of course yes. But it's equally axiomatic that a pitcher cannot *always* throw strikes. Doing so makes the hitter expectant—able to "crowd the plate" knowing the pitch will be in the heart of the hitting area. Mare's control was so surreal—he threw so *many* strikes—that even laughably overmatched batters sometimes got hits off him despite their ineptitude. Or maybe it was *because* of their ineptitude, we were never sure. There were afternoons when Mare resembled nothing as much as a riverboat gambler who had grown so bored with how easy it was to cozen the yokels he'd taken to more or less open public displays of how it all was done.

Bail finally just sat back and watched him, shaking his head—slouched morosely over his tobacco-flecked shoes at the end of the dugout. As overmatched as the hitters, he was finally reduced to little more than an occasional sardonic comment. "If that dildo ever th'ows another ball," he muttered to me once, "I'm gonna stop the goddam game and have it shrined in one of them little glass chests like a petrified hog's turd."

Mare. That the nickname fit him like a latex glove, and that he hailed from Mission Viejo, California, were about the only things any of us knew for sure about Arden Gilding. He was a lefthander who could (and occasionally did) throw right. He was a switch-hitter equally ineffectual from whichever side he was swinging. His thin voice and pale, hairless body—on those rare occasions when he set foot in the shower—drove players like Curt and Big Stick to the terry-cloth refuge of their towels. Behind the droopy surfer persona, there didn't appear to be a whole lot more.

His kookiness was compounded by the fact that nobody could understand most of what he said—especially Harry, whose Amarillo roots had left him so far from the lefthander's big-breaker beaches the pitcher might as well have been dropped from the moon. Listening to the two of them go at it at the end of an inning was like hearing Dennis Hopper and Slim Pickens try to negotiate the Camp David accords:

"*Got bent out there on that last one, Heddo. Fat-assed dude's a hodaddy. Guppin' gremmie. Rode the nose on a guppin' juiceball. But not to worry, Hedman. No problemo. Got bitchin' stuff today.* Bitchin' stuff."

"Goddammit, you dumb dildo—th'ow ever'thing down the coal chute and the bustard's finally gonna get 'holt of one I don't give a damn if he's fat as a ten-pound tick! That last ball hits you, you'd be layin' out there on the hill with a hole in your gizzard a blind pig could climb through without wigglin' a hair on his ass!"

I was still thinking about all of them, the motley crew I'd spent a spring with thirty years earlier, as the car rolled slowly into South Fork a few hours later. The sun was setting, and as I crept on toward the college, it broke free of the cloud cover for the first time in several days. I cranked down the window. Approaching the field where we'd played and practiced, I slowed further. Simply let the wheels roll on over the street beneath me. The car drifted to a stop just past the grandstand, its splintered bleachers needing paint even more than they had in 1964.

It was the same field. The same scruffy grass. The same balded rise where a few longhairs always lounged on sun-splashed afternoons to sneak a joint and chant good-natured ironies as we bumbled through another debacle. (*"We sting 'em, we wing 'em, there ain't no place we can't fling 'em. Gooooooooooooooo Bees!"*) But the field was limed for soccer, not baseball—an economy measure Pinchbeck had succeeded in pushing through a few months before his retirement in 1990. Mare's mound had long since been shaved, re-sodded—its spike-scarred rubber no doubt discarded in the same dumpster that held a bucketful of Harry's fragmented cigar butts. Harry himself had shuffled on until '92, when he too had retired, an old coach carrying a full load of phy. ed. classes and a thickening paunch.

As I stared out at the field, a handful of kids crested the rise, whooping and jiving—tossing a bright orange frisbee across what had once been the edge of the outfield. I stayed for a minute to watch them, remembering, then restarted the car and headed on toward the hotel.

I was thinking about a photograph. Not the famous photo—the *Life* shot—which to Pinchbeck's consternation had done more to make the name *Tabelard* recognizable across America than all the school's glossy ads and self-congratulatory claims of "innovative excellence." The picture I was recalling hung in Harry's office, above a battered duck decoy—a follow-up taken by the same photographer a few heartbeats after the loss string had finally ended. I'm not visible in this one—or rather I exist only as a pair of chubby legs protruding from a floodtide of intertwined bodies strung halfway back to the dugout. The bell tower soars toward a cloudless firmament in the background. An apple tree blooms. Harry kneels just up the third-base line—his gnarled hands raised toward the sky.

But it is not these I see as I move on through the town, reach the last traffic light, roll to a stop in one of the empty parking slots in front of the Red Rooster. What I'm remembering is a miracle. An image inconceivable ten seconds earlier on a team riven for years with loss-prolonged spite and dissension: our second baseman and shortstop are locked in a hooting, dirty-uniformed embrace.

Chapter 5

For several minutes, I sat in the car staring at the building in front of me. I still wasn't sure exactly what Curt's weekend renovation plans included, but one thing was as clear as the honking of geese piercing the fresh spring air a few blocks away. If my former coach needed as much attention as the old hotel where he'd hung out with his cronies every night back in the sixties, we had what he would have called "a job of work" ahead. Lifting my suitcase from the trunk, I stood for a moment peering up at the weathered sideboards, then moved on through the creaking front door.

The dusky interior was much as I remembered it—with a single, somewhat disconcerting exception: The lobby had disappeared. Where Bail and his buddies had slouched on swaybacked metal chairs over a smoke-smudged poker deck and long-necked, beaded bottles of Falstaff, there were now only storage shelves. I paused, trying to regain my bearings, then continued on to the front desk past rows of patched sheets and thin, graying towels.

Surprisingly in such an antique world, the clerk was both young and briskly efficient. Sporting a spotless green uniform that looked like a set of surgery scrubs emblazoned with a crowing, red-combed cock magisterially perched on a bedpost, he greeted me as if I'd stepped into the Holiday Inn.

"May I help you, sir?"

"I doubt it, " I said. "But you can try. I think there should be a room reserved for me. Shoemaker.... Jeff—make that Jeffrey—Shoemaker. One night."

"Of course. You'd be with the Knight party."

He cocked an eye to punctuate the pun, then leafed through an ancient, leather-backed registry as if it were the Gutenberg Bible. "Ah, yes. Here we are. We've got the pair of you in Number Twelve. Top of the stairs. Right hand side."

"The pair of us?" My sphincter tightened as I bent forward over the illegible page in his hand.

"Nothing we can do about it, I'm afraid. So many of you fellows are coming in."

He clapped the tome shut before I'd gotten a good look at the lettering beside my name, but the words I thought I'd glimpsed were *"Clark, Aristus."*

I took a deep breath—mouthed a prayer of silent gratitude. Bookie Clark had been our centerfielder. The team's only black. One of only a tiny handful on campus. He'd been so studious and reserved behind his taut skin and wire-rimmed glasses Allie jokingly accused him of spending words as if they were coins. From the years of Tabelard newsletters, I knew he'd risen from the grinding poverty of his childhood, through graduate school, to an endowed chair of ethnology at an eastern university. No roommate Curt could have assigned would have pleased me more.

I started up the stairs, replaying old memories of Bookie, whose greyhound speed had saved us bushels of runs and earned him the reverent epithet, "Amazing Grace," from Allie. It was a tribute that was etched deeper every time he loped from center into deep right to spear an uncatchable fly hit over the prostrate body of the stone-legged Big Stick. Of several such memories, I remembered one in particular—a diving catch so remarkable it had fired even the slack-jawed Bail Bond to the lofty heights of eloquence. Fondling Book's dog-eared glove after his return to the dugout, the reverent coach dubbed it "the place where triples go to die."

Unhappily, those same dark, finely-boned hands were less arresting when they held a Louisville Slugger. A lot less. If I remembered correctly, Bookie had gone through our entire season collecting fewer than a dozen hits—the majority of which were drag-bunt singles. So rarely did one hear the thwack of bat and ball when he swung away that Me—whose appreciation of good glove work began and ended with Sonny Liston—called him "Oh-fer" rather than Bookie—a derisive reminder of the number of times the lead-off man went 0 for 5. The centerfielder retaliated by quietly labeling his tormentor "Ofay"—a word only Allie appeared to understand—and by turning his frequent bases on balls and the numerous errors his speed engendered into the team's highest on-base percentage. Harry called him the most dangerous .125 hitter baseball had ever seen.

Aside from his skin color, what made Bookie especially exotic to teammates like Me and Hotplate was that he hadn't come to Tabelard simply in order to play baseball. He had in fact arrived on campus with no intention of playing at all. I might have considered the tale of how he ended up as a Honey Bee apocryphal if I hadn't been present the day it happened—a slushy March morning when the chain broke on his rusted bicycle and Bail noticed him hightailing it home with thirty pounds of books in his backpack. Bookie was returning to his room from the cloister he spent far more time in—the college library—and he was pedaling so fast across the common the coach had to chase him down in his car.

The ensuing hour's sales pitch got Bail what he was after—a centerfielder—but not before he'd had to go deep into his private well. He cajoled. Pleaded. Promised to replace his new recruit's campus dishwashing job with a couple of hundred dollars in aid money he'd somehow squirreled away from Pinchbeck's microscopic eyes. Even that might not have been enough if he hadn't finally offered to throw in a set of new encyclopedias Goodie had given him for Christmas. He'd received them the same Yuletide he'd presented her with an open-choke twenty-gauge Remington.

In detailing all of this, I don't mean to leave the impression that Bookie Clark disliked baseball. He just wasn't willing to abandon his library carrel for more than an hour a day to practice it. Or perhaps it wasn't quite that simple—was more than the love of learning and almost monastic self-possession he unfailingly displayed. Bookie drove himself—played the game—with an intensity I'd never seen before on a baseball diamond. But as our season of losses wore on, I came to feel, watching him, that it wasn't the game itself that fueled his resolve. One afternoon when we were walking back along the river after practice, I mentioned this feeling to him. He didn't respond—said nothing until we'd reached the dormitory—then quietly told me that for the first time in his life he hadn't played at all the previous summer. He'd spent it helping register voters in small Mississippi towns.

I'd reached the landing and found my hotel room—was turning the key in the lock—when I heard the stairs groan heavily behind me. I glanced back down the corridor. A mismatched pair of men stood staring at me a few feet away.

The taller of them was slightly stooped, snowy-haired, but the ebony skin still stretched as taut over his thin frame as it had thirty years earlier. The other, even rounder than when I'd last seen him, was equally unmistakable—a bowling ball in a business suit.

"Bookie!" I shouted. "Fat!"—their nicknames falling from my lips as spontaneously as the half-dozen steps I took in their direction. I was grinning like a two-year-old—and meaning it. I hadn't expected this first contact with old teammates would feel so good.

"Jeff?" Bookie responded tentatively.

His reaction took me down a peg or two. Not because it was reserved—he'd *always* been reserved. What deflated me was the irrefutable proof in both their faces of the age they clearly saw in my own.

But the letdown was brief—lasted no longer than it took for each of us to remark on the others' remarkable self-preservation, then move on to a modest summary of the current state of our affairs. In my case, the modesty was warranted. Bookie's wasn't. He'd just completed his fifth book. Lived and worked in Washington. Had spent the previous afternoon on a research project in the Library of Congress. I smiled at his embarrassed reluctance to say more about his achievements—then turned to the round man who stood beside him, his oval eyes fixed on my sloppily tied shoes.

"So Fat," I said, breaking the momentary silence. "What are you up to? Things going well for you too?"

"Goin' pretty well," the old catcher said. "Can't complain. I own a little company.... Clear Channels.... I spend a lot of time out on the road."

"*Clear Channels,*" Bookie repeated softly. "Pretty catchy name.... Some type of t.v. repair service?"

"Nope."

This time the silence was longer.

"We build organic waste solariums," Donnie finally added. "It's a good business. 'Specially the way sports are booming all over the country.... Football stadiums. Marathon races. Wherever a bunch of people come together without...you know...the proper facilities.... We're there to fill a need."

I looked at Bookie—deferred to the translating skills of a man who had spent most of his life in the reading room.

He was looking at me.

"Outhouses?" he ventured.

Donnie blew his nose. "That's what people used to call 'em. Back in the Dark Ages. The technology has improved a lot. The Japanese keep stretchin' us—pushin' us to get better. You can't sit around in this business or they'll kick your patootie—if you know what I mean. Any little hole we see opening up in the market, we try to fill it. Our latest is a boron model with push-button access and a translucent sun-roof."

"No kidding," I finally said, glancing at Bookie, who seemed to have been rendered temporarily speechless by the information. "It looks like you're onto something all right," I continued. "How did it all begin?"

"Relief Pitchers," he said.

I stared at him again. So did the scholar beside me—his Ph. D. notwithstanding. Donnie had clearly taken us to a level that required post-graduate expertise.

"Relief Pitchers?" I repeated.

"Yup. That's what you asked me, right? How it all got started? We pushed 'em real hard back in the 70's—mostly to campers and backpackers. You know, the hook and bullet crowd. A piece they did on us in *Outdoor Life* really got things moving. Our first load went in less than a week."

His round face glowed at the memory. Bookie's looked as if it had been coated with quick-drying cement.

It was clearly time to change the subject. I nudged open the door and set my suitcase down inside the room, half covering a nest of cigarette burns that clustered like spilled raisins on the carpet. "Great to see both you guys again," I said, turning back to them. Bookie still looked dazed. Clapping him on the shoulder, I added, "Glad to see they've got the two of us bunking together again tonight, Book."

The eyelids rose slightly below the clouded brow. "Bunking together?" he said.

"Sure. Didn't you know?.... You and me.... In this room here.... The guy downstairs—"

I stopped. My stomach began to gurgle. I nodded beseechingly toward the open door.

The dark brow furrowed deeper.

"That can't be, Jeff," he said. "The clerk must have misread the registry. I'm down in Number Ten with Don."

I didn't have the courage to return to the front desk—re-check the five or six letter name I'd misread as "Clark" penned next to mine in the ledger. Flopping down in the cramped, overheated room, I stared up at the water-spotted tiles on the ceiling. It wasn't death row, I reminded myself, as footsteps periodically creaked up and down the corridor. But I wouldn't have been stunned if the next rap on my door was the guy in green asking if I had any requests for a last meal.

When the fateful sound did come, a half-hour later, it wasn't a knock but the agitated scratch of a key in the door lock. I sat up. Slowly. Hoisted my legs over the side of the sagging bed.

"Layin' aroond on your butt, ay?" the intruder carped, peering through the gloom, stepping past my still unopened suitcase as if it had fallen out of a dumpster. He set his own bag down and switched on the overhead light. "Same old Shoemaker. Wastin' the better part of the day nappin'. Come on—it's time to get your fat rear oot and aboot!"

Pisser.

It was written in the stars. Predestined. From the moment Curt had assured me the old shortstop couldn't possible want to come.

"You're absolutely right, Blade," I said, rising wearily—addressing him by the one sobriquet that in the past hadn't inspired him to go straight for the jugular. "I been hangin' around here too long. Feelin' kind of logy. Think I'll take that advice of yours and go out for a walk."

I left him standing in the door, his sheared chin pointed after me like the whetted prow of an ice-breaker. I didn't look back.

Chapter 6

I walked that evening farther than I had ever walked.

Back through South Fork. Down its leafing gauntlets of cottonwoods. On toward the river and the little college that a century earlier had been carved out of the willows on its banks. When I finally got back to the hotel, it was almost nine-thirty. The young guy in green was still doing yeoman service behind the desk.

"Looking for someone, sir?" he asked solicitously as I started up the stairs.

"Not any more," I answered. "He's already found me. Tell Mr. Knight I appreciate the job he did in assigning me a roommate. I hope his own looks as sharp as mine."

"Oh it wasn't Mr. Knight," the clerk responded proudly. "He got called out of town for a few hours—left it up to me to decide on the bedding arrangements. I had a feeling you and the old fellow would hit it off."

"It hasn't quite come to that yet. But it might. Is he still up there?" I nodded toward the room.

He stared at me blankly, as if startled by the words.

"Why, no.... He's still at dinner. With the rest of them.... Where I assumed you had just come from. They're all over at The Weathered Nut."

Thirty years earlier, Allie had called it "The Withered Nut." That the old chophouse could still be serving meals surprised me even more than the Red Rooster's lingering dotage. Compared to The Nut's superannuated sideboards, the hotel's worm-holed timbers might have come fresh from the planing mill.

"How long ago did it start?" I said. "This dinner."

"Only a few minutes ago. There was some kind of problem, I think, involving your old coach. What's his name—Mr. Head? Mr. Hedges? He and Mr. Knight apparently had to spend longer than they'd intended over in Cranberry Bend."

I took a quarter of an hour to prepare myself, then slouched on around the corner to the restaurant, where an empty chair yawned conspicuously in "The Game Room" through whose pock-marked door a waitress directed me. Harry sat at its left. Sliding into it, I shot a quick glance around the table, checked to see who else Curt had been able to dragoon.

There were four of them.

Bookie. Fat Donnie. Big Stick. And the guy I somehow had to get through a night with back in my room. I was turning to say hello to my old coach, hand extended, when Curt's summoning voice arrested me in midstream.

"Jeffrey!"

Rising, the captain acknowledged my belated appearance as if he were issuing me a ticket for loitering.

"You've finally appeared," he said.

I shook his extended hand—then sat down and reached past a water pitcher for a piece of chicken. Across the table, Big Stick followed the stretch of my arm.

"Like unto a sluggard ass. The tardy man," he muttered—his gunmetal eyes tracking the drumstick as I lifted it off the platter. "Aggrieved the vitals of the old dog given to appetite."

Bending over his own plate, he shook his head censoriously before inhaling a heaping forkful of mashed potatoes and scalloped corn.

I stared at him for a moment, then turned once more toward my old mentor, who had given me a soft pat on the back as I'd dropped down beside him. His dome was bald. There were a few more folds under the beagle eyes. A cigar stub jutted familiarly above his grizzled chin.

"How you doin', Coach?" I said, feigning shock at his leathery features. "God, you're lookin' old. Looks like those poker games finally got the best of you." I could say it because in fact he hadn't aged all that much—didn't look a whole lot different from the last time I'd seen him thirty years before.

"Goddammit, I *am* old, Sonny," he shot back, re-christening me with the nickname he'd pinned on me the moment I walked into the gym an hour before the '64 season's first winter practice. "You boys are the ones what done it to me. You and all of them damn losses. Wouldn't been for you bustards, I might still have some hair left somewhere besides my crotch."

It was vintage Bail Bond. My memory looped back to the pre-game address he'd given before we took the field for the game that had finally terminated our four-year loss string. The speech had ended in a Knuteonian peroration Allie later transcribed and hung for the rest of the season above the locker room door: "Well boys," he'd said, "I don't guess your mamas are gonna stop lovin' you, even if we go out there and kick away another seventy-six of the sons of bitches. Which the way you dildos been playin', it looks like we damn well might could."

On that occasion, no one had said anything. This time, Pisser spoke up.

"Maybe we would have done better if you weren't always ridin' us, ay?" he muttered across the table. "It's hard to play decent when somebody's always plantin' doots in your head."

Harry removed the cigar from the corner of his mouth, knocking a half-inch of ash into what was left of his mashed potatoes—then just as carefully reinserted the stogie between his bicuspids.

"Plantin' anything in you bustards' skulls was about as easy as drivin' a two-penny nail through a block o' concrete," he said. "The sound of an idee bouncin' off of your noggins reminded me of a fresh cow pissin' off a flat rock."

"Nobody had to *plant* the doubts we had," Curt said hastily, glancing nervously around the table. "Four straight years of losses would put them in anybody's head."

"I didn't have any doubts," Fat Donnie countered, smiling over a heaping bowl of vanilla pudding. "I always thought it was the other team that was gonna go down."

"Hell of a lot of good it ever did us," Pisser croaked. "If you hadn't always been oot every night chasin' women, maybe you could have thrown oot a baserunner once or twice a year, for Christ's sake."

The oath hung rancorously in the air. I glanced at Big Stick, sitting a few feet away, his hunched shoulders tightening beneath his Servicemaster jacket. Somehow, he managed to hold his tongue.

Harry didn't.

"Listen at him," he said, biting down hard on his Dutch Master as he leaned across the table toward my nettled roommate. "Fella what cost us half-a-dozen wins givin' umpires the red ass—plus another five or six more 'cause he was always tryin' to kill that other dumbass playin' beside him at second on a double play. That's a good ten wins all that crap wound up costin' us. And them's just the ones I can recollect."

All of us stared at Pisser—remembering. He muttered something inaudible and peered into his soup.

"Speaking of Mr. Miller," Bookie offered drolly, trying to steer the conversation back into less troubled waters, "I've lost touch with him. Anybody know what he's up to now?"

"Robin?" Curt answered gratefully. "He owns a bar. In Oxford, Ohio. I tried to contact him like the rest of you, but the best I could do was leave a message on his answering machine."

"A *bar*," Harry said, rolling his eyes heavenward. "Can you 'magine it? That dildo—surrounded ever' day by nothin' but taps and bottles? I'll lay odds what he ain't drunk, he's broke."

"Me Miller," Bookie repeated, equally incredulous. "A *bar*. A pyromaniac with a book of matches in a gas plant."

"What?" Donnie said, his eyes widening beside me. "He works in a gas plant too?"

Big Stick's bass voice reverberated from the other side of the table. "A man given to spirits," he orated. "Sore afflicted in his innards. Forever dronkelewe."

Dropping a gnawed chicken wing on the table, he moved on to his dessert.

"*What?*" Donnie repeated. "I don't get any of this. *Dronkelewe?*"

None of us hastened to respond. Stick's big mitts had moved on to the bread plate—extracted what was left of the rye.

"I want to propose a toast," Curt said suddenly, his chair clattering across the floor behind him. Water glass hoisted, he lurched to his feet. "To Harry.... For all his years of devoted service.... And to the... to the success of our sojourn tomorrow. Our venture in Cranberry Bend." He raised the glass higher, smiling at the old coach, whose gaping countenance was still fixed on Big Stick. Bookie and I rose awkwardly to join him, glasses lifted. Wick's and Donnie's outsized frames took longer to get vertical, but eventually they stood too. Only Pisser remained where he sat.

Curt waited, his rueful eyes fixed on the old shortstop. Finally he reached disgustedly for his beer and hunched halfway up off his chair.

"To Harry," the captain's voice swelled again. "For all his tireless efforts on our behalf.... For guiding every man in this room down the road to where he is today."

A couple of us choked on our libations. Bail looked as if taking credit for where most of our roads had led us could make him an accessory to a capital crime.

None of it deterred our leader, who soared on.

"And lest we be chauvinistic," he said, "To Goodleaf. To Harry *and* Goodleaf...Their almost fifty years of...of lasting wedlock. May they find in their retirement homestead a wellspring of renewal.... A source of succor.... A lasting...a lasting...bond of...bond of—"

He almost got through it before he crashed, but when he went down he was a man without a parachute. Curt spiraled earthward on the failed wings of his rhetoric like a rock plummeting into the sea.

It was the guest of honor who rescued him. Harry came to his old captain's aid with a thorny self-deprecation that had lost none of its bite in the three decades since I'd last heard it voiced.

"I don't know about that *bond* you was fixin' to give me," the coach growled. "Seems to me I got one of 'em myself a while back, and it wound up costin' me a whole pisspot full of money. But I surely do 'preciate all the rest of it.... What you was aimin' at.... The fact all of you boys showed up here this evenin'. Some of you have come a hell of a long way."

We had finished our apple crisp, were silently sipping our coffee, when the door suddenly banged on its hinges and a burly intruder lurched across the floor, wedging his body between mine and Donnie's. A barrel thigh pressed like a cannonball against my right shoulder. A stubby arm bulged from an undersized t-shirt like a smokehouse ham.

"Christ," I said, looking up—startled into a blasphemy that doubtless went unchastised only because Big Stick too was gaping at the party-crasher across the table. "It's *Me!*"

"Damn right it's me!" the latecomer bellowed. "What the hell you assholes think you're doing. Eating without me. Donnie got so much snatch lined up for tonight, he couldn't wait?" A puffy hand fell heavily over the catcher's shirt collar—fingered the pair of glasses in the breast pocket of his suit. "How you been, Fat Man," the intruder went on. "Been doin' a lot of readin' lately? Other than menus, I mean."

Donnie sat goggle-eyed beside me—didn't respond. Didn't react even as the hand slid downward and squeezed a roll of flesh over his belt. I glanced at its pink, pale-haired companion—the fat fingers drumming the table beside my plate.

Me had been in the room all of thirty seconds, and one thing had already become as obvious as the large red wart that still rode the flange of his right nostril: He hadn't changed. Any space the old second-baseman occupied was sure to be jolted by several thousand volts of kinetic energy. The memory of a road trip suddenly flashed through my brain—a trip Harry hadn't made with us, a coaches' meeting requiring that he be at the ballpark several hours before the team bus pulled into the parking lot. Me had sneaked so many cans of Schlitz into his equipment bag we rumbled down the steps like a dozen caged rats on steroids. His rock-'em sock-'em fight chants as we rolled across the prairie had left even Mare's comatose brain in a state of hyperventilation. Unfortunately, after giving up ten unearned runs in the first inning, we proceeded to some even heavier hatchet work on each other. Three hours later, we expired twenty-six to two in a game that wasn't as close as the score.

I looked around the table, skittish, saw that the only empty chair was next to Pisser's. Me homed in on it like a laser—plopped down with the nimble grace of a ring-wise bull.

"Lizard!" he shouted. "You're the only one of these bastards who's got enough class to save a place for his old buddy. Damned good to see after all these years you haven't forgot your old double-play pard." Winking lewdly, he screwed an elbow into the shortstop's bony ribs.

"Robin, *Robin*," Curt said nervously—reaching over to shake his hand before Pisser could respond. "Good of you to join us.... None of us knew you were going to come."

He looked funereally around the room, clearly wishing it were bigger—a captain on the bridge of a ship about to go down.

"A plague and a pestilence," Big Stick muttered. "Goats and monkeys. Cursed the man given to spirituous drink."

"What did he say?" Me barked, his narrowed eyes darting around the table. "Is the Nutman talkin' about me?" He turned again toward the glowering rightfielder, temporarily reduced to a thin-skinned glare.

The same couldn't be said of Big Stick.

"You make mouths at me, sirrah?" he said evenly. "Ripe to be cudgeled, the winebibber who brayeth like an ass."

I stole a quick glance at Bookie, both of us clearly impressed that somewhere in his sacerdotal sojourns the Stick had gotten as fluent in the King's English as he'd always been in the Lord's.

"What's wrong with my mouth?" Me bulled his way back in.

He was on his feet now, wiping his lips—rocking on the balls of his feet as if he were about to launch himself headlong over the corn and chicken. Watching, Bookie also rose from his chair, his palms extended, joining Curt in a groping attempt to tamp down the fires. I turned toward Harry, who was slowly shaking his head.

The Blademan showed his customary restraint.

"He wants to know what's wrong with his mooth?" the shortstop hissed, bending toward Big Stick like a wiry fight manager goading his heavyweight back into action. "It's too big, ay.... Bigger than his brain is. It's a mooth that's been spootin' rubbish since the day he was born."

Curt stepped behind the little man's chair as Bookie put a restraining hand on Me's twitching right forearm. Harry's leg bumped against my knee as he rose.

"Now you all listen to me, goddammit!" he bellowed. "I've had enough of this bullcrap! ...*That's enough!*"

At the words, the room fell silent. The old coach stared long and hard at each one of us before he said anything more.

"I coached for close on fifty years," he finally continued, his voice softening. "That's a hell of a long time."

We waited for him to go on.

"Fifty years.... And I never had a bunch what could of done better than you fellas—if you hadn't always wore yourselves out haulin' around the red ass.... But you was only boys then. Boys got an excuse.... You ain't got no excuses when you're grown men."

He paused, cigar clenched in his jaw, then tilted forward, his left hand splayed on the table in front of me. The horny fingernails were as thick and yellow as the linoleum floor.

"You lost seventy-six straight games," he continued, his voice now little more than a gravely whisper. *"Seventy-six straight ball games without winnin' a goddam one of 'em...* And we had the best hitter what ever played for me...." He stared hard at Wick. "The two best glovemen." His eyes fell balefully on Bookie and Pisser. "And a bunch of other dildos which 'ever one of 'em could contribute somethin' to the cause, even if most days it wasn't nothin' more than gettin' under the goddam pitcher's skin." The basset eyes swept the room again, coming to rest on Me.

"All of that, I had settin' in my dugout—and we lost purt 'near a hunnert goddam baseball games in a row."

I was staring down at my own wrinkled hands as he wrapped it up.

"The van leaves for Cranberry at ten in the morning," he said, hobbling toward the doorway. "Any of you what plan to be on it, bring along your hammers—them ones made out of wood and metal.... The old place needs a lot of work."

Pisser was still steaming when I turned toward the wall in our room a half-hour later. I pulled the pillow over my ear in a vain attempt to tune out the harangue.

"Same old Miller, ay? Everything goin' great, then he shows up and starts curdlin' up the buttermilk. Droppin' thistles in the beans. Stirrin' up a hornet's nest stickin' his big ugly nose into oor doins.... Everybody gettin' along fine—and that pigsucker comes hornin' in on our shindig. I hope to God he falls oot of his bed and breaks his damn neck!"

Blade always did have a way with a metaphor. He should have majored in English instead of industrial arts.

Chapter 7

I was awake with the sun—roused to consciousness less by the clanging church bells echoing down the street outside my window than by the string of curses they inspired in my dyspeptic roommate. Eyes closed, I lay faking sleep as he shuffled testily across the floor to the bathroom—a dank coop whose clanks and gurgles during the night had made me consider rousting Donnie out of bed to ask if he'd sell me one of his Relief Pitchers. Hunched over the porcelain relics, the Blademan performed his morning ablutions to a hacking litany of grunts, coughs, and phlegmish oaths.

When the previous night's revelries had ended, not even our dauntless captain had suggested we reassemble at daybreak for another attempt at a communal bread-breaking, and I was prepared to feign a cement-headed stupor if that's what it took to prod my roommate off to breakfast by himself. It required less than that—barely—but at last the door slammed and he was gone.

I didn't twitch until I caught his voice in the street below—heard it carping now at someone else about the bonging of the bells and the blighted condition of his sleep-deprived body. Feeling a pang of sympathy for whatever hapless martyr had unwittingly replaced me, I risked a cautious peek out the window—saw a party of three about to disappear around the corner. Pisser's chin led the way. Pierce and Bookie trudged head-down a few steps behind it. They looked like a pair of privates being marched off to clean a latrine.

The poor bastards, I thought, glancing at my watch as I sank back into the pillow. There were still almost three hours until our appointed ten o'clock departure. And it was going to be tough for them to roll over and feign sleep in The Weathered Nut.

Two hours later I was dressed—about to slip out in search of another eatery—when a door banged open and footsteps thudded heavily down the hall. It suddenly occurred to me that I didn't know where our late-arriving bartender had managed to secure his night's lodging. I also realized I wasn't as hungry as I'd been a few minutes before.

When I finally joined the rumpled throng gathered out in front of the hotel at the stroke of ten, my stomach was growling, but I was breathing a little easier. No one appeared to have used his carpentry tools on any of the others. And it didn't look as if any more surprise guests had drifted in during the night.

It looked instead as if we had lost a member.

I did another quick head count—determined it was Big Stick that was missing—a realization I couldn't honestly describe as plunging me into a state of mournful bereavement. I didn't exactly want the Lord to call Wick home...but calling him back to Iowa wouldn't have troubled me a great deal.

Slipping in quietly behind Harry, I waited for further instructions—peered up the street at what I assumed must be our designated Cranberry conveyance. A battered rig that looked as if you could carbon date it back to the Stone Age hunkered down a few feet past the hotel.

"Where the hell *is* he?" the coach was muttering, winding his watch. "Any of you other boys seen the man?"

"I saw him at six," Curt answered. "He got up to go to church.... Some of you might have heard the bells."

"Christ yes we heard them," Pisser groused. "You think we're deef? But that was four 'ooers ago, ay. Even that crack-brained Moonie couldn't be in church that long."

"The hell he couldn't," Me said. "We're talkin' about the Nutman. It used to take him half an hour just to finish crossin' himself before he stepped in to hit."

"Not when I played with him," Donnie said, his own hand crossing his chest reflexively. "That must have been back when he was still in a state of gr—.... Before he got all screwed up, I mean." His plump paw moved instinctively upward—fingered the crucifix dangling beneath the open collar of his shirt.

"Got that straight from the holy fathers, ay?" Pisser spat derisively. "God speakin' through the mooths of his child abusers? Pig crap. That fool would be fine noo if he'd stayed a Loot'eran where he belo—"

"Goddammit, I don't give a rat's ass whether the man munches minnies or that damn Loot-fish what tastes like somethin' the sewer crew dug out of somebody's privy," Harry broke in. "How the man spends his time with the Lord's his own bi'ness. But right now the crazy bustard's takin' some of mine."

"He could be gone awhile yet," Curt added quietly. "From what I gathered last night, before we went to bed, when he was carrying on.... I'm sorry...when he was providing me with some useful instruction on the ways of the Brethren, I suspect four hours of worship may not be all that unusual for him."

"Four hours *every* Sunday?" I said.

"If I understood him, yes. Plus two or three more at their Inspired Text meetings on Tuesday night."

Bookie looked as dazed as I was. "Their *'Inspired Text'* meetings?" he said.

"That's what Wickliff called them. Apparently the 'Solomites'...his term for the faithful...assemble in a member's home every Tuesday evening to read passages they've somehow determined are especially sanctified by the Almighty. *Ecclesiastes*. Parts of Shakespeare. A fair share of Dante's *Inferno*...if I comprehended what he was saying.... I think there are even a few paragraphs from an anatomy textbook on the list."

"I need a cup of coffee," Bookie responded, stepping off the curb. The rest of us watched him cross the street—then trooped on toward the Weathered Nut behind him. Tight-lipped, we descended on the stools at the counter. Harry perched grumpily on the one with the clearest view of his van.

He was into his second cigar and third or fourth "Where the hell *is* that bustard?" when Bookie finally asked Curt the question I'd been too fainthearted to ask him ever since Me materialized the night before.

"Just out of curiosity," he said wryly, "are any of our other old mates likely to be joining us?" His dark eyes flickered over the burly barkeep muscling up over a jelly doughnut next to him, then drifted on toward the street.

"Same thing I've been wonderin'," Donnie added. "Seems like a couple more of our old gang oughta be here. I was really lookin' forward to spendin' a day or two with Hotplate."

"The hell you say," Me bellowed sarcastically, jerking an elbow into the receiver's ample belly. "You need another day with Plate like that dickhead in the White House needs another shitload of advice from his wife."

"I couldn't reach him," Curt mumbled. "You remember Roger. He's a very busy man."

"Busy doin' what?" Pisser cackled. "Drivin' aroond checkin' dumpsters for somethin' he can boil or fry under the hood of his car?"

"Quite the contrary," Curt answered. "This is going to surprise some of you—but Roger seems to have gotten away from cooking. Or at least, I understand he doesn't do nearly as much of it as he once did.... He's a lobbyist now."

"A *lobbyist*?" I grunted. *"Hotplate?"* Pisser's snort of disbelief was only a little more pronounced than my own.

"Yes. For the A.A.R.P."

Seeing my confusion, the captain added helpfully, "The American Association of Retired Persons.... I'm surprised you don't recognize it. We've all gotten old enough to join."

"I'm only forty-nine," I corrected him. "And I'm still trying to find a job I could retire from."

"Those friggin' old assholes," Me bellowed. "I know who you're talkin' about. They're always mailin' me a bunch of shit—tryin' to pressure me and the wife into joinin' 'em. Nothin' but a bunch of money-grubbers—milkin' you for a fortune in dues."

"Eight dollars a year?" Bookie said dryly. "I believe that's how much it costs to join."

"So what?" Me barked. "What good would any of it do me? Work my butt off so they can send me some boring magazine that tells me how to get a cheap set of false teeth?"

"I don't know," Donnie said reflectively. "From what I hear, it sounds like they know what they're doin'. Retirement-wise, I mean. They keep pushin' for all those bennies. Stuff that's gonna help us. None of us is gettin' any younger, that's for sure."

"It's true. They've done some good things," Bookie said, turning on his stool to face him, his voice measured. "But it's time they backed off a little.... There are a lot of young people out there.... And a lot of poor folks. Some of those benefits you mention end up resting on their backs."

"Screw 'em," Pisser muttered. "Let 'em work for 'em the way I did. Nobody emptied his pockets to help me oot when I didn't have any money. Anyways, most of them are so damned laz—."

"We won't go into that," Curt cut him off abruptly. He fixed the carpenter with a cautionary scowl, then turned again toward the black man as he hurried on. "I don't know why it failed to register, but somehow it never occurred to me all that time I was calling people that *both* you and Roger live in the Washington environs. Perhaps you could have reached him. Do your paths ever cross?"

Bookie hadn't taken his eyes off Pisser. Three stools away, I could see the long, finely boned fingers gradually loosen around his coffee cup.

He turned slowly to face his questioner. "Hotplate may have changed," he said softly, "but I can't see him spending much time in the Library of Congress.... I hadn't heard he worked as a lobbyist.... It's hard to believe."

"Oh he's a lobbyist all right. Although I have to confess, it probably never would have eventuated if Fate hadn't favored him with a serendipitous experience that began—I don't know—years ago...back when he started to cook for Julian Franklin. Remember him? The Housing and Food Service Director under President Pinchbeck?"

"That red-faced guy with the white beard?" I said, recollecting. "The one everybody always said went with Pinchbeck out to the Napa Valley and toured vineyards during spring break?"

"Exactly."

"Good Gawd," Harry grunted, rolling his eyes. He fumbled in the sagging pocket of his sweatshirt for a cigar to replace the one he'd knocked off his saucer. "'Magine it. That dildo and the Pinchpecker....

Out there sippin' wine. Nibblin' on them little itty-bitty bits of cheese. Drivin' around, the two of 'em, in that big...."

The watery eyes rolled heavenward, the image obviously too appalling to carry on.

"They did appear to enjoy the finer things," Curt continued. "I suppose that's the reason they asked Roger to cook the occasional meal for them. A few months after he graduated, Franklin hired him away from the Delta Chis."

"Did he give him a bath first?" I blurted, my addled brain groping to reconcile Plate's grease-spattered carcass with the dapper dean whose spotless apartment—at least according to Allie, who had once crashed a party there—fairly snowed with food and drink.

"Same thing I was wondering," Bookie added, stirring a trickle of cream into a fresh cup of coffee. Setting the spoon down with exaggerated care, he arched an eyebrow toward Curt and whispered with stage-voice irony, "Sounds like we're talking about another major *renovation* job to me."

The captain looked uneasily at Harry, then dropped his eyes, clearing his throat.

I leaned closer. So I wasn't the only recruit he'd had to wheedle, I thought, also glancing at Bail to see how much he knew of the reconstruction project targeted at his own person. I couldn't tell for sure, but he appeared oblivious—unaware of any repair effort other than that which explained half a dozen of us sitting in a coffee shop with claw hammers slung from our belts. The leathery face slowly seamed in a grin, then the coach suddenly began to chuckle, his belly quivering beneath the coffee-stained creases of his shirt.

We all stared at him, bewildered.

Curt said nothing—uncertain how to read a reaction he clearly took to be a response to his covert charity work.

To the captain's transparent relief, Bail bailed him out of his discomfort a split-second before he appeared about to confess.

"I was just recollectin'," the coach snorted, wiping his eyes, "what that bustard used to look like around the eighth or ninth inning. That fella Hodges, I'm talkin' about. All them shots he took off his shins down at third. Rollin' 'round in the dirt. Tryin' to work off all them stingers. I never seen the like of it. Hell, a pig would of give him room at the slop trough. He was the damnedest sight I ever saw, come the end of a ballgame.... But I'll say this for him—he had more want-to than any third-baseman I ever had."

I had begun to smile myself—initially at the memory of Hotplate's welt-raising tribulations around the hot corner—then at an equally vivid recollection of the last game I had ever played with him. It was our final contest of the season—one we'd wound up losing in the bottom of the ninth on a two-out, two-run blooper when Me and the lumbering Big Stick collided along the right-field foul line. But that we had been in position to win at all was due almost entirely to the epic base-stealing feats of Hotplate—a slow runner who, on that lone afternoon, had managed to pilfer seven sacks in as many attempts.

The images had gotten irrepressible, and I burst out laughing so hard the others sat gaping at me, waiting for a clarification. It took a while before I could speak.

"Remember that game Plate took his sock off?" I sputtered. "Stole all those bases? A few days after he got that—that big slideburn about six inches long on his shin?" I was about to continue, when the rest of them suddenly chimed in.

"It was so ugly nobody wanted to tag him," someone said. "The ball would be there waiting, but they'd refuse to touch him. That big sore. Just below his left knee."

"Blue and swollen."

"All scabbed over."

"With that white salve Allie gave him that looked like pus."

Our waitress, holding a coffee pot that seemed frozen above Bookie's cup as the commentary continued, suddenly set it down on the counter in front of him. Her blonde hair was still bouncing as she disappeared through the kitchen door.

"What a piece of work that crazy bustard was," Harry said, rubbing his fuzz-fringed crown at the memory. "He had all of 'em screamin' at the ump, time it was over. Tryin' to get him th'owed out of the game. But they couldn't find nothin' in the rulebook what said a player had to wear stockins' under his pants."

A row of heads nodded, remembering, as the coach took a long pull on his cigar. Nobody said anything as the waitress re-emerged, eyeing us warily—headed for a table at the far end of the room.

"Speaking of pieces of work," I finally said, looking at Curt. "What ever happened to Mare.... And have you...have you heard anything from Allie?.... You try to get either of them to come back too?"

The lawman was staring out the window, faintly smiling. It was clear he had to shift a mental gear or two before he could respond.

"I couldn't reach either one of them. But I didn't expect to. For all the rest of you, I at least had an address to go on. With Arden and Allison, I didn't have a thing. No one at Tabelard seems to have a clue of their whereabouts. All I could do was plant a few seeds in the grapevine.... There hasn't been anything on either of them in the alumni bulletin for years."

I wasn't surprised—at least where Allie was concerned. I had checked too.

"They were real travelers, both of them two," Me said almost reverently, glancing toward the street as if he expected them magically to appear.

Harry followed his gaze, then looked again at his watch, staring at the dinged silver relic as if it were broken. "Where the hell *is* that big dildo?" he moaned.

"*Mare?*" Donnie said, his round eyes getting even rounder. "You think *Mare* really might have gotten the word?"

Bail peered at him the way I remembered him doing one afternoon after he'd spent three hours trying to teach the receiver how to lay down a bunt. "Just go ahead and swing at the sumbitch," he'd finally said on that occasion. "Maybe the earth will start shakin' from all that weight you're carryin' and the catcher won't be able to see the damned ball." But this time the coach didn't say a word.

"It's still Sunday morning," Curt offered helpfully. "A lot of church services wouldn't be over yet."

Harry stared forlornly out the window. Spoons clinked against saucers. Cups slowly rose and descended from silent lips.

"Tell me about Jan," I finally said, my eyes on the scarred counter in front of me. "How did he die?"

Curt stared at me. "He fell out of a tree," he said gloomily. "I told you that on the phone."

"I know you did. But there's got to be more to it than that. I mean, Jan wasn't Baryshnikov, but he wasn't the clumsiest guy any of us ever played with either. Bookie only had to cover about half of left field for him. Let's face it—it's not like learning that Wick broke his neck falling out of a tree."

"I don't know much more than that single, tragic fact," the captain said. "He had a young wife. Was apparently having some marital problems. That's about it.... The accident occurred on his estate—up in the sand hills."

"His estate?" Donnie whispered.

"Jan was rich. You all know that. He'd made a lot of money back in the seventies—out on the coast—was shrewd enough to get involved early in the silicone chip trade with Japan and Korea. But he was a romantic—all of you should remember that too—and during the four years he spent at Tabelard, he'd come to have an abiding affection for cattle country. One day he decided he was going to retire here. Less than a week later he'd bought his ranch."

"A hymie livin' on a ranch?" Pisser cried, flipping his spoon on the counter to punctuate his incredulity. "Oot on the prairie? All by himself?"

Curt's eyes narrowed, and the room fell so silent I could hear his breathing. His voice could have sliced the uneaten doughnut in front of him as he went on.

"Jan was *Jewish*.... And he wasn't '*alone*'. Anyone listening would have heard me mention that he'd gotten married. It happened not long after he bought the ten thousand acres. As I understand it, he hadn't planned to retire on the place until he turned sixty, but when he met his bride he changed his mind."

"Why?" someone asked.

The captain didn't respond—was still staring at Pisser.

"I'm not sure," he finally said. "I've told you everything I know."

Harry's eyes remained on the empty street, where the occasional passing car or pickup truck was the only sign of activity. Turning toward us, he knocked the ashes from his stogie and cleared his throat.

"Jan wasn't much of a ballplayer," he mumbled. "You all know that. He couldn't of hit a curve ball if one of 'em floated past him like a mushmelon driftin' down a river. But he flat loved the game of baseball. Loved ever'thing about it.... And he was a damned good *man*."

The coach paused and glared at Pisser, then turned back toward the street. "'Least he was good where ever'thing was concerned except women. When it come to the ladies, he was blind as a three-eyed mole."

"What do you mean, '*blind*'?" Donnie said.

"I mean blind like a smart fella what sud'nly could never see nothin' any time he got around a critter wearin' a dress."

"I believe I know somebody like that," Curt murmured.

Bail looked at him—peered searchingly into the captain's stolid face—as the rest of us were also doing. If we'd just heard a gentle needle, we needed some time to assimilate it. Irony dropped about as often as slander from the big lawman's lips.

There wasn't much question what Harry thought he'd heard.

"Boys," the old coach resumed. "There's two ways you can look at the story I'm about to tell you. Whether there's anything you might could learn from it about livin' with a woman. One is, I've struck out myself so often, I'm hittin' about ott-fifty-five against 'em lifetime. The other is you're hearin' it from a man who's put in so many innings he belongs in the goddammed Hall of Fame."

A blue puff of cigar smoke drifted above his wrinkled pate, wreathing it as we reflected on the pair of options. He waited until the last ring dissipated in the ceiling tiles, then carried on.

"Like I said, Jan was a good man. And when he bought that ranch up on the Dismal, he had a hell of a good time for a month or two just diddlin' around on his land.

"He put in some fish ponds. Started a fruit orchard. Even had 'em build him a ridin' stable and a big swimmin' pool shaped like a pear."

"A *bear?*" Donnie said.

"A *pear!*" That thing what you eat.... What you used to look like anytime we could get you strapped into your goddammed gear!"

He shook his head, eyeing the catcher. Donnie slowly nodded as he went on .

"Shallow end was the neck. Other end was a lot wider and deeper. Biggest pool I ever seen—bigger'n that one they put in over in Ogallala. He prob'ly would of drowned in it if he hadn't gotten himself in even deeper when he met that little gal."

"Finally you come to the point, ay" Pisser muttered.

The coach ignored him.

"It kept him busy—I'll say that. Doin' nothin' but supervisin' all of them projects. Which was prob'ly good for him, take it all around. Jan was the type what always gotta be lookin' after somethin'. First few months, he was happy as a chinch bug in a flour sack—stickin' his nose into ever'thing up on that place."

"Just like Pinchbeck used to do, ay?" Pisser squealed, jabbing a needle nobody could have mistaken into an ancient sore spot. "He always loved to go snoopin' aroond, ay? Lookin' oot for you.... Tryin' to keep you from gettin' hauled off to jail."

This time Harry didn't ignore him—was stumbling off his stool—when Bookie defused the incident with a quick rejoinder. "Pinchbeck looked busy," he said, "but he could fool you.... He always seemed busier than he was."

Harry settled slowly back on his haunches—appeared to be considering the implications. I gave him some time to get his legs back under him, then meekly urged him to carry on.

He blew another smoke ring toward the roof.

"Tellin' a story to you boys reminds me of what it was like tryin' to coach you," he mumbled. "Used to be I felt sorry for m'self—couldn't unnerstan' how I got stuck suckin' back tit all them goddammed years back in the sixties.... I see it all clearer now. I was damn lucky we only lost seventy-six of them sumbitches in a row."

He took a long swallow from his coffee cup, then finally picked up the thread of his tale.

"Jan got married 'cause he was bored—that's the long and short of it. And when Jan got bored, he got crazy as a craphouse mouse. The only thing ever kept him out of trouble was he'd always managed to steer clear of women before.

"But this time he didn't. I ain't sure why. Somehow he took it in his head he wanted to get married. And a man what goes out *lookin'* to find a woman is like a three-legged dog what loves to chase cars."

"I don't get it," Donnie said. "He has trouble catching one?"

Harry pawed a book of matches out of his pocket. Stared blankly at his cigar. His face looked like a park ranger's the tenth time a ten-year-old has asked him how long it takes to hatch a petrified egg.

"Can't you understand plain English?" he said wearily. "Jan went *lookin'* for a woman. One of 'em he could marry.... I ain't talkin' the way you used to go out ever' night lookin' for 'em. He was tryin' to find one he thought he could live with. He wanted a *wife*. And he found one. One what left the poor bustard with a set of hoofprints up his tail."

I wasn't sure Donnie grasped this either, but his round head kept nodding as the storyteller plunged on.

"I tried to talk him out of it, o' course—stayed up a whole night with him one weekend when I was up on his place to do a little bird shootin'. But I could tell straight off I had about the same chance of gettin' through to that bustard as I did tryin' to teach you dildos the suicide squeeze. What I mean, it's like I said—he was blind. Ain't nobody could of talked any sense into him at that point. He kept jabberin' there wasn't nothin' could make him happy 'cept marryin' this little gal about half his age he'd met 'bout a week or two before.

"Now, I'd hunted up in that country for years, so the fam'ly she come from happened to be one I'd come to know a little. Fam'ly name of Swiver. They ran an old motel I used to stay in before some crazy bustard with a hot stove-poker went out and burned the damn place down.

"Anyways, gettin' back to what you asked me, I'll say this for Jan. He might of been blind, but he damn sure found himself one hell of a looker. That little Marylou Swiver could of made a fresh-cut steer think all he'd had was a bad night's dream."

"Bullshit," Me muttered. "You're shittin' us. If she was that good lookin', why would she marry an old coot like Jan? Next thing you'll try to tell us is that after he kicked off, she tried to get the Lizard into the sack."

"Shut your trap!" Pisser squealed defensively. "Always runnin' your dirty mooth—"

"Now hold on here!" Harry silenced them. "I ain't finished. I never said she went for him—or even that she was all that het-up about gettin' married. But Jan was rich. And he treated her nice. And she never growed up around nothin' like the things Jan could knock her socks off with ever' time he brought her up there to his prop'ty. Get some idee of all that, you ought could see why her mama and daddy wasn't 'xactly real discouragin' when they heard the man had proposed to her. Hellfire, all of 'em was Swivers. I've known Swivers for goin' on forty years, and I ain't never met one of 'em yet what had a pot to piss in."

"Too bad they never ran into my roommate here," Bookie said, winking, draping an arm around the portly creator of the Relief solariums. I cracked up, but the others sat confused—clearly unaware of their old teammate's inspired entrepreneurial feats.

"Sorry," Bookie added. "Just jivin' with my bunkie.... It's an inside joke."

The cropped hair was still bristling above Pisser's rabbit ears, but the banter seemed temporarily to have taken the bite out of him. Chewing his lip, he glared at the gun-shy waitress as Harry moved on.

"Anyways, like I was sayin', I tried to talk him out of it, but he went ahead and married her—which turned out to be one of the dumbest damn-fool things I ever seen a smart fella do. Jan was close to fifty. She couldn't of been a day over twenty. So right from the beginnin', it was one of them screwball mixed marriages you're always readin' about. Diff'rent ages. Diff'rent backgrounds. And for damn sure two diff'rent ways of lookin' at things up on that ranch.

"It all went to hell in a hurry, is what it did. And the way I see it, neither one of 'em was really to blame. What I mean, that poor bustard knew 'bout as much about ranchin' as he knew about women. And now that he was married to this little Swiver gal, he had a hell of a lot more int'restin' things occupyin' his mind than ridin' around fixin' fences or checkin' the water-level in his stock tanks. If you dildos are followin' me. So he went out and hired this cowboy—this big strappin' young buck—to more or less look after things.

"Well, I don't guess I have to tell you what the fella wound up lookin' after. What I mean, if you're gettin' my drift here. It fin'lly got so obvious, even a man blind as Jan was couldn't help but get suspicious. And then the crazy bustard got even crazier than he'd been before.

"It like to drove him out of his head, he got so goddammed jealous. So he started spyin' on her—wouldn't leave her alone more than half a minute. Purt' near kept her locked up all day in that big new house. Got to the point he was doin' more fencin' work than the cowboy. And his wife fin'lly wouldn't put up with it no more.

"I ain't sure how much fire there was beneath all that smoke, leastways back at the beginnin'. What I mean, back before he fired the cowboy and hired this fella to take his place what was old enough to be her granddad. But you can bet the farm that *after* he did it, he damn sure had a few reasons to think he was bein' burned. Now that little gal was up there all alone—just her and Jan and the old man—nothin' else for her but the cows and twenty-odd sections of ranchland. For a woman her age, it wasn't near enough.

"That's purty much it....

"He kept spyin' on her. She give him more and more reason to think he needed to. Finally he got so crazy jealous he did somethin' about as pure-dee dumb as anythin' I ever saw a grown man do.

"He wrote her a letter, is what he did. Wrote it with his left hand—tryin' to make it look diff'rent so she wouldn't rec'nize the handwritin'. Then he signed the thing '*Your lover*' and told her to meet him out in the fruit orchard that night when the moon come full.

"Well, a little after dark, he climbs up in this big old tree what had been growin' there for years—the only tree within ten mile of the place before he put in all of them store-bought ones. He must of set there for hours.... Fell asleep waitin'.... Nobody heard him hit the ground."

No one stirred.

"He fell out of a tree," Donnie finally whispered. "Jan Merchant. Fell out of an apple tree and killed himself."

"Pear," Harry corrected him. "It was a real big one. 'Bout a hundred yards from that goddam swimmin' pool."

There didn't seem much the rest of us could add. We might still be sitting there, perched on the creaking stools, shaking our graying heads while other moons rose over the sandhills, if Bail hadn't suddenly jumped up and started toward the door. I turned to stare after him. Big Stick was trudging up the street.

"Fin'lly," the coach growled back at us. "The crazy bustard must of wore out his welcome with the Lord."

Wick in tow, we headed back down the street toward the van, whose battered hulk rested near the far curb like the tottering corpse of a dead elephant. It had four sagging bench seats. The left tail-light was shattered. A homemade bumper sticker had been taped to the rusting rear beneath the dangling bulb.

I paused for a moment, studying it . A cracked baseball bat, barrel drooping over a pair of scuffed balls, had been sketched to form what appeared to be some type of crude logo. A few crayoned letters were scrawled above it. *"Old Coaches' Lobby,"* they read.

Bookie had noticed it too. So had Donnie. They stood beside me puzzling out the words.

"Old Coaches' Lobby?" the receiver murmured—waiting for one of us to provide some enlightenment. "I've never heard of them."

The scholar and I were just as befuddled. Imagining Hotplate as a lobbyist was one thing. He'd hired on with Julie Franklin, the sultan of suck-ups, and Plate had already shown us how much influence a running sore could have against even the most recalcitrant opposition. But Bail Bond? The Bail we knew was to political-action organizations what Jethro Clampett would be in a roomful of the latest from Giorgio Armani. It just didn't square.

The others had moved on past the three of us, had begun to climb in the door, when Bookie spoke up.

"Hey Coach," he said. "Come back here a second.... What's this thing you've got stuck on the rear of your van?"

Harry stopped—checked his watch impatiently. Finally he hobbled back toward us, scratching his head.

"What the hell are you talkin' about?"

"That thing," I said, pointing.

"What thing?"

He took a step closer, following my thumb, then mumbled, "That sticker up above the tailpipe?"

"Right," Bookie said.

Getting no response, he added, "It's not an organization any of us have ever heard of.... When did you get interested in politics?"

Still there was no response.

"What kind of damned goofy weed you boys been smokin'?" the old man finally said. "You know I'd sooner have the hoof n' mouth disease than get anywhere near all o' that bullflop. *'Politics'*? What the hell you mean?"

I nodded again toward the sticker. "The 'Old Coaches' Lobby'," I said. "If they're not political, what do they do?"

Dawn slowly broke behind the leathery eyelids. He bit off the end of a fresh cigar and spat it in the street. "Ain't a *they*," he said. "It's a *it*.... It's what a couple of us started callin' the van after those gov'ment dumbasses screwed ever'thing up with their 'renovations'."

"Their *renovations?*"

My voice joined Bookie's in the mock falsetto, both of us warbling it toward our captain's ear. But the lawman had already slid into the van—was out of earshot. Only Donnie was left to gape at us. He and Harry. The coach eyed us as if he were contemplating the nearest road to the state hospital for the insane.

"Okay," Bookie continued, wiping the grin off his face. "I'll bite. What 'renovations' are you referring to?"

The coach took a beleaguered step toward the door, then turned and gestured back up the street toward the old hotel we'd spent the night in. "The ones they done in the Rooster, you dildos. Ain't you noticed the lobby ain't there no more? That's what them politics of yours gets you. The sumbitches said it had come to be a fire hazard. A couple weeks later they went and closed the damn thing down!"

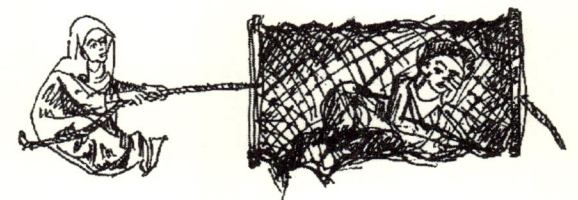

Chapter 8

It started to drizzle as we followed him toward the van, and the horn blared twice above the sputtering roar of the engine. Trotting up to board, I did a double take—then shot a dubious glance at Harry. There was no mistaking the bullet head and thick shoulders hunched over the steering wheel.

"Me's driving?" I gasped, rattled to my shoe soles. Unless he'd undergone his own renovation—one that would have ranked just below Pisser being awarded the Nobel Peace Prize—our old second-baseman was the last person I wanted ferrying me to Cranberry Bend.

"It's my fault," Harry growled in confession. "I left the keys in the ignition. Like I always do. And that dildo jumped in soon as he saw." He rolled his eyes at the beer-keg leg pumping the gas pedal, the knuckled fist clamped on the gear shift—clearly contemplating the same visions that were lurching through my head. "I hope to hell the Preacher put in a word for us before he got out of that church."

Jaw clenched, he climbed in beside the driver—began to fumble unfamiliarly with the tangled clasp of his seat belt buried under a pile of spent shotgun shells. Curt, Donnie, and Big Stick occupied the seat immediately behind them. The third was empty, and I slid into it—found myself next to Bookie's already buckled-up frame. Pisser sat alone in the rear.

Me had us rolling before I slid the door closed. The latch had barely clicked shut—we were already half a block up the street—when Curt suddenly clambered off the seat, shouting *"Wait! Stop it! Stop the van!"* Me shot a glare over his shoulder, then hit the brakes so hard Donnie pitched forward and caught him in the neck with a flying elbow. The rest of us bounced and jostled behind.

"What the hell!" Me fumed, rubbing his head. Pisser cursed and moaned. Curt was already out the door, moving with such resolve it occurred to me he might be about to write the driver a ticket for reckless driving. But he jogged on up the street, his arm raised—back toward the hotel where the green-clad clerk stood beckoning from the doorway. The two of them spoke animatedly for a moment, then disappeared inside.

"Good God almighty!" Me groaned. "What the hell did that damn dickhead forget to do n—"

He was brought up even shorter than he'd been a few seconds earlier—this time by sterner flesh than Donnie's adipose elbow. Big Stick had leaned forward, his eyes gleaming—had clasped the nape of the driver's neck with the thick, unyielding fingers of his right hand.

No one said anything. Even the blasphemer behind the wheel was silent, his freckled skin slowly turning the color of oatmeal above his earlobes. I leaned forward, peering at him. He had the look of a man who had tasted of the wormwood—felt his tongue cleaving unto his jaws.

The rest of us remained in a decidedly contemplative posture for at least a minute. The big rightfielder didn't release his grip until Curt slid the door open and rejoined us—sank into the litter of shell casings next to Don.

His visage was as pale as Me's.

"It was the airport," he murmured distractedly, wiping the rain off his forehead.

He looked around numbly at the rest of our expectant faces. His eyes were glassier than the man's behind the wheel.

They finally fell on the old coach in the seat ahead of him, as if checking to see that he'd managed to get himself fastened into his safety belt.

"You're not going to believe what I'm about to tell you," he said. "I'm not sure I believe it either.... Arden has just flown in."

"*Mare?*"

The response was choral—followed by shocked, stupefied silence as a half-dozen brains struggled to process the news. It was clear Curt had been right. We didn't believe what we'd just heard.

"*Jesus,*" Me croaked—to which even Big Stick didn't react, sharing our collective acknowledgment of a phenomenon roughly equivalent to the Second Coming. The only sound was the still-running engine's wheezing ping.

"Head for the terminal," Curt said at last. "The main gate.... He wants us to pick him up on our way out of town."

I could have counted on one hand the cosmic influences I thought it would take to lighten the legendary lead foot of Me Miller—who had once put his '51 Dodge through Pisser's front door after he'd skated it across his lawn and a half-frozen pool full of goldfish. But Curt's announcement proved to be one of them. He drove us toward the airport at the creeping pace of a horse-drawn dray.

Behind him, the mood had grown even more reflective. No one said anything, lost in thoughts that no doubt ran, as mine did, toward the single season we'd spent with the flaxen-haired pitcher. The atmosphere was a little like what you might expect at an ammunition depot if someone mentioned that Wile E. Coyote was back in town.

I didn't know what anyone else was remembering—even a few days with Mare left too many possibilities to contemplate—but my own mental images kept returning to how little I actually knew about the guy. He could seem so simple, or so complicated, that Harry's *"Where's Choirboy?"* at the start of practice came to take on existentialist connotations. The only givens were his slouching insouciance and surreal faculty for throwing strikes.

What he *seemed* to be, the majority of the time, was a spaced-out California surf bum. But he could also remind you of a beat poet. Or Dr. Strangelove. Or occasionally even Max von Sydow playing Christ in the year's most pretentious film, *The Greatest Story Ever Told.* With Mare, you were always guessing—which explained the silence that had descended on the van as we pottered on toward the airport. We were all trying to conceive what cargo we were about to pick up.

South Fork being South Fork, I assumed the left-hander couldn't have arrived on any airline I had ever heard of. It could have counted all its four-legged residents and still come up shy of twenty thousand occupants. It was a safe assumption, but it was my only accurate one. Mare hadn't, in fact, come in on a commercial flight at all. When we pulled up at the Quonset hut, the chucker was slouched by the doorway. The jet on the landing strip was his own private Lear.

I was still gaping at it when—more numbingly—the van door opened to a Wall Street banker. At least that's what appeared to slide into the seat beside Bail. The arms were still long. The pale frame still flaccid. The blank vacuity of his face as impenetrable as I remembered it. But the saffron hair was sleek and rakishly feathered above a suit and silk tie that were straight off the pages of *GQ.*

I couldn't have been more jolted. Nor more disappointed. A single glance at my fellow pilgrims told me most of them felt the same. Except for Big Stick, whose expression never changed—it always looked as if it belonged on Mt. Rushmore—their expectations appeared as deflated as mine. Donnie looked as if he'd dropped in on a Grateful Dead concert and smelled smokeless tobacco, or come across one of Casanova's capes and discovered he was five foot two.

I hadn't seen Mare for three decades—nor, as far as I knew, had anybody else in the van. He'd dropped out of Tabelard after the '64 season, just as I had, neither of us making it beyond the rank of freshman. The difference was that in the ten days that followed our last game, I had at least hung around long enough to go through the motions of taking finals. Mare hadn't. He'd headed for a Rolling Stones concert in Omaha—astoundingly, in retrospect, one of the first the group had played in America—and never been heard from again.

But he was here now. In the flesh. Considerably more flesh than he'd carried three decades earlier. The doughy body settled deeper into the sagging seat as a leather bag appeared over the coiffed hair and passed from hand to hand back toward the rear. Barely larger than a briefcase, it looked to be made of eelskin, and I studied it for a moment before Pisser snatched it from me. His beady eyes were so intent I was sure he was calculating how he might open it. Finally, his attention diverted back to the owner, he dropped it beside him on the seat.

All of us were waiting for our new arrival to speak. To say something—*anything*—in conclusive proof of his incarnation. It was clear nothing but a few syllables in that inimitable goat's voice would fully convince us it was our former mound ace who was rolling with us now out of the airport. From what I could see of his gelid eyes, they remained about as expressive as a glass of gin.

It was Bail—or a combination of Bail and the squat driver beside him—who inadvertently managed to evoke the magic utterance. As we neared the airport exit, the van's wheels slammed hard over a set of speed bumps, lifting the shaken coach roofward over the gear shift our new seating arrangement had put between his knees. "Goddammit Badger!" he shouted, "You go over another one of them things like you did that last one, and I'm gonna start soundin' like Choirboy here." (*"Badger"* had always been his personal sobriquet of choice for our pugnacious second-baseman, while *Choirboy* was the appellation he'd usually reserved for those rare afternoons when Mare hadn't driven him up the dugout wall.)

We were another half-mile up the road when the pitcher finally responded.

"The day you and me start soundin' the same," he drawled, "is the day I'm checkin' my fat ass off the planet.

"Anyway," he added, glancing down at the old coach's privates, "from what I been hearin', Goodo hasn't left you a whole lot to worry about down there."

"Damn straight!" Me roared, gunning the engine—his hand sliding over the gear shift in an obscene mime that played on for several seconds between the coach's knees. "Goodie's got the jewels—took 'em just like all of 'em will if you don't let 'em know who the hell's boss from the beginnin'." Chortling, he buried his elbow in the coach's gut as the van accelerated up the road.

"What did he say?" Pisser gibbered behind me, stabbing a finger between my shoulder blades. "What's that fool talkin' aboot up there noo?"

Having trouble hearing them myself through the pelting rain and the rumbling cough of the van's overtaxed engine, I waved his hand away angrily and leaned forward over the next seat. The few words I'd heard Mare utter had been more than enough to confirm that at least one thing about him—his reedy voice—hadn't changed at all in the years since he had vanished. But I wanted to hear more. If *what* he had to say remained as mesmerizing as the high-pitched cadences that still penetrated the consciousness like trilled clarinet notes, another road trip with the old hurler was something I could almost look forward to.

Bookie obviously felt the same way—had leaned even farther forward than I had—as had Donnie immediately ahead of me. The same couldn't be said of Big Stick, sitting beside him, who seemed to have been rendered narcoleptic by Mare's sudden appearance. Whether it was because even a world-class flake looks normal to another one, or because his morning devotionals had left him a tad shy of shut-eye, I wasn't sure. Whatever the reason, we hadn't advanced more than two miles up the potholed highway before the craggy head began nodding—then lolled back on the seat. Almost at once the old rightfielder began to snore, which contributed further to the cacophony of road noises. The jangling concert reached its crescendo when Me pulled a harmonica from his pocket and began to play what I took to be a bartender's goosed-up version of *Stand by Your Man*.

It all added up to the most frustrating half-hour I'd ever spent. The van rumbled along, lurching through the rain, and I could pick up only occasional snatches of a front-seat conversation that steadily grew more and more animated. Mare's hands moved faster, Harry's eyes grew wider, Donnie's body hunched farther and farther forward until even my sight-line was sealed off by his upholstered flanks. And the little I did manage to hear only made the frustration worse.

Improbable as it seemed, Mare's stunning metamorphosis to corporate respectability appeared to be true—true at least in the sense that a frog no longer resembles a tadpole. But beneath the upscale sheen, it soon became equally obvious, the same lunatic heart was still pumping the same electrodes into the same demented brain. Aside from his radar fixation on the strike zone, what had always set the pitcher apart was his talent for making the most outrageous utterances sound as if he were simply noting a moderate change in the weather. And from the wisps of conversation that drifted back to me, I didn't need Harry's bulging eyes to convince me that this faculty remained vintage Mare.

From where I sat, I could only imagine how the conversation had begun. Most likely, Harry had ventured some innocuous opener after the three-plus decades in which his ace lefty had turned up missing in action—no doubt some such Bailspeak as "Been ridin' 'em hard out there, Choirboy?", or "What the hell you been doin' with y'self all these years?" And Mare had told him. Told him the way only he could tell him. Caught him up on his life as if it were no more eventful than that of the local custodian who'd spent thirty years pushing a broom.

I picked up just enough of the interchange to trace a sketchy profile of the pitcher's career.

A career which—for lack of a better term—I suppose would have to be described as innovative merchandising.

Mare had apparently begun peddling silicone penis implants—then moved on to less pedestrian ventures—all of which he described with the same routine matter-of-factness that once characterized his descriptions of twenty-foot waves and topless bars.

"*Veronicas*," I heard him say at one point (adding a clarifying *"handkerchiefs"* only after Bail scratched his stubbled chin in confusion). "Little scraps of cloth with a picture of Christ's face printed on the front of 'em. We're sellin' 'em all over now—'specially to illegal aliens—along with stamped hot-wax seals in both English and Spanish. They guarantee that the cloth that touched his face was red, white, and blue."

Harry's orbs bulged further.

"It's a license to steal," the left-hander continued. "Pure guava. I could move a million of 'em if I really wanted to work."

The coach started coughing. Me slid into *Pennies from Heaven*. For two or three maddening minutes, I couldn't hear anything else from the front of the van. When the interference subsided, one more fact about our recent arrival's life became as transparent as the glaze over Harry's dilated orbs: the pitcher was an equal opportunity agnostic.

The targets of the labors he was now describing were the type whose only contact with an alien came when they paid the cleaning woman, or asked for another coat of wax on their car:

"...*Fortunate Falwells*. That's what we call 'em. Little statues made out of plaster and plastic. They sell out in five minutes at bass-fishing tournaments. N.R.A. meetings. Anywhere in the country you find a bunch of Republicans. Every one of 'em comes with a testimonial from some famous dude guys like you always recognize. I'm talkin' big enchiladas here—the Jesse Helms types—dudes willin' to brag about all the good shit that started happenin' to 'em soon as they put a *Falwell* on their desk or up over their dashboard: Pat Boone. Newt Gingrich. A whole bunch of other hodaddies I can't remember that play golf."

"What did he say about Jesse?" Pisser hissed in my ear. "Is he spootin' trash aboot Helms?"

"Poke me in the back one more time, and I'm going to tell Me you called him a liberal," I shot back, slapping his hand off my elbow. I wasn't prone to violence, but a man can take only so much.

Mare was piping on two seats ahead of me. I hunched forward to catch as much as I could.

".... *Rush of Wind Balls*. Our latest item. One of the highest grossers we've ever put out on the market. Bitchin' sales all over the country.

I'm talkin' *chillin'*. Been that way from the first day we started our Wind Ball campaign."

"What the hell is it?" Harry wheezed.

"Trick item—like a Whoopee Cushion. Takes 'bout half an hour to make a whole shitload of 'em back in the factory. All it is—I'm talkin' just the parts here—is a big balloon with a little tin reed that vibrates anytime somebody pulls down the handle on your toilet. Costs less than a dime to make. But stick it in your tank—it makes the sound of a flatus that won't quit. Doesn't stop till the bowl fills up again with water. I mean, it just keeps on poppin' away. Sounds like an old woody with a hole in the muffler. We started out chargin' a buck for 'em, but we couldn't keep the guppin' things in stock. So we jumped the price up to seven-fifty. And we're still ridin' the nose. I mean, it's gnarly. Ever'body from L.A. to the Big Apple's gotta have a Wind Ball. I'm either gonna have to build a new plant, or switch some of my dudes off of the Falwells. Think about it. *The Rush of Wind Ball.* Simplest thing I ever come up with. But it starts pumpin' out those big flatuses as soon as you hook it up to the john."

The rain was drumming harder, Wick was snoring louder, and Me's harmonica had reached the final bars of a tune I took to be either *The Hallelujah Chorus* or the Ohio State fight song. I couldn't hear anything more until the van wheeled through a construction zone a few hundred yards short of a bridge.

Me barreled to a skidding stop just short of the abutment, where a woman in work boots and a yellow slicker stood waving her arms and shouting. A red flag flapped in her hand. The van had halted less than a yard away from her, and she glowered at us for several seconds after the dripping flag dropped to her side.

We were so close I could see the rain trickling down her glasses. Me's knuckles tightened on the steering wheel.

"Shit!" he said. "Look at that crap. Anywhere you go anymore, there they are. Screwin' things up. Blockin' your way."

"I don't know," Donnie said, staring at the bridge. "Not where I come from. I get out a lot, and I think the roads are better now than they've ever been."

The ham-hock neck slowly swiveled in the driver's seat. "I'm not talkin' about the road, you dumb dickhead. Take a look! They got a god—" He stopped suddenly, shot a glance at the still slumbering Big Stick—then finished the denunciation. "They got a goddamn woman for a flagman!"

"So what?" Bookie said evenly, just loud enough for the driver to hear. "She seems to be doing well enough.... Got you to stop, anyway. I've known doors and walls that couldn't get that done."

No one laughed harder than Harry. "And alls she had to do it with was a little old piece of red cloth," he cackled. "Waved it in his nose and stopped him dead in his tracks. Just like a bull."

"Allie used to do that," I chipped in. "Remember? When Me or this redneck sitting behind me started one of their tirades, she'd cool their heels like El Cordobes. She even had that red cape, come to think of it—the one she said she bought on one of her trips to Spain. Hemingway would have loved her work."

"I doubt it," Bookie said. "El Cordobes didn't wear a skirt."

"Neither did Allie," I responded impulsively, flushing as I said it. The image of her in jeans and sweaters hadn't faded. I added, "At least not most of the time."

"Elko who?" Donnie said.

"Allie wore a skirt, but it was always up aroond her neck, ay," Pisser smirked, filling the air with innuendo. "Only reason I could fight her off was I was a married man."

Bookie and I glanced at each other like a pair of waterfowlers—our silent expressions saying "Do you want to take this one, or should I?" Charitably, he let me fire away.

"The closest Allie ever got to any part of your anatomy was the time she clipped you across the nose with her fist," I said.

"I remember that one!" Me roared. "I was standin' right next to the Lizard. He tried to tell her part of her job was washin' his jock."

"Well, I was right!" the shortstop squealed. "She was the student manager, wasn't she? What the hell other reason was there for lettin' a woman hang oot with the team?"

For what had to be the first time in their truculent history, Me's ruddy noggin nodded in agreement. Big Stick was still sleeping, but even his rasping snore seemed to offer assent.

Harry shook his head. "That gal was the best thing we had goin' for us," he said. "Lots of days, she was about the only thing.... Someday you boys are gonna get some sense in your thick skulls and rec'nize that."

"Like hell," Me said, his puffy palm slamming the steering wheel. "The day I think a goddamn woman's the best thing I got goin' for me is the day I turn off football and start watchin' that bunch of fruits in the Ice Capades. I'd rather look at some fairi—"

The diatribe was aborted by a sharp rap on his window. The driver rolled it down peevishly—found himself peering into the dripping face of the flagwoman, who turned and pointed across the bridge.

"You might as well shut your engine off," she said. "We've got a Cat stuck in the mud on the other side of the river. It'll be awhile before you can cross."

Me glared at her, then cranked the window up without answering. "Shit," he said. "See what I mean? Give 'em a job like that and they screw everything up."

"I don't guess she's got a lot to do with what's happenin' over yonder," Harry said, his tone sharp enough that it bought us a few moments of silence. Gnawing his lip, Me stretched a grudging hand toward the ignition and flicked the key. The engine coughed and died, but the windshield wipers continued to labor across the glass.

The nine of us sat in the van, peering out at the rain. It seemed to be lessening, but the clouds still hung like wisps of gauze over the river. The other end of the bridge looked to be less than a hundred yards distant, yet its skeletal ribs loomed eerily in front of us—gray and ghostlike through the early afternoon gloom.

"So who's that Elko guy you were talking about?" Donnie said.

Getting no response, he tried another tack.

"I'm hungry.... When are we gonna get to a place where we can eat?"

Still no one answered.

"Town of Jerome's only a few mile up the road," Harry finally mumbled. "If we ever get across this bridge, we'll stop and let anybody what wants to get a bite."

More silence followed. The only sound was the measured click of the wiper-blades across the windshield. Mare was staring at them as if hypnotized. Or he seemed to be. I couldn't tell what the pale, colorless eyes were riveted on. It might have been the rain. Or the spectral bridge across the river. Or the flag that drooped wetly from the woman's hand.

It suddenly struck me that the pitcher hadn't said a word since we stopped. The last thing I'd picked up in my frustrated eavesdropping was a spiralling catalogue of items that ran from *"ProsPerot Panties"* to *"Condoms for Christ."* I wondered what had turned him so silent. Sitting beside me, Bookie had clearly noticed the change too.

"Mare," I said softly, unable to see his face, hoping to get him to open up again now that I could hear him. "Back in the cheap seats here, we couldn't make out much of what you were saying earlier. I didn't even catch where you flew in from."

But the manic phase had run its course. He barely turned to acknowledge the question. When he finally answered, the thin voice was as hollow as his eyes.

"I was in a city a while ago," he murmured. "It might have been this morning. Or yesterday morning. I was sitting alone in a bar, near an airport. Sometime. Somewhere.

"The bar was empty. Just the bartender. Myself. Three young guys sitting at a table behind me. No one else. It was so early in the morning they hadn't turned on the lights or the music. The room didn't have any windows. The only light was a shaft of sunlight streaming in through the door.

"But the three dudes behind me were already drunk. Hot-tempered. They kept slamming their bottles on the table and cursing. All of them were gambling. They'd bought a stack of pull-cards—the kind that pay off if you match three apples or cherries. The floor under the table was littered with them—losing cards they'd ripped up and thrown away in anger. As they drank more, they bought more of them, which brought more losing, which made them do still more drinking. And the more they drank, the louder they swore.

"All three of them were tanned. Big muscled. They wore expensive clothes—the kind you see in health clubs and fitness centers all over the country. They looked good in them. They knew they looked good in them. They were three young men who loved beautiful bodies.... Their own bodies—and the bodies of beautiful girls."

The rain had stopped. But the far end of the bridge had disappeared behind a gray veil. Mare's voice seemed to be coming from somewhere inside it as he went on.

"They kept on gambling. Drinking. Then suddenly the wail of a siren cut through the room. All of us turned toward it—sat staring at the shaft of sun in the open doorway. A police car slowly passed by it, moved on down the street, followed by a hearse.

"The windows were black. A red ribbon lay on the hood. Five or six cars brought up the rear, their headlights shining dimly in the sunlight.... Most of them were also draped in red.

"We watched until the last car vanished—sat staring once more out at the street—couldn't hear anything now but the disappearing wail of the siren. Gradually it faded too, warbled one last note, and was gone.

"The three dudes turned back to their beer.

"'Want to know what all of that means?' the one nearest me said, jerking a thumb toward the door as he lifted his bottle off the table. He tipped the beer to his lips and drained it—set the bottle down—made another mocking nod toward the street. But he didn't say anything more. Simply waited. Waited until the one across from him finally said, 'No. You tell me. What does it mean?'

"The first one turned toward me, sneering—then spelled out the answer with the middle finger of his right hand.

"'*A.... I.... D.... S*', he said slowly. '*Another Incurably Dead Sonofabitch.*'"

The words sucked the last breath of air from the motionless van. A half-dozen pair of lungs inhaled audibly.

"No, Arden," Curt whispered, shaking his head. "Not.... Not now.... Not here."

Mare ignored him. The rest of us sat transfixed.

"The three of them ordered more beer. Bought more pull cards. Kept drawing one loser after another. But now the curses, the fists on the table, were followed by a drunken chant whenever they tore up a card and threw it down with the others on the floor: *"Another Incurably Dead Sonofabitch!"*

Curt said nothing more. No one did. Mare had leaned so close to the dash his forehead was almost touching the windshield.

"Some time later, we heard another sound from the street—the tap of a cane quietly echoing down the sidewalk. The three dudes turned again—sat facing the door—turned silent as the tapping grew louder, closer to the bar. Suddenly the doorway darkened. An old man in a white, hooded sweatshirt stood facing us. He stood there for several seconds, blocking the sunlight, the rays glinting around his hooded head like a crown.

"He hobbled toward us—drew nearer—tapped his way across the floor toward the table. I could see that he was poor. Sick. The sleeves of his shirt hung over his emaciated body like bat wings. I could barely see his face under the hood of the sweatshirt. A big patch had been sewn on his chest. Over the heart. It was a pink triangle. Pinned to it was a thick gold star."

The voice had gone so soft I could barely hear it. Behind me, as it faded, Pisser's sibilant wheeze pierced my ear:

"What was it? What did he have pinned on his sleeve?"

"Nothing!" I hissed, slapping his hand away.

"The old man stood at the table, bent over his cane, his eyes burning down the hood of his sweatshirt. In the shadows, they were all I could see of his face.

"The dudes had stopped gambling. They were getting uneasy—began to edge away.

"'Get your ass out of here, you old scumbag,'" the one nearest me swore at him. His hands shook as he reached for his beer.

"'Christ yes,' said the one across the table. 'Jesus, check the skin on him. He looks like he just crawled out of the grave.'

"The old man didn't respond—leaned even closer to the youngest one's face.

"'Get the hell away from me!' he shouted. 'I'll break this bottle across your fucking face!'

"'No need of that,' the stranger murmured. 'You can see I'm old. Frail. Worn down by too many years of traveling.' He paused, then nodded toward the floor. Tapped his cane across the cards that littered it. 'You clearly love to gamble—the three of you.... I have a wager to propose.'

"The three eyed one another.

"'What kind of *'wager'*? the one nearest me grunted. He lifted the bottle clutched in his fist—threatened to shatter it on the old man's head if the answer didn't satisfy him. But the answer did satisfy him. Satisfied them all. Pleased them so much they set their bottles down and began to howl with laughter. The stranger had offered to arm-wrestle each of them. Promised to give them the gold star on his chest if even one of them won.

"They banged their glasses on the table, punched each other's muscled arms, hooted with drunken laughter until tears streamed down their faces. But the old man said nothing more. He simply bent over his cane—his body shrinking deeper into the oversized shirt that covered his withered shoulders. Suddenly the loudest of the three stopped laughing. Stretched his hand toward the silk triangle and snatched the star.

"'Jesus!' he cried, jerking his hand away. 'The damned thing's sharp!'

"His fingers were bleeding. He lifted a napkin off the table, cursing, and wiped away the blood. 'What the hell would we want with the fucking thing?' he shouted. 'What's it good for? Some filthy old shitbird's star?'

"'Maybe he's the local sheriff,' the youngest one answered. 'Come in here to clean up the town.'

"'Plans to gun us down,' the third added. 'Whoever's left after he arm wrestles one or two of us to death.'

"They howled even louder as a sinewy hand emerged from the sweatshirt—unpinned the star and tossed it heavily on the floor.

"'Solid gold,' the old man whispered as it thudded. The three turned silent again as the words echoed through the room.

"'It's yours if you can best me.... I insist on but one thing: We clasp the star between us as we wrestle.... That's part of the wager. We hold it between us—keep it pressed between the flesh of our hands.'

"The one who had cut himself bent down cautiously—lifted the star off the floor—tested its color and weight. The others did the same, passing it from hand to hand.

"'All right, we'll do it,' the leader snarled when the six points had circled the table. 'Put the goddammed thing wherever you want.' He clasped hands with his friends in silent agreement, then added, 'Set your sorry old bones down here', kicking the empty chair beside him across the floor.

"A few moments later, the first pair of hands locked—the one tightly muscled, glowing with health; the other shriveled, pale as parchment, mummified. And yet there was strength in it. The younger man's face contorted with rage as the sharp points pricked deeply. His chest heaved with exhaustion when the spidery fingers at last touched the table under his fist.

"The other matches were even more fierce. Left the beefy young bodies gasping for air when the old man's withered arm finally gave in.

"The moment the three bouts were finished, the stranger rose. He bent to pick up his walking stick, steadied it in his bony grip, then shuffled away from the table at the same creeping pace he had approached it. Reaching the doorway, he turned for a final look back—peered down the tunnel of his hood at the victors. A moment later he was gone. The tap of his cane grew more and more distant, until it too faded. There was only the silence of the empty street."

No one in the van moved, said anything. We simply waited for the incredible narrative to end.

"I looked back at the table—at the star—lying in a pool of blood where the old man had surrendered it. Blood seeped through the napkins. Trickled down the sides of the bottles. Glistened on the arms and faces of the three young gamblers. They were laughing drunkenly. Hysterically. Tears streamed from their eyes as they clung to each other in triumph. Their bodies were smeared in a river of blood."

For the first time since he began, the pitcher turned away from the bridge. He sat now staring through his window into the trees.

"My God, Mare" Donnie whispered, crossing himself. "Is that story true?"

The pitcher's hand lay on the dash, fluttering slightly, pale and limp as a wounded bird. It stayed there through a few more clicks of the wipers, then rose toward the door.

"I have to piss," he mumbled, swinging the door open and slouching through the ditch toward a willow thicket on the riverbank. The rest of us sat staring after him, gaping at the small opening where he'd disappeared.

He didn't return. I began to think he'd done exactly what he'd done thirty years earlier—yielded to some feral instinct and struck off for whatever terra incognita he could find. Donnie and Curt talked about going after him. Pisser and Me cursed. Harry shook his furrowed dome in tight-lipped concern.

Beside me, Bookie hadn't moved. His eyes remained as riveted as Mare's had been on the rain-streaked windshield. Me had switched off the wipers, but the black man seemed to be looking beyond them—appeared to be staring at the threads of fog hanging over the bridge. Or it could have been at the stoic flagwoman who still stood a few feet away.

I can't repeat the story he went on to tell, for I followed it closely only at the beginning. My mind kept drifting back to the grim narrative that had obviously provoked it—and to what could possibly have happened to its teller out in the woods. Yet I heard enough to know that under any other conditions, what my seat-mate described would have been spellbinding. It came, like the story before it, in a voice so quiet and uninflected it seemed less like spoken language than a surfacing dream.

No one questioned that this tale was true, every word of it, though its harrowing events had occurred a number of years earlier—back in the summer before the centerfielder had first arrived at Tabelard. It was the summer he'd spent in Mississippi, assisting with voter registration—helping out with civil rights work wherever he could. What Book had experienced then was the focus of his story. Or more accurately, the life of a young black woman he'd met one night in a country church was what he revealed to us. Her name was Zelda Gray. She was eighteen. Poverty had forced her to accept a job as cook and housekeeper for a rich cotton grower named Mr. Walters. What the narrative described were the countless ways he had proceeded to brutalize her—ways appalling even by the grotesque standards that prevailed in the bayou backwaters of 1963.

It was too much to absorb—the two stories together—too much for my overloaded brain to take in. And I wasn't alone. When the second tale ended, my companions sat slumped in their seats—appeared only a little less benumbed than the big rightfielder who had somehow managed to remain asleep through both of them. Drained by his narrative, Bookie himself had sagged back wearily on the seat next to me—lay motionless with his eyelids closed.

"You okay, Book?" I said softly.

The lids flickered, but didn't open. His dark hand slowly lifted and brushed my arm.

"I'll be all right," he said. "I'm just.... Thanks for asking. I'll be okay."

"I'm going to step out and get some air," I said. "You want to come?"

"No.... You go ahead. I think I'll just lie here for a time."

I bent forward to slide the door open, but Curt's hand was on the latch before I could reach it. "I could use some air too," he said desperately. It was clear the past few minutes had demoralized him. His frame drooped as if a block of granite had been dropped on his strapping shoulders. I couldn't refuse his earnest, "Mind if I tag along?"

My spirits plunged further as Pisser climbed out immediately behind him, cursing under his breath. I was on the verge of giving up the whole idea, feigning a twisted ankle, when the little man brushed on past us into the brush—presumably to perform the rite befitting his nickname. He'd made so many trips to the bathroom the night before in our hotel room I'd finally asked him if he'd ever considered a prostate transplant.

Curt watched the wiry back disappear behind a cottonwood, then set off in the opposite direction, toward the bridge—where I was more than happy to follow him. He paused when he reached the flagwoman, his big hand touching the bill of his cap. "How are things going, ma'am," he said.

"Not a whole lot better," she answered, taking a few quick steps up the blacktop. We watched as she waved a small truck to a stop behind the van. That we'd been the only vehicle stalled on the road—for what had seemed an eternity—said more about the route to Cranberry Bend than I wanted to contemplate.

The woman gave the trucker what I assumed was the same bad news she had given Me, then turned and splashed back toward us down the rain-puddled highway. For the first time I noticed that the fog had lifted completely—had given way to a warming sun.

Back at her post, the worker shed the slicker and folded it neatly beside her thermos and glistening lunch pail.

"Weather's improving," Curt murmured, though his face still looked as if he expected a deluge lurked behind the nearest sandhill.

"They say it's supposed to clear off," the woman said. "Now if we can just get that damn rig out of that mudhole." She pulled out a pack of cigarettes and extracted one, holding the pack toward us, then dropped it back in her jacket pocket when both of us declined.

"Sorry about this hold-up," she continued, lighting the cigarette and jetting a stream of smoke toward our vehicle. Pisser was crawling back in through the side door, his haunches hunched like a foraging rat. Through the windshield, I could see Me's narrowed eyes fixed on the flagwoman's face.

"It couldn't be helped," Curt said. "Not a thing in the world you could do about it. We're the ones who need to apologize. Occasionally our driver there gets a bit...a bit uncivilized."

The woman grunted, but said nothing. The three of us stood listening to the quiet flow of the river, studying our feet, before my sidekick spoke again.

"I've had a little experience with road problems," he offered diplomatically, clearing his throat loudly in embarrassment. "Would you mind if my friend and I took a stroll across the bridge?"

He nodded past her—toward the knot of men and machines a few hundred yards beyond. "I'd just like to have a gander at it.... You have my word, ma'am—we'll stay out of their way."

She looked into his face, as I did—felt the well of good will beneath the transparent discomfort. He'd gotten over the shoal water—the making of a request that might have been taken as pushy. The lined face relaxed a little as he carried on.

"I'm a highway patrolman. Down in Arizona.... I probably should have mentioned that first."

She blew another puff of smoke, measuring him, then slowly bent to pick up her lunch bucket. "What the hell," she said. "Go ahead. It ain't no skin off my nose."

The first day I'd ever set foot in Nebraska, three decades before—been dropped out of the sky on the little prairie airport where we'd picked up Mare an hour earlier—I'd heard someone describe the river that flowed past the campus as "a mile wide and an inch deep." I thought of that now as the two of us crossed it, walked on in silence, staring at the water that tinkled like a pocketful of coins over the copper sand.

The description was an exaggeration, but not by much. The Platte here was even wider and shallower than I remembered it in South Fork—its channel less a river than a lacing of silver ribbons between islands that had just turned a mid-April mint green.

It felt good walking. I would have been happy simply to carry on across the bridge, past the construction blockage, on up the potholed highway to the little town Harry had mentioned. I'd almost forgotten I had a companion. We were halfway across the river when he broke the spell.

"It's lovely here," he murmured, his eyes following a flock of cranes settling soft as a white blanket over a sandbar. "You tend to forget that when you're away awhile.... Find yourself remembering only what it looks like from the Interstate."

I didn't respond. Simply kept walking. After a few more steps he spoke again.

"I needed to get away from it," he said. "All of it—back in the van.... The squabbling. Robin's driving. Those two stories Arden and Aristus told." His pace slowed, and I reluctantly slackened mine to match it, hoping the moment would pass. But we advanced only a few more steps before he suddenly halted, his hand on the bridge rail. He stood now staring down at the water below.

"None of it's going quite the way I hoped it would," he said reflectively. "We should have been in Cranberry Bend by now—well along with the work."

I'd forgotten the hammers we'd tossed in Harry's tool chest on the ride to the airport. Pulling mine from my belt as I eyed Pisser, I had felt a little like it must have felt checking in your six-shooter at a saloon in Dodge.

"I don't know exactly what it is," Curt continued. "The fellows aren't.... it's not exactly that they're not cooperating. But the old wounds have obviously never healed over.... That disappoints me, quite frankly. I thought thirty years would be more than enough time."

"I wouldn't worry too much about it," I said. "We'll get by."

"I'm not so sure." He turned toward me, frowning, then slowly bent and picked up a handful of pebbles. One by one, he began tossing them into the river. "I'm not sure anymore," he repeated. "I have to confess it. That will probably surprise you, coming from me."

It did, and I said so. Three decades earlier, I'd never seen anything kill his resolve.

He tossed another pebble toward a sand bar. The stone dropped in the water, a good twenty feet short.

"A few things about you haven't changed," I added, commiserating. "You still don't have an arm."

His face creased in a rueful smile, but little of the gloominess lifted. I picked up my own pebble and tossed it toward the sand.

"I thought I could pull it off," he said. "I truly did. Thought we all had gotten old enough that it would finally work." He flipped another stone after mine—then opened his palm and let those remaining trickle through his fingers. They splashed in the water below and disappeared.

"Now the highway's blocked," he said resignedly. "It's an omen even I'm not blind enough to fail to see."

"I don't know," I mumbled.

I had no idea what else to say to him. Disillusionment was written across his high cheekbones and chiseled nose—his tight skin burnished a dark bronze in the sunlight. I remembered he'd once told me his grandmother was a full-blooded Arapaho.

His eyes continued to stare vacantly out over the shimmering river. First Mare. Then Bookie. Now even the big lawman seemed to be haunted by its hypnotic flow. Studying him, I felt compelled to add something to ease his distress.

"Doesn't seem to me it's much of an omen," I said. "Bulldozers are probably blocking half the roads between here and Lincoln. Most of them are old Cornhuskers with bad knees."

The quip didn't noticeably lighten the mood, but he did start on over the bridge—his shoulders still sagging. I plodded on with him, saying nothing more.

"I was back here a while ago," he said after a long silence. "Maybe that's why I consider all of this an omen.... Things turned out pretty badly then."

"What do you mean?"

He stopped again. Turned to face me.

"It was ten years ago.... Or was it eleven? It was the year of our twentieth class reunion. You remember, we were going to...."

He paused, catching himself in mid-sentence—glanced at me with that solicitude in his face that never seemed to fail him even in his most self-absorbed tribulations. "I'm sorry, Jeffrey," he added. "I sometimes forget that not everyone on our team was a senior in 1964."

"Some of us were never seniors.... Somehow we managed to survive. Carry on."

"Well, as I'd begun to say, a decade or so ago I was back in South Fork for our twentieth reunion. Coincidentally, that year I happened to be the chair of the Alumni Association. I suppose they chose me," he added, dropping his eyes, "because back in '64 I had somehow been elected class president."

"Not to mention Homecoming King—and Halloween Hive Drone—and vice-president of the student council...just to list a few I can remember. It's a good thing you were also captain of the Honey Bees. Otherwise there wouldn't have been a crown big enough to fit your head."

It was a gentle barb, and he took it as gracefully as I knew he would—barely pausing before laboring on.

"Anyway, I'd done a fair amount of preparation. Spent a lot of time organizing. I thought I had arranged everything about as efficiently as I possibly could. It took a year for us to do it, all told, but things went so well I approached the reunion feeling extremely optimistic. When the wife and I flew in on Friday morning, I was confident it would be one of the best commemorations in the history of Tabelard."

"I take it that means it wasn't."

He shook his head, his shoulders drooping as if I'd dropped another Sisyphean boulder on the load he'd toted out of the van.

"I mean, I was sure we had taken care of *everything*.... Hand-inscribed invitations. Flight schedules into the Denver airport. Community sings with our director of activities.... We'd arranged communal meals. Private rooms in Pinchbeck Hall. Even color-coded, perfumed name tags for the accompanying husbands and wives."

"I think I'm beginning to understand," I said.

The irony escaped him. He nodded his head appreciatively and went on.

"We even transformed the walls above the three gymnasium entrances into shrines to the graduates' past glories—marks of achievement by every returning member of the class. The idea was that each of them would enter the banquet hall to orchestral fanfare and a spotlit illumination of his or her most notable accomplishments in life."

I remembered a few of the notable lines I'd once penned for Hallmark. Dropping out of school felt better than it had in a long time.

"So they hated it," I said understandingly.

"Hated it?" He looked at me in bewilderment. "On the contrary...they *loved* it. Wondered how we'd ever arrived at ideas so inspired."

I stepped back—felt my face whitening—a petrifying image rising from my brain like a chimera. "You don't have something like this planned when we get to Cranberry," I gasped. "Do you?.... You wouldn't do something like that for the guys on our team?"

He stared at me, still more dumbfounded—looked as if I'd checked in from the lunatic fringe. "You're teasing me," he said uncertainly. "You're pulling my leg.

"You had me going for a moment there, though, Jeffrey," he added. "I have to admit it." A faint smile played wanly across his lips. "Think of it. A *Portal of Achievement* for players who lost seventy-six games in a row." He walked on, shaking his head.

I exhaled in profound relief.

"I still don't get it," I said, trotting to catch up to him. "I thought you said the reunion hadn't gone well.... It sounds to me as if it went about as well as you could have hoped."

"It did," he said. "It did.... Up to that point."

He paused, then repeated, "Up to *that* point.

"We all had a fine time at the banquet. But after the banquet, we were all primed to have a ball."

This time I was the one confused—uncertain whether *he* was being ironic. *"Having a ball"* was the kind of idiom that dropped from Curt Knight's lips about as often as the revelry it signaled seemed to interrupt his life.

"What does that mean, exactly?" I ventured. *"Having a ball."*

His eyes narrowed, and he moaned a pained "Jeffrey, *Jeff*-rey." I had to repeat the question twice to convince him I wasn't putting him on.

"A *ball!*" he finally answered. "What else could it mean?.... A big dance, with a decorated ballroom and formal attire and a top drawer orchestra that plays anything you could want, from waltzes to the foxtrot. The wife and I were really looking forward to it. So were all of the others. Especially after all the earlier festivities had been such a success."

"But it didn't go well?"

"That is the understatement of the year, Jeffrey," he murmured. "It truly is. The understatement of the year."

"So what went wrong?" I tried again, more wary, but still curious.

"It was all my fault. That's what's so hard to handle. Certainly I would have felt bad if it had been someone else. But I'm sure by now I would have put it behind me. I don't think I'll ever fully get over it as it is now—the knowledge that I was the one responsible. It's taken ten years simply to come this far.... Simply putting this thing together with the six or eight of you fellows pretty nearly did me in."

I had never lamented more the length of someone's convalescence. If I'd been a little luckier, he might not have recovered at all.

The feeling was accompanied by a pang of guilt, and I tried to make amends.

"I'm sure it wasn't you. I've been to a few reunions," I lied. "They hardly ever seem to turn out very well."

"It's kind of you to say so, Jeffrey. But it was definitely my fault. Most definitely mine. In the end, there wasn't even a dance *to* turn out badly. I'd feel some considerable relief if there had been."

"What do you mean, there wasn't a dance? Didn't you just say that was what hadn't turned out the way you'd planned."

"There was *supposed* to be a dance. In downtown South Fork. At the old Legion Club a block up the street from the Red Rooster. We'd spent all morning decorating it—really sprucing the place up. It looked wonderful. Almost regal, in fact."

"And?"

"Unfortunately, there's no '*and*.' Only a '*but*'. I had arranged everything, but I'd gotten the date wrong. It was the fourth of May—not the third, as I'd designated.... Somehow, I misread the calendar on my desk."

"Couldn't you simply reschedule? Pay another night's rent on the ballroom?"

"No. It was out of my hands at that point. The rest was a matter of fortune.... Bad fortune, unfortunately. I had made the error, but an ill-fated booking conflict compounded it. The hall had been rented for that night."

"Rented to whom?"

"A group of Shriners. A chapter from Scottsbluff. Over a hundred of them—the Sandhill Sultans, I believe they call themselves. They were already there with their wives and girlfriends when we arrived, out on the floor, dancing to their own local orchestra. Most of our class had taken the limousines I'd arranged—there were about a hundred of us too—but it was such a lovely spring evening a few of us had decided to walk over from the college. It's less than a mile—perfect walking distance—and by the time we reached the ballroom we were quite intoxicated with the atmosphere.... You can imagine the letdown when we arrived to find the situation in the hall."

"Why couldn't you just share the floor?" I asked. "If it's the building I walked past last night, it's good-sized—plenty big enough to handle a dance for a couple of hundred couples."

"That might have happened—seemed about to happen, actually—even by the time those of us who had walked finally arrived at the front entrance. Unfortunately—and I blame myself for this too, since I hadn't been there to prevent it—things had escalated considerably in the half-hour since the first of our limousines arrived."

"Escalated?"

"Yes. As I mentioned, those of us who walked over had become rather intoxicated with the evening. The festive atmosphere. The smell of lilacs. The big silvery moon rising over the Platte. But a few of our earlier arrivals had simply gotten...well...intoxicated. It didn't help matters that some of the Shriners were in that condition too."

"So what happened?"

"Well, as I indicated, despite the inebriation and the growing hostilities, it appeared that cooler heads had prevailed by the time those of us on foot arrived.... Our sergeant-at-arms and their High Potentate had even shaken hands.

"Then the incident occurred that turned the tide. Threw everything into a cocked hat. Made all of us realize how the best laid plans of mice and men...."

He left the cliché hanging, his eyes glazed. Ten seconds later, I completed it for him. The sound of my voice seemed to jar him a little, but he remained silent. Once more I prodded him to go on.

"The *incident?*" I said.

"Yes. The incident.... I did my best to stop it, but we'd arrived a few seconds too late. The two young men had thrown down the gauntlet. The battle had already been joined."

"Wait a minute. I thought this happened ten or twelve years ago, when the class you graduated with would all have been forty. *'Young men'* seems a little self-deluded to me."

"These *were* young men—no more than twenty-one or twenty-two. Hot blooded young men to boot. As Latins so often are, where matters of the heart are concerned."

I said nothing, simply let him roll on.

"Unfortunately, they were both fond of the same girl. I'd met one of them. He was one of our limousine drivers. A Mexican-American who had made his mark—I discovered this later—on that year's varsity fencing team at Tabelard. Pedro Palomino was his name, as I remember. The other was a Puerto Rican.... Jésus Arcita. He was tending bar for the Shriners, but he was also a Tabelard student. I'm fairly sure he was a fencer too."

"Bees with real stingers, ay?"

I caught myself as I said it, and blushed. After less than twenty-four hours, I was already starting to sound like my previous night's crop-haired roommate from the north.

"Disregard that," I said. "Sorry to interrupt."

"It's quite all right. Fortunate, in fact—for I see I may have misled you. There were no weapons involved in the conflict. Only fisticuffs. Unfortunately, there were plenty of the latter.... Especially after Oswald got involved."

This time I was the one who stopped walking.

Pisser?" I shouted. "He came to that reunion too?"

"Why, yes.... He's one of my classmates.... I'm surprised you weren't aware of that fact."

"I *was* aware of it, dammit! But when you called me four days ago, you led me to believe he was some kind of hermit who lived so far up in the tundra his closest neighbors were woolly mammoths. You didn't tell me he'd been down here before!"

My old captain looked past me—we were only a few feet from the end of the bridge—then turned back and put his hand apologetically on my shoulder. "I'm sorry if what I said conveyed that impression, Jeffrey. I truly am. It was completely unintentional, I assure you.... I suppose I was thinking that, after what happened to him back then, he almost certainly wouldn't want to return again."

"What was it? What *did* happen to him then?"

"Well, as I'd begun to tell you...things escalated. There was a battle. And...and I suppose it's only accurate reporting if I call him one of the ringleaders. He came out of it with a broken nose. A dislocated arm. Assorted other bumps and bruises I won't go into. Several of our other fallen warriors were nearly as bad off as he."

"And the Shriners?"

"They took some losses too. They clearly did.... Although I'd have to say that...insofar as a melee of that kind can ever be said to have a winner...one would certainly have to conclude that they took the measure of our men. Toward the end, as I circled the hall attempting to restore order, everywhere I looked someone in a fez and cowboy boots appeared to be clutching the lapels of a tuxedo. It still weighs on me.... It was a painful thing to see."

"That our guys lost, you mean?"

"Oh no. *Everybody* lost. One way or another. Some of us just show a few more scars." He stared morosely down the highway, where the machine was mired in hip-deep mud.

I told him again he wasn't to blame, but it didn't help.

"Now you see why I take that as an omen," he said, nodding toward the Caterpillar. "It can't bode well."

"Okay," I said. "Call it an omen. "But look at it this way. It probably stands for stuff you've already gone through since you got here.... After last night and this morning, how much worse can any of it get?"

Hearing the growl of an engine as I finished, I looked down the road. Another Cat crested the hill and rumbled toward the immobilized hulk in front of us. "See what I mean?" I added smugly. "Our luck's already starting to change."

We watched the big machine roll to a stop—move into position next to the smaller one. Curt took a quick step closer, then suddenly dropped to his knees, studying the work.

"Sucked up all the way to the belly pan," he murmured. "They'll have to hook the cable to the drawbar.... No wonder they couldn't get it out."

He rose to his feet again, but didn't move. We stood there for several more minutes, supervising the extraction, before walking back across the bridge.

The others were waiting when we arrived—had congregated outside the van in varying postures of annoyance and monotony. Bail sat between Bookie and Fat on the bridge abutment. Big Stick was reading Scripture. Me stood glaring up the road at the flagwoman, who stood now near the last car in a line that still numbered no more than six or eight. I was relieved to see that Mare had returned too. His lank frame was slouching against the van, his pallid face expressionless as Pisser harangued him from a throne-like perch on a tree stump. Seeing us approach, the old shortstop scrambled to his feet and redirected his fire.

"It's aboot time you two come back, ay! Runnin' off like a couple of rabbits. Leavin' the rest of us to rot oot here in this godforsaken muckhole! Where the devil you been?"

I said nothing—waited to see if this outburst would prove churlish enough to break my companion's seemingly inexhaustible forbearance.

It didn't. Apologizing for the length of our quest, he proffered a prediction of imminent liberation from the grime-caked leviathan that stymied us. Then he just as solicitously herded us back into our rusted transport, which was soon coughing its way over the potholed bridge.

Chapter 9

On the scale of naive assumptions, what I'd said to Curt about fate already having dealt him his sorriest hand quickly proved to rank with the purchase of a lifetime ticket on the Titanic. We hadn't passed the crater-sized mudhole the Cats had vacated before Me and Pisser were at it again.

There were only a couple of differences from the first leg of our voyage: The events of the last hour had made all of us even pricklier. And Big Stick had finally risen from the dead.

If there was a triggerman for what erupted next as we rolled on toward the tiny town Harry kept insisting lay just around every bumpy bend in the highway, it was the flinty firebrand sitting behind me. But our bullet-skulled driver definitely had his moments. And our resident ecclesiast occasionally weighed in from Sinai too.

In the van's volatile atmosphere, it didn't require much tinder to get the conflagration started. All it took was an innocent question from Donnie. He asked what kind of restaurant we were likely to find in Jerome.

Predictably, the query inspired some pointed jests about the catcher's eating habits—which led to a more scurrilous set of anecdotes about his other bodily appetites—which blew us on with the relentless inevitability of a prairie wind to the incendiary issue of our still national-record losing streak. We had barely cleared the river bridge before we were pinned against the etched-in-bedrock fact that no baseball team in history had ever lost as many consecutive games as we had.

The question was how it could have happened—who was responsible—the most to blame for letting our "adversaries" (as Big Stick put it) "have dominion over us" seventy-six times in a row. I could still see the flagwoman through the mud-splattered window behind Pisser's cropped head when the old shortstop poured on the fuel.

"Field, hit, and run, ay? That's it. The three things you've got to do if you're goin' to play the game of baseball. Nothin' personal against him, but we had to go oot there with a catcher so fat he couldn't do any of the three.... If he hadn't got pulled for a pinchrunner the day we finally did manage to win one, we'd have lost that game too."

"Bullshit!" Me shouted over the road noise. "So the Fat Man hurt us more often than he helped us. At least the fucker got on base ten or twelve times a season. When you got on, Lizard, they stopped the game and took your bat out to have it bronzed."

"Lot you could tell, ay?" the shortstop shot back. "You couldn't see any farther than those red lines dancin' across your eyeballs.... Most of the time, you were so drunk we could have put a pig oot at second and been better—"

The van careened wildly off the edge of the highway as the driver spun around—his right leg swinging suddenly out over the gear shift. Bodies slammed against doors—bounced off other bodies—banged heavily into the seats ahead of them. Harry clawed frantically at the wheel, bellowing. He released it only when Me dropped back into the driver's seat and the vehicle somehow righted itself on the road.

"*Good God almighty you dildos like to got us killed!*" the coach roared. He massaged his knee and right shoulder with a trembling hand—then checked the sorry condition of his cigar butt. Throwing it disgustedly on the floor, he fumbled for another, barely able to light its quivering tip.

"What the hell difference does it make how we lost all them games?" he went on, brandishing the smoldering stogie in the direction of Pisser. "We lost 'em, didn't we?.... Who did what—or didn't do what—or what we might could of done if we had it all to do all over...them things don't mean a rat's ass at this point. The question is, what are you boys gonna do *now?*"

"I'm going to tell the *troot!*"" Pisser shot back, taking courage from the fact that the van driver would presumably have to cross four seats and seven bodies to reach him. "I didn't come all the way doon here to listen to his lies, ay? My battin' average might not o' been high, but I could get on base when it coonted. That hothead's the one that was the easy oot."

"I wasn't all that fat back then," Donnie said.

The van rolled on as we turned to look at him, momentarily silenced by the non sequitur.

"You were waxing fat," Stick finally bellowed. "Like unto a wether's haunch, the girth of your loins."

"The weather's what?" Donnie said, blinking.

"The weather's *paunch!* " Pisser spat. "You were fatter than a damn storm cloud. It's a figger of speech. Listen to the man!"

"I still don't get it," Donnie said. "What does it mean?"

"You don't get it because you never picked up a book in your life. You were always oot eatin'. Always chasin' women.... There wasn't a day went by when you could lay off either one."

"Seems to me he laid off his eats and the ladies about as well as you laid down a bunt whenever we needed to move a runner along," Harry mumbled from the front.

"What? What was that he said?" This time the bony finger jabbed the shoulder next to mine.

Bookie didn't move for several seconds. Then he slowly turned and fixed the crabbed face with a glacial stare.

"What he said, honky, is that you never learned how to sacrifice."

Pisser turned ashen—leaned back on his seat. But the pause lasted only long enough for him to refill his lungs.

"That's a crock of garbage!. I could lay the ball doon whenever I needed to. But how often was that, ay? You were hittin' ahead of me. How often did you get your lazy ass on?"

The cut sliced deep. I felt Bookie's arm tense beside me—saw the long muscle in his thigh twitch beneath his sweatpants. But he held his tongue. He didn't say what we all knew—that despite his anemic batting average, the walks and skittish fielders' errors that his speed generated had given him a higher on-base percentage than anybody on our team except Wick. It was Bail who refused to let the distortion rest.

"Now just a damn minute, Oz. That's the biggest load of bullflop I've heard since the night that Shriner did a two-step all over your chin and you said you'd run into a doorknob. Fast as Aris could move back then, he didn't need nobody to move him over.... Anyhow, if I recollect rightly, most of the time I had you hitting last."

"That's a lie!" Pisser retaliated. "Mare *always* hit last."

Harry tongued the cigar deeper into his cheek—shot a glance at the slouched, expressionless figure staring out the window beside him. Since his harrowing tale and solitary trek into the woods, I hadn't heard the pitcher utter a word.

"Choirboy don't count," the coach said. "Whoever was in the lineup ahead of Choirboy was the last hitter we had."

He turned back toward Pisser. "Most games that was you. Which it ought to help answer that question you was askin' earlier—how we lost all them games in a row."

Even our thick-skinned old coach was getting rankled. I peered up the road past him—tried to see the town, which I was beginning to suspect might be a figment of his imagination. Nothing stretched ahead of us but blacktop and prairie sky.

Behind me, Blade was temporarily silent but seething—no doubt honing his verbal cutlery. It was Big Stick's turn to weigh in again.

"Woeful the man whose testicles are crushed.... Aggrieved beyond all men, the milksop in the barn."

This time I was as befuddled as the round man sitting ahead of me—whose "What does that mean?" hung pendulously in the air.

No one responded. The van rolled on. But on the horizon at last there loomed the sign of habitation I'd been desperate to see ever since we'd crossed the river. The dim outline of a grain elevator rose into the colorless sky.

In the flood of relief that followed, I was thinking only of deliverance—had forgotten Donnie's question. The pilgrim behind me hadn't. His voice carried past my ear to the seats beyond like the white heat of an acetylene torch.

"What does it mean? I'll tell you what it means, ay? It means you can't win if you don't have balls, and the man in charge has to have 'em just the same as his players. It's what Gilding was talkin' aboot earlier.... The old man on our bench lost his jewels."

What happened next probably took less than thirty seconds, but it unreels in my brain like the creepingly clicking frames of a home movie. From the seat directly in front of me, Curt rose—reached forward—put his hand on the driver's beefy shoulder. "Stop the van," he said. Startled, Me pivoted to look at him—then braked to a stop on the edge of the road.

The captain had the side door open before we'd stopped rolling—had quickly stepped out, crooking a finger in my direction. Seeing the expression on his face, I hopped out behind him, confused. He stepped past me without speaking—back into the van—stood now in the tight space I'd just vacated. He gave a wordless nod to Bookie, who read him at once, and the two of them each hooked a hand under Pisser's bony elbows. In a single motion, they hoisted the wiry body off the seat and proceeded to carry it, crab-like, to the shoulder of the road.

None of us looked back as we drove on. No one spoke. The van rumbled up the highway like a meatwagon late for its next delivery. The pair who'd just lightened our load wore the impassive look of a couple of stevedores who had just deposited a crate of lemons on a loading dock.

Two minutes later we passed the buckshot-peppered sign that marked the western edge of the prairie oasis Harry had promised. Me rumbled on to the tavern. Slowly rolled to a stop. Turned the key and killed the van's sputtering engine. But even he didn't immediately climb out.

A dog barked. A fly bounced drunkenly against the windshield. Sparrows pecked at a cigarette butt on the dirt-crusted sidewalk outside the tavern door. They were the town's only visible signs of life. When the spell finally broke, it was in words so soft I'm not sure anyone else in the van heard them.

"All these years," Bookie murmured. "And we still can't get along."

Chapter 10

We had made it to Jerome. A town so tiny it would be flattered to be called a backwater. So remote I half-expected the stagecoach to roll up at any moment with the county's first schoolteacher or crop of mail-order brides.

I peered out the window, down the treeless streets. Three tottering edifices rose toward the clearing sky in a progressive scale of debilitation. The grain elevator. A weathered church spire. And in the square, just across the road from where Me had parked us, a silver water tower whose peeling sides bore both the town name and a hand-scrawled, barely legible "RAVENS, '53."

A cockroach couldn't have found any privacy in the flatiron environs, but there was ample space for the eight of us to put some distance between ourselves. Me slammed his door and headed for the bar. Mare went roaming. Big Stick toted his Bible in the direction of the church. Donnie mumbled, "I gotta get something to eat" and waddled up the weed-cracked sidewalk to what was obviously the town's lone beanery. Bookie—whose sweatsuit and worn Nikes afforded him a less sedentary option—slid past me and drifted toward a boarded-up grocery on the corner. Palms pressed against its cracked facade, he did a few stretching exercises, then jogged on up the street. Curt stood watching him, shading his eyes, until the runner had disappeared around a corner. Then he turned and walked slowly in the other direction—back down the road over which we had just come.

Harry hadn't moved in the front seat. I remained in the rear. The two of us were the only passengers who hadn't vacated. A flop-eared dog suddenly materialized out of an alley and trotted up the street past us. Stopping to sniff a splintered lightpole, it lazily hoisted a back leg.

"Not much of a town," I said.

Bail followed the dog as it loped on past the van, then turned back toward the windowless tavern, reaching over to pull his keys from the ignition as he studied it. "Ain't what it once was," he mumbled. "Back in the days when the railroad ran through here reg'lar. Jerome was a hell of a town way back when."

I doubted it. It looked less like a place Time had forgotten than one it had never dropped in on. But the words, and the sigh that accompanied them, brought home to me just how many years the old coach had seen.

'Want to get something to eat?" I said, easing out of the van. I wasn't hungry, but I didn't want to leave him there alone.

"No. I think I'll just set a spell," he said, swinging his bum leg toward the curb and climbing stiffly down onto the sidewalk. "That park bench over yonder looks kind of invitin', out there in the sun."

I followed his gaze toward the town square. Found myself silently agreeing with him. "Mind if I join you?" I said.

The sun had already begun to dry the sandy ground, and we ambled across the sparse, patchy grass to the slatted bench that faced both the cafe and tavern. From where we sat, the street's only other occupied building seemed to be a barbershop whose cracked sides looked as ancient as the bench we'd squatted on.

"That has to be the last place in the country that still has a barber-pole," I said, startled by its red and white piping despite all the foregoing marks of anachronism. "It's hard to believe there's anybody left in this burg who still has enough hair to clip."

"There's a few of us," Harry said, his palm sliding instinctively over his weathered dome. The gnarled fingers lingered for a moment, then dropped to the bench between us. The basset eyes were staring back down the road we'd traversed.

Again my own gaze followed his. Neither of us said anything more for some time.

"What the hell gets into him?" I finally asked.

The old coach didn't answer—simply shook his head.

"Some fellas just seem to be born with the red ass. Oz is one of 'em. Go back and talk to his mama, she'd prob'ly tell you he chomped her teats off with his gums."

"Maybe," I said. "But I don't remember him being quite *that* cantankerous.... And anyway, it seems to be mostly when he gets around Me that he goes berserk."

Harry glanced at the bar across the street—no doubt envisioning the fireplug who even as we spoke was bending his elbow, readying himself for the next round.

"Why is that?" I added. "I mean, the two of them seemed to hate each other before I ever got to Tabelard.... Were they *always* like that? From the first time you ever saw them play?"

I was remembering a windy afternoon thirty years earlier—a game we could have won but wound up dropping as the streak moved into reaches no team before us had ever visited. We'd nursed a single-run advantage into the ninth, when Pisser backhanded a wicked one-hopper in as pretty a play as I'd ever seen a shortstop execute—then rifled a throw toward second that should have been the game-ending force out. He fired it so hard at Me's thigh the ball ricocheted into the right-field corner as both runners circled the bases. We went down five minutes later on three consecutive strikeouts, losing six to five.

Harry continued to peer down the road, into the shimmering haze, where Curt trudged on—a lone speck on the horizon. When the old coach looked back at me, a long puff of smoke curled above his face as he spoke.

"The year Badger started playin' for me, Oz had already been around a season or two—had had time enough to settle in at shortstop. And for a few games, they paired up better than any two fellas I ever put out on the field. They wasn't friends. It ain't likely anythin' but a rattlesnake has ever been a friend of Oz's. But they got on good enough to make some plays I never seen anybody else make in this country, before or since.

"We'd lost about twenty in a row at that point, as I remember, which wasn't surprisin'. Most of the bustards I had to send out on the field with the pair of 'em couldn't of told a horsehide from a horse turd. But the school was gettin' bigger, and I'd beat the bushes a little, and I knew I'd fin'lly rustled up three or four stud ponies what wouldn't fall over on their ass ever' time they saw a goddam curveball."

The baggy face rose toward the church spire, and a stream of tobacco juice arced past my shoes.

"I had the Preacher by then. And Curt. So I was purty sure the streak wasn't gonna last too much longer. The Preacher wasn't much with a glove, o' course. He couldn't of caught himself a cold in a meat locker. 'Least he couldn't if he had to move his rear more than ten foot to get where the goddammed germs was. But when he wasn't hunkerin' down with the Lord, the big bustard had learned to hit the hell out of a baseball. And Curt was a good captain. He held us together. Even got that dumb dildo Hodges to where he was only kickin' dirt on the umpire once or twice a game."

"Hard to believe," I said, remembering the Hotplate I'd played with. The coach brushed away my doubt with a dismissive wave of his hand.

"This was all before Badger got booted out of his dormitory," he said. "That was the thing changed all of it. Badger gettin' booted out of his room."

"I'm afraid you've lost me," I said. "Me lived in Perkyns Hall—just like we all did. At least everybody except Pisser. He had that place just outside of town. That old three-story house surrounded by trees."

The coach nodded glumly as I said it. His face looked as if I'd reminded him he was due for a procto exam.

"That house was the other thing changed ever'thing," he said. "Hadn't been for that house, the two of 'em might never of started goin' after each other. Hadn't been for that house, Oz might still treat Badger the same way he treats ever'body else."

"Like that dog did that light pole," I said, nodding across the street where a few minutes earlier we'd watched the canine pass.

"Sure. But that'd be an improvement. The crazy bustard ain't never treated Badger that good since he caught him tryin' to diddle around with his wife."

I rose off the bench, then sat down again. Bail blew another cloud of smoke into the afternoon air.

"You're going way too fast," I stammered. "I wasn't aware of any of this.... All I knew was that the two of them never got tired of riding each other. Go back to the beginning...what you said about Me getting kicked out of the dorm."

"It was a couple years before you played for me.... Badger's first year, if I recollect. He got caught in the hallway with a can of beer in his britches. Well, they let him stay in school—the Pinchpecker would prob'ly of put him up in a brewery if he had to, rather'n sacr'fice the bustard's tuition money—but for the rest of the year, they told him he couldn't stay in the dorm."

"What did he do then?"

"Just what I was tellin' you. It was just about the time Oz bought that house—the one you was talkin' about—with the three stories and the fish pond and that big outside stair up to the attic deck. He'd just bought it a month or two before."

"That's something else I never understood," I said. "How a college student could afford to buy a house like that one. I mean, Pisser was older than the rest of us, and he had those odd jobs—but a *ten-acre farm?*"

"He had some jobs, all right," the coach said cryptically. "I won't take nothin' away from him—Oz has always been sharp, and I don't guess he ever come up short on whatever he worked out with that old carpenter what hired him—but I never could figger out how he could salt away more workin' twelve hours a week for that dumbass than I was bringin' home from the goddam school."

"That part of it doesn't surprise me," I said, being honest. "Pisser was so tight, his rear-end squeaked. And if I remember, he didn't spend four hours down at that poker table in the Red Rooster every afternoon."

I glanced at him, saw his face curdle. "Besides," I couldn't resist adding, "it doesn't sound like the guy he was working for was quite as vigilant as the one keeping tabs on you."

"You got that right, Sonny," he mumbled, jetting another stream of tobacco over his shoetops. "Oz been tryin' to pay for his house workin' for the Pinchpecker, he couldn't of bought himself a goddammed three-penny nail."

"You still haven't told me how that old place figures into all of this," I reminded him, trying to steer him back on course. "What does it have to do with Me?"

"He lived with him."

"With who?"

"With *Oz!*.... Ain't you been followin' any of this what I been tellin' you?"

I suppose it was a logical question, given the words I'd heard come out of his mouth, but the syllables still refused to register. Imagining Pisser and Me sharing the same lodging was akin to discovering that J. F. K. had slept with Khruschev.

"You're telling me that the year before I came to Tabelard, Me Miller lived in Ozzie Reeves's house?"

"That's right. Up on the second floor. Just above the room with that big bed Oz tried to get that little wife of his to spend most of their time in.... You do recollect that back then Oz had a wife."

He offered the last with the deliberateness of a sixth-grade teacher asking the class clown if he remembered the city where the Boston Tea Party had been held.

"Of course I remember he had a wife," I said. "That was always even harder to fathom than the house.... Not just that he could find somebody willing to marry him—but that she turned out to be such a knockout. What was her name? May Ann? May Jean?"

"Mayleen."

"Right. May*leen.*"

Lean. Jeans. Tight white blouses. Black headbands. A come-hither face with cherry lips and big, long-lashed blackberry eyes. I might not have recalled her name, but there was little else about her I'd forgotten. Mine were a set of associations I had no doubt would have been equally vivid for most of my old teammates.

"How *did* he marry her?" I repeated. "Jan I can understand. He got rich. And even if he hadn't, those New York smarts of his would have impressed almost any girl from the country. But *Pisser*? I mean...."

The thought wasn't one that led anywhere I'd ever been.

"She come off the farm too. That's the first thing. Oz brought her down here with him—down from up North when he come back to school the beginnin' of his soph'more year. Ain't so surprisin' if you've ever been up there. That little gal might not of seen more than eight or ten men in her life."

"But *Pisser*?" I repeated. "How many women do you know who'd marry that guy if the only other one they'd ever seen was Toulouse-Lautrec?"

"Who the hell's Lou the Dreck?"

105

The watery eyes turned toward me. The cigar drooped from the grizzled jaw.

"Anyways," he went on, "you're askin' *me* to tell you about women?.... What it is makes 'em tick?"

He looked as if I'd asked him to explain the federal tax code. Stymied, I nudged him back toward less thorny ground.

"I have a feeling I know where this is heading," I said. "Me needed a room, and Pisser had one to rent him. But the lady of the house wasn't exactly the type to inspire domestic tranquillity. It was a *ménage à*—.... Call it a recipe for disaster. Am I right?"

"You don't know the half of it."

I waited for him to fill me in.

"There was trouble from the beginnin'. That won't su'prise you, knowin' them two. It'd be odds on for trouble if you left one of 'em alone in a house with a potted plant. Put the both of 'em in it together, with that little gal—" He left the thought unfinished, presumably on the assumption that for even such a chowderhead as the one he had the misfortune of addressing, it wasn't necessary to post a tote board on a sure thing.

"Like I said, Badger had to find a room, and what with all the scrapes he'd gotten himself into, his suitcase wasn't 'xactly bulgin' with letters of rec'mendation. So Oz had him by the short hairs, is what he had. Give Oz that kind of a leg up, and he'd screw ever' nickle out of you he could."

"What you're telling me is that from the moment Me moved in with Pisser, he was royally pissed."

"I suppose you might could put it that way," the coach said, cocking a shaggy eyebrow, "if you was of a mind to be crude."

"Okay. I'm still with you. So what happened next?"

"Well, that little Mayleen was shiny as a penny. Frisky as a spring colt. Skipped around that big house like some itty-bitty little mink playin' on a riverbank. And you know the Badger. Nobody ever accused him of bein' short on want-to when it come to women. 'Specially when somebody had stuck a burr on his butt the way Oz'd done.

"Anyways, wasn't long before the Badger was shaggin' her. Tryin' to get her tail to quiverin'. But she'd only been married a little while— just long enough to tickle him a little. Not quite long enough to start diddlin' around.

"Oz didn't know that, though. Leastways, the way he was actin', he didn't. He got damn near as jealous as Jan did. And the Badger, bein' the Badger, did ever'thing he could to stick the needle in as deep as he could. Off-color jokes. Winks and pinches. You name it, he done it. Most of it right in front of the poor bustard. I was up to that house one evenin', tryin' to calm him down, when the Badger come bargin' in and started raggin' him like a deerfly on a bluetick's rear. It wasn't a whole lot diff'rent than it was last night in the Nut—or the way he used to get a pitcher's goat by rubbin' his crotch and grinnin' up toward the bleachers at the bustard's girlfriend. I should of suspended the both of 'em, is what I should of done, but we had a game the next day and I thought it was time maybe we was finally gonna win one. The team we was playin' didn't have sheep dip.... Hadn't won a game all year."

I didn't have to ask.

"Let me guess," I said anyway. "When it was over, the only streak that had ended was theirs."

"Thirteen to three, if I recollect."

"Let's back up a minute," I said. "Why didn't Pisser evict him? Simply have him thrown out of his house?"

"He tried to. Even saw a lawyer. But sometimes a foxy fella like Oz winds up lookin' down the wrong end of the foxhole. When the Badger moved in, Oz had made him sign a lease.... He was stuck with him till the end of the year."

"Right.... So I take it things got pretty bad."

"*Bad?* Callin' that year bad is like sayin' Pierce is carryin' a extra couple of pounds above his pecker. You damn better believe it got bad. I've got to give that little wife of his credit for that."

"Mayleen?.... She made it worse? I thought she was trying to fend off both of them."

"She was tryin' to defend off both of 'em, all right. But the way she done it was like tossin' a soupbone in between a couple of shorthairs. I don't blame her. She had to do somethin'. But it's thirty-odd year ago now that the thing happened, and the two of 'em still don't show no sign of lettin' up."

"*The thing,*" I said. "What thing?"

He gave me the same schoolteacher glare he had five minutes before.

"I'm sorry," I added reflexively. "You have to remember, I came to Tabelard after all of this occurred."

"That ain't no excuse," he mumbled, scratching his ear. "There ain't nobody in South Fork even now what don't know ever'thing about that evenin'. Hellfire, half of 'em wound up there—out there laughin' on the lawn beside Oz's house.... Wouldn't su'prise me to learn even the Pinchpecker was back there somewhere, sneakin' around in the crowd."

"You're forgetting that I was a scrub. A benchwarmer. We don't get to see much action—even in the replays. You may never have had to tell anyone else this part of the story, but you're going to have to tell it to me now."

He glanced at his watch.

"I'll fill you in best as I can," he growled. "Even though it's been so long ago I'm prob'ly gonna be a little shaky on the de-tails. What I do know for certain is that she had ever'thing set up so perfect neither one of them dumb bustards had a prayer."

"Mayleen?"

He closed his eyes.

"The first thing she done was bat her lids at Badger and tell him he'd fin'lly pe'suaded her it was okay for the two of 'em to hop in the sack. But they had to wait until Oz was out of the house. She wouldn't do it otherwise. And he'd have to get all decked out in a disguise."

"A *disguise?*"

"She told him it was 'cause Oz was so terrible jealous she was scarified.... Wouldn't meet him unless he come up to the attic at midnight, wearin' a set of woman's clothes."

"You can't be serious! Me Miller? In *drag?*"

The hooded eyes didn't open. Sunlight gleamed across the hairless crown.

"She didn't have to drag him into nothin'. How many times I got to tell you, Sonny? This was the Badger. He was the goddamndest dildo for diddlin' I ever seen. He had the hots for her so bad by then—and he was so het up at Oz—he'd of wore Pinchpecker's lace undies if that's what she told him she wanted. Anyways, alls she made him promise was that he'd wear some clothes she was gonna leave up in his room for him. She didn't tell him what kind they was. The only other thing she told him was that they had to wait for a night Oz wouldn't be home to sniff it all out."

"If he was as jealous as you say he was, that could have been a hell of a long time."

"It was the next night."

"The *next* night?.... What did she do, lock him up in the garage?"

"What she did was, she took all them duds she'd bought to give to the Badger and dolled her own self up in 'em. Put on a pair of sunglasses. High-heel shoes. So much rouge and lipstick she looked like a damn Christmas tree ornament. Then she sashayed on down past this house where Oz was doin' some shinglin'—wigglin' her rear end and givin' him the eye."

"She did this to Pisser? Her own *husband?*"

He paused.

"Y' know, Sonny," he said. "I commence to see why you could never hit a goddam curveball.... You got to *wait,* son. Wait on the pitch."

"Roger," I said, then added as an afterthought, "but he couldn't hit one either.... Roger, I mean.... Hodges.... Forget it. What happened next?"

He settled back on the bench, shaking his head.

"Oz fell for it, o'course. Hook, line, and sinker. Saw her prancin' around out there on the sidewalk, and like to dropped his crowbar off of the roof. So later that afternoon—when she sent him the note—she had the both of them horny bustards primed."

I bit my tongue. Didn't say *"What note?"* Simply let him tow me on to whatever port he was headed for.

"It was the damndest thing you ever saw. I got a gander at it after ever'thing was over—when Oz got back from havin' his arm splinted up in the hospital. She'd signed it *'Melody'*. Wrote how she'd seen him play. Said she loved the way he swung his big ole bat—same as she liked the way he carried that big hammer ridin' up the leg of his britches.... Told him he owned the best pair of ball-'n-tackle joints in town."

He turned away, clearing his throat, his face aflame.

"It was the biggest pile of bullflop I ever seen."

"I don't doubt it," I stammered. "What's hard to believe is that Pisser fell for it.... Somebody who swung the bat the way he did...."

The thought trailed off, lost in memories of the shortstop at the plate—his thirty-ounce toothpick flicking foul after foul into the seats.

"I told you what happened to Jan. It was the same thing with Oz.... A woman can blind a man. Put a hell of a pair of blinkers on him. Besides, you saw that little filly. Saw how much run she had in her. It wasn't no su'prise to me."

"But she was his *wife!*"

He looked up at the sky.

"*You* know that. *I* know that. Ever'body 'tween here and the goddam Colorado state line pro'bly knows it. But *Oz* didn't know it. That's the whole point I been tellin' you!"

"Okay," I mumbled. "So she wrote a note and got him going. I still don't see what the *point* of it all was. What she went to all that trouble *for*."

"That's 'cause I ain't come to the point of it. You keep interruptin' me before I can."

He waited.

I waited.

Finally he went on.

"Once she'd got him all hornified, she went home—this little Mayleen did. Took off them clothes and slipped 'em into the Badger's bedroom—'long with another note she'd wrote on that perfumy kind of paper what women use when they want to get a man's glands to gallopin' good. This one said she'd meet him at midnight, up in the attic, when her husband was sound asleep from all his roofin'. Then, after she done all that, she waited till Oz got home from work and told him she was goin' to Denver for the weekend to visit a sick friend.

"She only had one thing left to do."

He glanced at me dubiously. Paused again. Then turned slowly and peered back down the road toward the river. There was no sign of either Curt or the peevish pilgrim we had jettisoned .

"She packed up her suitcase," he went on. "Made it look like she was leavin'.... But the Tay Hay was as far away as she got."

"The what?"

"The *Tay Hay*.... You remember it. Little motel with a red roof. Used to set a mile or two out west of town?"

I'd never heard of it.

"Strange name," I said.

"Like I told you, it was a goddammed motel. A place to '*hit the hay*'.... I s'pose that's what the hell they had in mind when they named it. Think about it. You're s'posed to be the writer.... Though I'm commencin' to see why you still ain't."

"Anyways, the name ain't important. Even the fact it was a damn motel ain't important. She sure as hell wasn't out there 'cause she wanted to get a good night's sleep."

"She was going to meet a lover," I said, confident I was finally catching on.

He turned his shuttered eyeballs toward the sun. "I don't see hows I can make this any simpler for you, Sonny," he moaned. "I already told you she hadn't been married long enough to be out there doin' any diddlin'. I ain't sure how much of that she ever did, to be perfec'ly honest. What I mean, she didn't hardly have time to do a whole lot of it—seein' how her and Oz didn't stay married much longer than another year or so. A woman ain't—"

"Why did she need a motel room then?" I cut him off defensively. My brain felt like a lead balloon.

"She had to have a place to spend the next two or three hours, that's why."

I tried to absorb the monosyllables, which were flowing now in the molasses creep teachers use to try to teach a slow learner. The pace didn't pick up appreciably as he went on.

"Like I said, Oz thought she was off to Denver. Try to recollect and it might come back to you. Besides, she needed to use the telephone."

I nodded my head.

"She just about had it all set up now. Only thing left was to call Oz, do a little heavy breathin' into the telephone, and ask him if he'd got the note she sent. Well, she laid it on even thicker this time than she had before, o' course, and he lapped it up. Which it shouldn't su'prise you, knowin' him and the Badger. Neither one of 'em could see jack straw when their gonads got to trottin' good. And that little Mayleen had managed to work 'em up to a flat-out run. Time she hung up, Oz thought he'd talked her into meetin' him...pe'suaded her to come on over to his house a little after midnight. Only problem was, she told him she knew he was married. Which made her worry his wife might could come bargin' in.

"I ain't sure, but I'm guessin' it took her awhile to get the dumb bustard to come up with the answer she was waitin' for. Even a cuttin' horse what's good as she was is gonna have some trouble when the critter bein' moved don't have sense enough to go where he ought. But she fin'lly corralled him. Steered him where she wanted him. She'd meet him up in that ole attic—which had an outside stair."

"You still with me?" he said, squinting into the sun.

"I think so," I lied. "Sure.... Go ahead."

"An idget could follow the rest of it. A few hours later—gettin' on toward midnight—the Badger puts on the wig and dress she left him and creeps up into the attic, where o' course there ain't nothin' waitin' for him but some cobwebs and a few bug-eyed bats. There wasn't even a chair to set on. Wasn't nothin' for him to do but flop down on the floorboards. Only thing he's got to keep him company is a bottle of Jim Beam he'd slipped into his purse. So the two of them killed a little time together—him and ole Jim did. Settin' up there in the light of the moon.

"Now, while all of this is happenin', Oz is waitin' downstairs, listenin'. Got them pointy ears of his rose up like a pair of antenny—them beady eyes fixed on the kitchen clock. Comes about twelve-thirty, he hears the Badger's bottle clatterin' across the floor, and he thinks it's this Melody gal what's fin'lly climbed up there in her high-heel shoes—ready to make a little music.... Thinks she's snuck up that outside staircase just like he told her. Is waitin' for him to join her, just the way they planned.

"It didn't take him a hell of a long time to get up there, you can bet your tail on that. Back in them days, Oz could be quick as a rattlesnake's tongue whenever the spir't moved him."

"Which was about once every ten games," I cut in—trying to give my spinning brain a few seconds to catch up. "The Oz I remember was always so busy pissing and moaning about how banged up his body was, he never got around to using it."

"He damn sure used it this time. Leastwise he was willin' to. This is one time he was damn sure willin' to give it ever'thing he had.... Problem was, the game he had in mind to play didn't turn out quite as easy as he'd intended. Not by a long shot. But he didn't have a handle on that yet.

"He's feelin' even cockier than he did before, in fact, now that he's up in that attic—peekin' through the door."

"Let me see if I've got this straight," I ventured. "A man built like a wrecking ball is sitting up there waiting for him, swinging an empty bottle, and Pisser's feeling *confident* about the way things are shaping up?"

"But *he* ain't seeing a man. How many times I got to give you the poop on all this, Sonny? This whole story what I'm tellin' you? What *he's* lookin' at is this little Melody gal what wrote him a love letter and give him the cootchie-cooie over the telephone. Anyways, the Badger's not *settin'* there.... And he ain't holdin' no bottle. If you'd been listenin', you'd recollect he dropped it and was layin' there drunk on the floor."

"With a wig on."

"Right."

"Wearing makeup."

"Sure."

"And a woman's dress."

"You ever heard of a men's one?.... Forget I asked you that. They prob'ly do got some of 'em over there in that goddam place where you're livin' now."

Bail wasn't a man you could debate. I shut up and let him carry on.

"*Course* it was a woman's dress.... And it was a real slinky one. And all the hair on that gold wig had spread out on the floor like a damn pile o' corn silk.

"What it all comes down to, Sonny, is that Oz's got his nose stuck against that crack in the door, gapin' in at a woman he has ever' reason to think is ready to have herself a high old time.

"So he takes a step inside. Starts whisperin' to her. Says *'Wake up, my love',* and *'I'm here, my sweet,'* and *'Don't be afraid, it's your honeybun comin' oot of the dark to find you.'* He give her a whole goddam wagonload of such-like kind of cowflop. I couldn't begin to recollect it all."

"'*Recollect*' it?.... Wait a minute.... I don't have a fix on this either. You mean you were *there?*"

"No, 'course I wasn't *there.* But she was. What I mean, this Mayleen...Oz's wife.... She'd managed to get up there in time to hear him. She'd been parked out back for over an hour, just waitin'—sneaked back in the house when she saw him pass by the kitchen window on his way upstairs."

"So she told you all this?.... That's how you know so much about the whole thing?"

112

"What the hell.... You think *Oz* or the Badger was gonna fill me in?"

He had me. I had to confess.

"Anyways, she seen all the rest of it.... Seen Oz tiptoe on in. Get down on his knees. Crawl up to the Badger like he was about to get those bony hands of his on the crown jew'lry. Heard him start whisperin', *'We've got the hoose to oor'selves, ay? Rise up my lovely one. Open up your arms!'*"

I didn't stop him this time only because my jaws had frozen. Pisser and Me—in a remake of the *Song of Solomon*—with a voice-over from Festus Haggins. My head spun.

"So the Badger twitches a little," my informant went on. "Starts to wake up. Begins to get his bearin's just about the time Oz has commenced to start gettin' down to the partic'lars. He feels those skinny hands tuggin' at his dress—thinks Oz's wife is climbin' all over him—has slipped on up them stairs just like she promised him she would.

"Only it's better than she promised. A whole bunch better. He's got 'aholt of the horniest damn woman a man ever had the dumb luck to find in his arms.

"All of this carries on about ten seconds.... Just long enough for him to run one of them ham-hock hands across the little darlin's face. Which I person'lly got to thank the good Lord for. I don't even want to cog'tate what might could of happened if it hadn't been after midnight—late enough that even Oz had sprouted a whisker or two since he'd last run a razor 'cross his chin.... God only knows what the two of 'em could of ended up doin' together otherwise.... We're talkin' goddam Pinchpecker country.... That's what we're talkin' here."

It was clear the coach had reached his own mind-boggle threshold. Mercifully, I figured his narrative couldn't have much longer to run.

"Well, when the Badger felt that pointy jaw, he reared up off the floor. Started roarin' like he'd backed up into a horse-crippler. I mean, he damn near come out of his shoes."

"The high heels, I assume."

"Goddammit, no!.... His own shoes.... You've seen the Badger. How the hell is he gonna get them feet of his into a pair of things that little Mayleen gal was able to fit into.... You got to *think*, Sonny. Think about all this, what I'm tellin' you."

"I am thinking about it! That's the problem. I mean, didn't you say he got into her dress?"

His lip twitched, and his hand clutched my thigh. "You gettin' the dirty-mouth on me here?" he said.

I stared at him for a moment, uncomprehending—slowly began to repeat the question. "Didn't he get into her—

"*Hey!*" I shouted. "Wait a minute! I mean, he was *able* to put on—to slip into—her clothing.... Isn't that what you meant?"

His fingers slowly loosened. "You can buy a dress what stretches," he croaked. "Shoes don't stretch.... Even them women Cind'rella's sisters couldn't stretch a pair of shoes."

"I believe it was only one."

"Like hell it was. There was two of 'em. My mama used to tell me all about 'em. Both of 'em was ugly as a three-tongued toad."

The few hairs remaining on his reddening dome had sprouted like hen hackles above his ears.

"Forget it," I said. "Let's get back to the story.... I take it what you're telling me is that Me and Pisser shared an epiph—...a moment of mutual surprise."

He stared at me.

"Callin' it a *su'prise* is like sayin' I'd of been su'prised if you could of ever kept your shoes tied," he croaked. "Or the Preacher said somethin' so's a person could understand him. Or Choirboy got ahead in the count and didn't th'ow a goddam—"

"Okay! I take your point," I derailed him. "The two of them were more than surprised. Were perhaps, one might say, even a trifle miffed."

He raised his eyes again—stared up at the church.

"Son," he responded quietly, brushing twenty-minutes of cigar ash off his sweatshirt. "Let me put it to you this way.... Tell me if I'm goin' too fast for you.... The two gentlemen we been discussin' commenced to fight like hell."

"And that's how Pisser broke his arm," I countered. "See?.... I was listening. A while ago you said he wound up in the hospital.... I assume that means it must have happened in the fight."

"It didn't happen in the fight.... It didn't happen at all. He broke his *nose* in the fight. He *dislocated* his arm when he fell off the roof."

"The *roof?* How did he get up there?"

"Well, I suppose if you want to get techn'cal, it wasn't the roof. It was that deck he'd built up at the top of the staircase. But it sure as hell was high as a roof. And it took him just as long bouncin' off all of them steps on his way down."

I mulled it over for awhile, staring down the road, where I thought I could make out a pair of figures creeping toward us through the midday glare.

"There are a couple of things I don't understand about all of this," I finally said. "If it happened when you said it did—sometime after midnight—how did a whole crowd of people end up out there, laughing at Pisser? Wouldn't they have been asleep? And why would they laugh at a man who had just brok—*dislocated* his arm?"

"You still ain't thinkin'," he answered. "You played a year with Oz and the Badger, know what they're like when they start goin' after each other. Shouldn't su'prise you they made enough of a ruckus to get just about ever'body in town out of bed. And you know Oz's disp'sition. Should su'prise you even less that a few folks wouldn't 'xactly start sobbin' with symp'thy when they saw what had happened to him— 'specially since that wig of the Badger's wound up layin' under his pointy chin. Anyways, he was back on his feet in no time, jabberin' like a jaybird, threatenin' to call the police and have the whole damn passel of 'em arrested. And the Badger was still up on that landin', stompin' around in the moonlight like a little boar hog wearin' that polka-dot dress.

"Take all that into consid'ration, I'm guessin' you'd of laughed too."

I looked away. The two shimmering figures I'd seen approaching had detached themselves from the horizon—were clearly Curt and Pisser trudging in over the old overland trail. Harry put his arm on my shoulder before I could stand.

"Don't take me wrong, Sonny," he said. "It ain't quite as bad as it sounds.... Folks got Oz to the hospital; helped him get the lease broke; even made an effort to help him get a handle on his marriage.... It even seemed to help a little, 'least for a while there. What I mean, they managed to help him patch things up for a time with his wife. But I doubt a county-fair mule could of pulled hard enough to keep the two of them together more than another year or so. Folks give it an effort, though, is what I'm sayin'. Hell, *I* give it an effort.... I damn sure tried to do ever'thing I could."

Seeing the look on my face, he paused before going on.

"I can tell what you're thinkin'.... Havin' Harry Heddes for a marriage couns'lor is like havin' Choirboy teach you how to hit."

He was right. But I couldn't say that to him. The beagle eyes looked too forlorn.

Neither one of us said anything more for some time.

"Speaking of conjugal bliss," I finally ventured, trying to lift his spirits, "Curt tells me you and Goodie haven't exactly been sharing the honeymoon suite."

This time it was the coach's gaze that drifted down the road toward the mismatched pair of wayfarers, the smaller one's hands stabbing the air.

"No we ain't," he said.

"At least you're not in jail," I said, groping for a bright side. "You're still sleeping in your own bed."

"That's what bothers me.... It's diff'rent this time. She ain't never done nothing like this before."

The road was empty except for the two men walking. There hadn't been a car over it since our van had rolled into town.

"What do you mean?" I said.

He didn't respond.

"That's what gets me, Sonny," he said at last. "I ain't got no idee.... I keep tryin' to scrabble it out in my head, what the hell's got into her. And ever' time I do, it turns out more cockeyed than the time before. Fryin' your brain tryin' to make sense out of a woman is like...is like.... I don't know.... I guess maybe that's the point of it. I don't know what the hell it's like."

It was the first time I'd ever seen him come up empty reaching for an idiom. He was clearly in a lot worse shape than I'd thought.

"She didn't say anything to help you out?"

"Not a whole lot.... Said I was a '*dinosaur*'. A '*relic*'. Blind as a bat 'cause I was too '*full o' sin*'...*full o' scent*—.... I don't know what the hell the word was. That's part of the problem. She started takin' these damned classes at the college. Usin' all these high-falutin' words you had to haul around a goddam dictionary just to unscrabble out. I ain't sure. I was full o' somethin', anyway. That's all I know."

"*Phallocentric?*"

He gaped at me as if he'd nodded off for half a minute on the park bench and woke to find himself sharing it with Einstein.

"Godamighty!.... You understand 'em! You got a handle on where she's comin' from!"

I rocked back on the creaking slats, raising my hands in protest—hastened to disabuse him of the notion. "Just a lucky guess," I sputtered. "I live in a university town.... You pick up a little of the jargon, no matter how dense you are."

"But you got some sense about it...some idee what all of it means!"

"I'm not sure what you mean by *it*."

I was beginning to feel pinned—pressed to elaborate on the one subject in the universe which I felt least qualified to venture an opinion on. Even after thirty years, Allie's old t-shirt, "*Freud Should Have Asked Me*," made sense only on some subliminal level I had no illusions I knew enough about women to tap.

"I'll tell you what the hell it means," he said. "It means what the hell's got into 'em?.... So many of 'em.... Look around you, Sonny. Women ain't the same anymore."

"There's no denying that," I stammered, half-hypnotized by the jabbing tip of his cigar butt.

"Well.... I don't understand it.... That's what I want you to tell me. Why the hell they're so diff'rent now."

Things were getting cloudier, not clearer. Even in such a Stone Age outpost as the one we'd wandered into, I couldn't believe a man could be as out of touch as my old coach appeared to be. Unsure where we were heading, I offered a tentative response:

"Start with rape.... Ongoing wage inequality.... The fact there's not a street in the country they can walk down at night and feel safe when they're alone.... Those are a few of the reasons.... I'm sure if Goodie were sitting here with us, you'd hear a lot more."

He waved his hand dispiritedly.

"I don't mean all that. I ain't bright—but I see them things. And I don't feel good about any of 'em. They're things the country's got to change—got to set right—or we ain't gonna have a goddam country to worry about much longer. But that's not what I'm drivin' at."

"I don't think I'm the man to help you, then," I said, meaning it. "I can't tell you anything more."

"Ain't you married?" he asked.

"Not anymore," I said. "I *was* married.... It didn't work out."

He nodded sympathetically. "But you live around these kind of women. Work around 'em.... Got some idee of what makes 'em tick."

"They're not watches," I said, my eyes on the road. It might have been the first time anybody but his mother had ever seen Pisser approaching and wished he'd pick up the pace.

"You know what I'm talkin' about," my inquisitor said. "Don't start pussyfootin' on me. There's somethin' diff'rent about 'em now. Damn diff'rent. 'Specially them women what go to school...commence takin' all them cockamamy classes. It don't come right away, but sooner or later, it happens. Even to a woman old as Goodie is."

"I don't know," I mumbled. "What kind of classes does she take?"

"That's what I want you to tell me! She's had a pisspot full of 'em—said she was gonna get the degree she never got when I started coachin' and we had our fam'ly. God only knows what the hell she's takin'. I ain't a genius, but seems to me at least the goddam *name* of a class ought to be somethin' a man can understand—even if he can't make head or tails out of anythin' else about it.... *Economics. Organic Chemistry*. Names like that.

'Course I been 'round long enough to know there's always gonna be a few 'xceptions. Hell, I even got roped into one of 'em once myself. They made me teach that *'kinesiology'* cowflop. Which it turned out okay 'cause I fin'lly figured out it had to have somethin' to do with your goddam muscles. But what the hell kind of class is *Gynandrogy?* Or *Valorizing the Vagina?'* Or *'Motherness, Otherness, and the New 'F' Word'?* And don't tell me I should ask Goodie. Ever' time I tried to, she turned colder on me than a witch's tit. That's what I mean...what them goddam courses'll do to 'em. I think the last one she took had some name like *'The Fallacy of Patriarchal Bi—Bi —...what the hell.... Bi-somethin'—Thought.'"*

"Binary Thought?"

"See! There you go again! You *do* understand it—talk the same kind of language they're talkin'. I don't give a damn if you have struck out a time or two with 'em—you can goddam sure hep me now if you try!"

"All I know is a few of the buzz words," I countered. "I'm just as lost as you are. Dropping a 'myocardial infarction' on somebody doesn't mean you're ready to stick a scalpel into his heart."

"One is not born a woman, one becomes one," he croaked.

I gaped at him, stunned. Searched for a clue in the bulldog jaws working over the soggy cigar butt.

"*What?*" I said blankly. "What did you just say?"

"'*One is not born a woman, one becomes one*'.... That's what I mean. That's the kind of stuff she's been layin' on me. It's what I been tellin' you. How the hell is a man like me supposed to understand a goddam 'xpression like that?"

He had a point.

"So that's what Goodie's been picking up in these classes she's signed up for?"

"It's just the beginnin'. There's a whole craploard of others. '*I now pronounce you woman and husband.*' That's one of 'em. Or, '*Ask Will Rogers' wife*'. That's another one. Flop like that. She nails me with 'em ever' night at dinner. Sets there rollin' her eyes at me, like I'm dumb as a goddam post.

"What the hell. Maybe she's right, I don't know. I mean, I wouldn't have a clue what I was s'posed to ask Will Rogers' wife if I did happen to run into her. I didn't even know the bustard was a married man. "Anyways, that'll give you some idee where she's comin' from. It's got so bad she's even started tellin' dirty jokes."

I didn't believe it. Goodie Heddes—at least the Goodie Heddes I remembered—was Mamie Eisenhower with bigger biceps. Imagining her telling an off-color joke was about as easy as envisioning Big Stick telling someone he was having a hell of a hard time getting up to go to church.

The beleaguered husband saw the skepticism in my face.

"Whaddaya call that useless little flap of skin at the end of a penis?" he blurted.

I stared at him harder. The jut of his jaw would have made Churchill look weak-chinned—irresolute. His eyes appeared to wobble in his head.

I didn't react. Was growing disoriented. Felt my own eyes start to swim in the prairie sun.

"*A Man!*" he croaked.

The words barely escaped his throat as he said it. His fingers locked in a vise-grip on my knee.

"Now you tell me," he wheezed. "If that ain't a dirty joke, then I damn sure ain't never heard one.... And to top it off, she told it right down in the Weathered Nut when I was settin' there having coffee with the boys."

It took me awhile to respond.

"*The boys,*" I finally uttered. "I assume they're the same bunch of guys you hang out with in the *'Old Coaches' Lobby'.*"

"A few of 'em, sure. Matter of fact, we'd just come from there when she told it. Been out on a little quail hunt down on Hubie Fryar's bean field. Had us a hell of a shoot before Mac Melibee's knee give out on him.... Didn't make it back to town till close on nine."

I rose off the bench, unsteady—took a few lurching steps across the sidewalk. Curt and Pisser had finally made it in.

Chapter 11

I waited on the curb as the pair approached.

Curt's eyes looked even glassier than Harry's. Pisser's darted from side to side in slashing syncopation with his hands. Curt was tight-lipped—said nothing. The old shortstop's mouth was motoring faster than Me had had us moving in the van.

"You threw me oot! *Threw me oot!*" he squealed. "Left me to rot like a dead skunk on the highway. Don't think you're goin' to get away with it! None of you better have any doots on that score!"

The lawman glanced at me as he passed, shellshocked—but kept on walking until he'd reached the bench behind me. His big frame collapsed next to Harry like sand draining down a well.

Pisser too marched past me—on up the street—the wizened joints of his body still jerking like a marionette's. He didn't stop until he'd reached a battered phone booth on the corner of a gas station a block away. The rusted pumps didn't have bubble tops, and as well as I could tell, the swinging sign didn't promise Regular at thirty cents a gallon. Otherwise, the place provided no visible evidence that the second half of the twentieth century had arrived in Jerome.

I trudged back to the bench and flopped down between Curt and Bail. "I assume he's calling his lawyer," I said.

Curt's eyes drifted toward the phone booth. Behind the dusty glass, Pisser's right hand was slicing the air like a machete in a cane field. The captain looked away—didn't reply.

"His lawyer or his doctor, one," Bail responded for him. "He's the damndest fella I ever run across for threatenin' to sue somebody ever' time his joints ache. Damn good thing he ain't a lawyer himself. If he was, he'd pro'bly of been workin' for one of them greedy sumbitches in all that baseball strike arb'tration cowflop, tryin' to screw another hunnert million out of the other side."

A snowfall of tobacco ash put a coda on the diatribe.

"We should have left him back at the bridge," I muttered. "Dumped him in a cockleburr patch crawling with sand fleas. If he's going to sue us, I don't want to feel shortchanged."

The salvo of spleen clearly surprised them—as it did me. But I'd suddenly run out of patience. Felt my skin prickling in the heat.

Wiping the sweat out of my eyes, I glanced up the empty street—saw a solitary runner eating up ground in a liquid lope toward us. I could feel the others' faces drift toward him too—their eyes as rapt as mine on the black skin glistening in the sun.

"Ain't that somethin'," Harry said, his voice a reverent murmur. "Damn fella looks like he could go out there right now, don't he? Float under a fly ball just the way he always did—let it settle down in his glove comf'table as a chicken egg in a nest of hay.... Hard to believe, after all these years."

Watching Bookie run, I recalled the most astonishing catch I'd ever seen him make—a play that had snuffed an almost certain game winning, ninth-inning rally a few minutes before our 76-game slide had finally ended. There were two outs. The bases were loaded. He'd chased down a ball hit so deep into the right-field power alley that Bail had turned away and thrown his cap at the dugout wall, conceding defeat. Mare, who'd thrown the pitch the hitter hammered, had simultaneously turned his back on the soaring sphere falling earthward almost 350 feet from the mound. But he'd turned away in his familiar no-sweat, end-of-the-inning slouch toward the bench. When Bookie speared the drive—made a levitating, over-the-shoulder grab that turned his uniform into six feet of grass stains—the pitcher was already halfway to the dugout. As he sprawled on the seat beside me, I gaped at him in disbelief.

"When that ball left the bat, it was gone," I said to him. "Even God thought it was going to clear the bases.... How did you know he was going to run it down?"

Mare looked at me as if I'd asked whether they ever got any waves on the Banzai Pipeline. "Dude had it all the way, man," he said. "Had that cherry wired."

The three of us watched as the runner slowed, staring at the phone booth as he passed it—then suddenly stopped and walked back to the shattered door.

"That's big of him," Curt said gratefully. "I hope he has more success than I had."

"We all seen him pull off some mir'cles," Bail responded, "but I don't recollect even that fella ever managed to walk on water. He's got about as much chance of gettin' Oz off that telephone as I got growin' another head of hair."

We waited, watching. Thirty seconds later, Curt sank back on the bench as the runner slid the door closed and loped on up the street.

He dropped to his knees beside us, panting slightly, then flowed into some warm-down exercises on the scruffy grass. The sweatshirt crept up his stomach as his back arched. The washboard flesh had loosened a little, but a finger would still have rippled across his ribs.

"You've stayed in good shape, Aris," Curt said softly.

The athlete paused in mid-contortion—let his leg fall back on the sand. "Not really," he said. "Most of the parts you can't see have gone to hell."

The rest of us said nothing. Curt would have had reason to—he still looked as if he too could pull on his old uniform and not evoke more than a few raised eyebrows—but Harry and I had reached the stage where the struggle every morning was to look down on a bowling ball, not a helium balloon.

"I hate jogging," I said.

"I don't much like running," the black man murmured. The correction was neither defensive nor arrogant—simply a statement of fact.

"I've never understood that," I responded, genuinely curious. "Why do so many people do it then?.... *Run*, I mean."

"Good question."

A long leg lifted off the ground. The almond eyes closed in the high midday sun.

"I don't mean to be disingenuous... less than honest," he said. "On some atavistic level, I suppose I'd even have to admit that I love it.... Have it in my blood."

The leg rose higher.

"My great-grandparents were brought over from Kenya.... My heritage is Masai. But I can't say that's why I run as often as I do."

"Why, then?"

"A lot of reasons.... I suppose you could start with ulcers. High blood pressure. Cholesterol."

Harry was shaking his head—looked as if he were about to fall off the bench in a fit of apoplexy.

"What's wrong, Coach?" Bookie said.

"Goddam, I wish you wouldn't of mentioned that," he answered. "Makes me feel the same way I did the first time I saw DiMaggio peddlin' a cup of coffee on t. v."

The runner smiled in mid-stretch.

"We get old, we get old.... We wear the bottoms of our trousers rolled," he reflected.

"Bull crap," Harry fired back. "Maybe you might—but you'd be the only one I seen doin' it lately. Them bustards playin' now wear their pants so goddam low 'round the ankles it looks like there ain't nothin' above their shoes but some itty bitty strip of duck tape. Six-million dollars a year, some of them dildos are makin', and most of 'em look like they can't afford to buy a goddam pair of socks."

The old center-fielder slowly stood, wiping the sweat off his forehead.

"I'm hearin' you, Coach," he said.

Fifteen minutes later, Pisser was still cutting cane in the phone booth. No one else had rejoined us. Harry was several gravely arpeggios into "What the hell's keepin' the rest of 'em?"—accompanied by headshaking scowls at his watch. Finally, Curt rose and started across the street.

"I'm going to check on Robin," he said. "I'll also try to persuade Donnie to be a bit more expeditious finishing his lunch."

The rest of us glanced at each other. "I don't think I'd crank up the Lobby just yet," Bookie murmured in his wake.

The captain reached the curb, started across the street, then turned and took a few steps back in our direction. "If Arden comes back in," he said, "it might be wise to discourage any further perambulations.... At least until we arrive in Cranberry Bend." He started again across the road, had almost reached the tavern door, then paused once more.

"One more thing," he added, nodding toward the church across the square behind us. "It would be useful if one of you fellows could fetch Wickliff.... shepherd the big fellow back to the van."

He disappeared inside.

The rest of us remained on the bench, not moving.

A full minute later, no one's posture had changed.

"*Fetch Wickliff,*" I finally said. "*Shepherd him back to the van....* A bookmaker wouldn't make that better than even money if the three of us were the Holy Trinity.... Maybe that's what we look like to him, sitting here in the sun."

"Feels more like Larry, Curly, and Moe to me," Bookie said.

He rose wearily as he said it—wiped away the sweat that still trickled down his brow. Bending, he touched his toes a few more times—then looked across the desolate square at the church.

"I'll go after the lost sheep," he murmured. "I'm afraid you two are on your own with the Mare."

Harry and I watched as he trooped past the water tower, continued on until he'd reached the chapel. Staring up at the cobalt sky, he did half a dozen deep knee-bends, then trudged on up the stone steps and went in.

"Poor devil," I said, feeling guilty.

Harry wound his watch.

He held it up to his ear.

He peered up the empty highway—then back at the still occupied phone booth. "We got 'bout as much chance of gettin' this crew to the pars'nage before sundown as we got gettin' inside of it once Goodie sees who's standin' on the stoop," he said. "What the hell we're gonna do then, I ain't got no idee. There ain't no Red Rooster in Cranberry.

There ain't even a boardin' house.... I been tryin' to get that through the dildo's head all along."

"*What?*" I shouted, a bead of sweat blurring my left eye.

"He 'pears to think alls we have to do is show up on the doorstep. Stand there holdin' our hammers. And she's gonna commence actin' like a cow what finally starts givin' good milk after ten years with the hoof and mouth disease."

"*Your wife?*"

The words grated through my throat like a pair of lug nuts—barely cleared the phlegm in my windpipe. He didn't appear to notice. Simply carried on.

"I don't know where we're all gonna end up, that's the thing of it. Ain't so bad for you boys...but I'm too damn old to be sleepin' out in somebody's pasture. If I'm layin' there tomorrow mornin', all stove up, starin' out at one of Mutt Manciple's farrowin'—"

"Who? *Whaa—?*" My hand clamped on his flailing left arm—brought him to a stop—force achieving what my paralyzed voice had failed to accomplish. Gathering myself, I framed a question and put it to him as unhysterically as I could, enunciating every word:

"You're telling me we're all heading for Cranberry Bend...to work on this building you bought...but Goodleaf doesn't know we're coming...and we don't have a place to stay?"

"Not if she don't let us in that church, we ain't. And the odds of that happenin' are 'bout as—"

"*Wait!*" I said, tightening my grip on his elbow. "You mean to tell me Curt brought us in here from all over the country...arranged for us to drive up there...even had us cart along enough tools to build a goddamned airplane hanger—*and your wife's not going to let us through the door?*"

He blinked at me.

"A tick on a dog's ass," he said.

I stared at him wildly. "*What?*" I shouted. "What in God's name does that *mean*?"

The look in his face changed—passed from incomprehension to impatience as he glanced down again at his watch.

"What the hell you think it means?.... Same as it's always meant. We got a lot a crap starin' us in the face."

I let go of his arm—remembered the story our captain had told me on the bridge an hour before: how he'd arranged everything for his class reunion—down to the most minute detail—then screwed up the date.

"Why didn't he call her?" I said numbly, my eyes drifting toward the phone booth down the sun-parched street. "He could have stopped all of this.... Just by picking up the telephone."

I already knew the answer. The old place had no phone, and Curt's unshakable faith had convinced him he'd be able to breach even Goodie's rock-ribbed defenses once we arrived.

I was half right.

"He *did* call her," the coach said. "Yesterday afternoon—after him and me drove over to Cranberry to talk to her. She pulled the curtains down when she seen us.... Told him it was a waste of time."

I sank back on the bench, staring up the street at Pisser—wondered how he'd respond to the idea of a class action suit. Bail Bond had revved up again beside me—the prospects for our night's lodging getting bleaker with every "Shep" and "Doke" whose bovine hostelries he took considerable pains to describe. I slumped lower. Let my chin fall on my chest. Closed my eyes.

It was relief akin to the singing of angels when the crusty voice was gradually obliterated—gave way to an approaching motorcycle's high-throttled belch and roar.

I didn't move as it geared down—rumbled nearer—came to rest a few yards from my outstretched legs. To whoever it was that had arrived, I wanted to remain what I was sure I had to appear—just another drowsy old gaffer lazing out his string on the liar's bench in Jerome.

The motorcycle's thunder decrescendoed into a string of hard, flatulent pops, rose in a surging vibrato—then suddenly died. A few blissful seconds of silence followed, trailed by a series of equally soothing sounds filtering through the warm afternoon air: a kickstand's metallic clank; the pleasant squeak of oiled leather; the jingle of a chain.

"God, Sugar," a throaty voice resonated. "I'm sweating like a pig."

"A chauvinist pig?" a woman coyly responded, tittering.

I opened my eyes.

The bike was a Harley Davidson—coral red—its handlebars pitched and flared like the upthrust head of a stallion. Next to me, my suddenly mute companion peered at it with his mouth agape. What didn't flash an eye-blinding scarlet glittered in a silver array of pipes, plate covers and polished spokes.

The pair sitting astride the machine was no less arresting. Both were helmeted, sheathed in leather—the driver in a crimson ensemble only slightly more muted than the flashing metal that gleamed beneath his bulging thighs. His rider, who perched behind him with the chic delicacy of a fashion model, was clad from head to boot-polished toe in jet black. A tail of golden hair fell beneath her shoulders, the impressive width of which were accentuated by the studied daintiness of her posture. A second look confirmed that she was in fact a large woman—half a head taller than the brawny driver whose outsized waist she still held.

"Good Godamighty," Harry murmured. "Would you look at that?"

We watched as the pair slid off the seat, glanced our way—then whispered something to each other, laughing. The biker stretched his muscled arms. The blonde bent demurely toward the mirror, unbuckling her helmet, taking pains not to break a nail.

A strand of hair drifted across her cheek. She brushed it fetchingly back in place—an instinctive gesture that looked faintly familiar to me. Plucking a small makeup kit from her pocket, she went to work on her face.

The biker studied her for a moment, then shook his head indulgently—and sidled past her toward the van.

I looked back at the woman, who appeared to be applying mascara. Her forehead was as wide as my hand.

I did a double take. Then another. It couldn't be. Yet the longer I stared, the more unmistakable the identification. *"Tina Egland,"* I whispered in disbelief.

"Whats'at?" Harry said distractedly, still eyeing her companion— who stood now with his hands on his beefy hips just behind the van's back bumper. "What'd you say?" The biker was clearly occupying as much of his attention as the blonde was mine. He took a step forward, clamping down on his cigar.

"What the hell's that bustard think he's doin'?" he squawked. "Snufflin' around my vee-hickle!.... Lookee there! Now he's openin' up the goddam door!"

"That's Tina!" I said, grabbing his arm.

"Look at that sumbitch!.... He's climbin up 'hind the wheel!"

"That's Tina! Tina *Egland!*.... Tina Egland from Tabelard!"

"Who the hell's Teener Egland?" he growled, stumbling over the curb. "Look at that big bustard! *He's tryin' to steal my van!"*

"Wait!" I shouted after him. "You remember! She was the campus queen. The Pi Phi president! Allie always used to call her *'Priss'*—"

But I'd been abandoned. The coach was hobbling across the street, advancing on the red menace—his cigar jutting from his jaw like a stubby lance. I watched as he approached, flapping his arms disjointedly. He mumbled something I couldn't hear—then backpedaled in a cautious crouch as the intruder slid off the seat and took a sudden step toward him. He still hadn't removed his helmet. Its dark visor italicized the brawny bravado that palpitated from the skin-clinging red leather like plasma from an outsized heart.

Bail retreated another step—took a second look—then retreated some more. The biker paused. Then with stunning dexterity for one so hefty, he leaped toward the old coach and began pummeling him on the arms. Dazed, I stood frozen as the pair nearly tumbled into the street.

I'd finally taken a few steps forward, faintheartedly considering how I might effect my old skipper's deliverance—when it became obvious that a rescue effort wasn't necessary. The mauling was affectionate, not hostile. Locking the coach's bald crown in a bear hug, the biker began laughing so convulsively he wasn't able to continue thumping the rounded shoulders with his free arm.

Harry wasn't yet aware of the sentiment.

"Goddam!" he barked, stumbling backward. "What the hell!.... Take it! Take the damn thing!.... Here's the keys!"

He was fumbling in his pocket when his assailant finally let up—released his grip—slapped his crimson thighs in an ear-piercing cackle so infectious I began to laugh with him. When he'd recovered enough to speak, the biker made a last bearish swipe across the coach's burnished crown, then unsnapped his chin strap and doffed the helmet. Flipping it toward his companion, he winked and took a step toward her. The blonde I was even surer I recognized set the helmet down demurely on the motorcycle's seat.

I looked back at the biker.

The dark hair was short. Flecked with gray. The broad face was florid. Mischievous. Smiling. An unforgettable gap split the white, otherwise perfect front teeth.

"*Allie!*" I gasped.

Harry staggered back another step—then lurched forward drunkenly as I pulled up beside him. Both of us stood now between the two women, wide-eyed. Their red and black leathers gleamed in the sun.

"If I were half the man you thought I was, Shoeoff," the biker grinned at me, "I'd say something really clever now. One of those inspired jock terms of endearment like 'How the hell you hangin'? But women's speech is impoverished. It's another thing we lack. We're the lackeys of lack—have you ever noticed? Or maybe it's the daughters of deprivation.... Anyway, you'll have to content yourself with 'How have you been?'"

"Fine," I said. "Fine.... Just fine."

I would have babbled on like the village idiot if Harry hadn't taken me off the hook. He'd recovered enough from his recent pummeling to begin to gibber on his own.

"I'll be a— Well, I'll be damned," he said, turning to me. "You're right. It *is* her. I'll be goddammed if it isn't. Ain't that somethin'? *Allie*. Here in Jerome. Sure as you're born."

"Hey coach," she said, waving a hand in front of him. "Look at me. I'm over here. I'm not a ghost."

He turned back to face her, shaking his head.

"No you ain't" he croaked, clearly still not quite believing it. His goggle eyes moved up and down her ample body. "You damn sure ain't no ghost, that's for certain.... I don't know where you been hangin' out all these years, but somebody been feedin' you good."

Allie chuckled—rubbed the coach's own paunch in retaliation. "Tina," she shouted over her shoulder. "Check this out. This is the man that's accusing me of putting on weight." She peeled off her jacket as her companion nodded primly—tossed it on the seat next to her gleaming helmet. "Grab that arm," she ordered Harry. "Go ahead. It won't bite."

Bail didn't look convinced, but gingerly did as commanded—eased a single finger into the brave new world.

"Well?" Allie said as he drew it away.

"Well, what?"

"Well...what do you think?"

"About what?" Harry said, glancing at the still extended digit as if it had contacted a chunk of plutonium.

Allie sighed and looked at me. "How many of you are there here?" she said, changing the subject.

"Who?" I answered, clearing my throat. "People in Jerome?"

She stared at Tina. "See what I mean?" she said.

The one-time princess of preciousness spoke the first words I'd heard her speak since the pair's arrival. The voice had lost none of its breathy warble in thirty years.

"I thought they might have changed a little bit," she lisped. "I mean, I've changed.... At least a little.... Haven't I?"

"You're changing, Sugar," the biker responded. She nudged Harry in the ribs. "As this old fart used to say, you're showin' us some want-to.... It's a start."

Grinning indulgently, she turned back to me.

"Speaking of want-to...I still want to know. How many of you boys are we talking about?"

I stared at Harry.

He stared at me.

"*Men,*" she said. "Honey Bees. Old jocks that rode in on this wreck of a van."

I did a silent calculation.

"Nine," I said. "Counting Bail."

"Eight," he corrected me.

Allie rolled her eyes again. Turned toward Tina. I was doing my own mental reconfigurations. That the two of them had arrived together continued to astonish me—was even more shocking than the unveiling of the burly biker as our old student manager and dugout nemesis. Three decades earlier, Allie Bathgate and Tina Egland were the antipodes between which American womanhood labored for identity. Seeing them in tandem now—in a place like Jerome—was akin to witnessing Gloria Steinem roll into a Tailhook reunion with Tammy Faye Bakker in tow.

"Which is it?" Allie pressed. "Eight or nine?"

I repeated the mental arithmetic—arrived at the same figure. "It's nine. At least it's nine if Mare hasn't deserted us.... Count 'em," I said to Bail. "You'll see."

"Mare's with you?" Allie gasped. "My god! And I thought this was going to be a challenge before." She stared down the road, across the flatiron fields—then up at the ramshackle water tower. "Think of it. Mare Gilding.... Here."

"Who's Mare Gelding?" Tina said.

The rest of us stared at her as if she'd spent the last half-century under a hair dryer.

"Gilding," Allie said. "Though Gelding isn't bad.... A lot of the time you couldn't tell."

It was the kind of impulsive remark you think you hear something in—then spend months convincing yourself it was all in your imagination. For a flickering instant, I suspected she must once have carried a hidden torch for the guy.

"I never heard of him," Tina said.

"Anything's possible," I said, trying to clear my head, which had undergone more jolts in less than a day than it had in the previous three decades. "If you can believe it, Harry seems never to have heard of you."

"Not *that* possible," Allie said, glancing at me. "Either side of it.... I hadn't spent a week on campus before I knew who both of them were.... I mean, how could I help it? The two of them were legends in the hallowed halls."

"I don't think Bail spent a lot of time in those environs," I said. "Unless the halls you're talking about are those old lobby corridors down in the Red Rooster. And I doubt if Tina spent many of her nights in The Weathered Nut." I turned to her for confirmation.

"The weathered what?" she said, her long eyelashes blinking.

Allie stared at her for a moment, then turned away.

Despite my scouring of the alumni bulletins, I knew even less than Harry did about where she had been the past thirty years—the uncharted roads she had traveled. But it was apparent there had been a lot of them. The high prairie sun exposed the hard miles in her face.

She remained one of the most attractive women I had ever seen.

"This is hopeless," she snorted. "Nine. Eight.... I still don't know how many of you boys we're dealing with."

"Let's take it one by one. Shoe, you're here—at least physically. So is Harry. And Mare's apparently out there somewhere—doing something—being Mare. In deference to Tina, I won't ask you what it is. Then there's our Knight Errant. I assume he's with you, since it was his message that worked its way to me.... That's four of you. Who else?"

"The Fat Man," I said. "Bookie. Big Stick.... And then there's your favorite double-play combination.... Not to ruin your day."

For several seconds she didn't respond—simply stared up the street at the phone booth.

"That's nine," she finally acknowledged. "A full lineup." She turned again toward Tina, rolling her eyes.

"Think of it," she said. "All that testosterone.... Eighteen old balls.... Eighteen, at least, if you're willing to give Mare the benefit of the doubt."

She looked back at Harry.

"I'm afraid you've lost a step, Bail. I hope you're not still trying to do your own income taxes. There definitely seem to be nine of you schlepping around here—not eight."

"That ain't what you asked me," he said.

"What isn't?"

"How many of us are here now—settin' around on our rears."

"Sure it is."

"No it ain't.... You asked me how many of us rolled up in the *Lobby*. And there wasn't but eight of us what come in that way."

"The *Lobby*?"

"Don't ask," I said. "All he means is that nine of us started out in South Fork, but by the time we got this far we'd...how can I put it diplomatically...we'd encouraged one of our number to avail himself of a short sabbatical. Technically, he's right. Only eight of us arrived in the van."

"Who'd you dump?"

As she nibbled her lip contemplatively, I realized the answer wasn't quite as obvious as I'd assumed. Even back in '64, if we'd had a Pain-in-the-Ass Award, we wouldn't exactly have been shy of candidates. I finally nodded down the street toward the phone booth, which showed no sign of going unoccupied anytime soon.

"The Blademan," she said.

"You got it."

I'd just begun to update her on his exploits—when she suddenly put her hand on my shoulder and stepped into the street. Bookie was descending the church steps—alone—and she trotted on toward the square to meet him. Harry and I watched, nudging each other in the ribs, barely containing ourselves until the inevitable moment when she came into the centerfielder's ken. Neither of us spoke, but it was clear we were both anticipating his stunned reaction to the big-muscled biker in the red leather pants.

We kept waiting.

And waiting.

The two met next to the water tower. Nonchalantly hugged. Then began chatting as if they'd chanced on each other walking to the local grocery store.

"I don't get it," I said.

"They must of seen each other lately," Harry said, caught as off-guard as I was but recovering with his characteristic dispatch. "Don't su'prise me much. She was always the damndest one for knowin' people— goin' places—of anybody I ever seen."

I wasn't satisfied.

"Tina," I said, stepping toward her. "Has Allie been someplace recently where she might have run into Book?"

"Who?" she said, the doe-eyes widening.

"Sorry.... *Aris*. You know. Aristus Clark."

"I don't know what you're talking about. I've never heard of him. *Dommage*."

I looked away. The pair under the tower showed little sign of returning. I decided to try a different tack.

"What have you been up to, Tina?" I ventured as delicately as I could. "I have to confess.... I was a little surprised to see you pull up on... on a motorcycle... with Allie. As I remember from my one year at Tabelard, you weren't exact—...you didn't quite seem the type back then."

She frowned, and her body stiffened.

"What exactly are you asking me?" she said.

Unthinkingly, I rephrased the question—blurted a *"What do you do now?"*—knowing even as the words turned to stone on my lips that they would not—*could* not—seem simply conversational to a woman. Asking a man what he did carried little more freight than inquiring what part of the country he'd grown up in. I'd foolishly loosed a lot more loaded set of possibilities here.

"What do I do?" she pounced. "How does one answer that?.... I do a number of things."

"What's your occupation?" I scrambled. "That's all I meant by it.... If it's not being too intrusive to ask."

Her expression left no doubt that it had been. She appraised me coolly for several seconds before turning away.

"I own Virgin Blush Cosmetics.... You've probably never heard of us."

She was right. I nodded noncommittally—and plunged on. "Did you meet Allie through your business?"

"I knew Allison at Tabelard," she said icily. "It wasn't a question of *'meeting'* her. We weren't close back then, of course.... We were too different. But we're *women*.... We had contact."

She emphasized the last two syllables as if administering a history lesson. It irritated me more than it should have—a touchiness she clearly noticed as I went on.

"I believe *'meet'* can mean 'a chance encounter'," I said testily. "Has been known to convey the sense of bumping into someone accidentally.... But I'm a man. An old jock. It's ninety percent certain that I'm mistaken. Permit me to rephrase the question.... How did you and Allie happen to come together for this trip?"

I hadn't set out either to act like a prig or to irritate her, but I'd succeeded at both.

"I'd rather not answer that, if you don't mind," she snapped, stepping into the street.

The centerfielder and the woman in question still stood by the water tower. Tina kept walking. Bookie smiled and nodded politely when she reached them, holding out his hand. My antagonist seemed to shake it hesitantly—nervously—whether out of diffidence or continuing annoyance I was too far away to tell. The three of them chatted briefly, then drifted back toward us—Tina's right arm looped under Allie's left bicep. Catching my eye, she let the ringed, manicured fingers slip downward and clasp the biker's unresisting palm.

"Alchemy," I murmured.

"Whats'at?" Harry mumbled.

"It has to be alchemy.... Some kind of mystical hocus-pocus.... Nothing else could have changed her that much."

"You're talkin' about Allie, I gather," he said, "though I ain't never heard nobody call her—what the hell was that name again? *'Alkie? Alk'nie?*.... I can't believe you don't recollect her real name's *'Allison'*."

"Whatever her name is, she's changed," I said. "Remember how she used to feel about Tina?.... Outside of Pisser and Pinchbeck, nobody else in the school inspired so many of her shticks."

"I don't recollect 'em," he croaked. "Like I said before, I never heard of that Teener woman. But I can still see Allie usin' that stick you're talkin' about on the Pinchpecker's backside. Funny as hell when she got it goin'. Damn near beat killin' snakes."

"*Shtick*," I corrected him.

"That's what I said.... *'Stick!'*.... It's a Yiddish word.... Little fact I don't guess you ever run up against. Comes out o' the show bi'ness. They used to—"

He ground to a stop. Squinted at me. "Why the hell you gawkin' at me like that?"

"Sorry," I backpedaled. "It's just that...I have to confess...it surprises me—the depth of your cultural erudition. Must be all that time you spent in the bowers of academia. I guess a lot more things rubbed off than I'd realized."

"You talkin' 'bout Tabelard?" he growled.

"Sure."

He sluiced a stream of tobacco juice over the curb, then wedged the cigar stub deeper between his molars.

"Don't be such a shenozzle," he said. "I learned a hell of a lot o' things back in them years, all right—but they damn sure wasn't in your halls of acanemia. I picked up my Yiddish from Jan."

Across the street, Allie, Tina, and Bookie had sat down on the park bench we'd vacated. Tina had shed her jacket. Her hand was still cradled inside Allie's arm.

"I never understood that," I said, turning away. "Jan, I mean.... How he wound up at a place like Tabelard.... People came there from all over the country, sure. But you could have leafed through a closet full of files in the Admissions Office and not come across more than a half-dozen Bees who weren't full-blooded WASPs. Then there was Jan.... Stuck out here in the plains."

"I told you dildos all 'bout that earlier. He wound up buyin' himself a ranch here. Don't look to me like he thought of it as bein' *'stuck'.*"

I didn't respond—was looking at Allie laughing—at her mesmerizing face turned up toward the sun. It seemed to radiate warmth.

"I didn't know Jan very well," I plowed on. "Didn't really know him at all, I suppose, if you come down to it.... All I mean is...there must have been times he got awfully lonely out here."

The old coach slowly raked his toe across a crack in the sidewalk.

"Sure there was," he said. 'Specially at the beginnin'. Before he knew he was gonna get a chance to play a little ball for me. It was baseball brought him here...and baseball kept him here.... I know that for a fact."

"He came from Brooklyn," I murmured—which is a non sequitur only if you were born after 1955.

Harry didn't respond. Turned away and peered down the puddled street, past the still occupied corner phone booth. Mare was shambling toward us, three or four blocks away.

"He come from Brooklyn," the old coach repeated softly. "Where once on a time they used to play ball."

Chapter 12

A door creaked open down the street.
I turned as Donnie stumbled out of the cafe, rubbing his eyes in the sunlight, a candy bar in his hand.
"Looks like the flock is recongregating," I said.
Harry checked his watch. "We ain't got that dildo off the telephone yet," he grumbled. "And God only knows how long the Preacher's gonna be hunkered down over in that church." He waggled a horny thumb toward the far side of the square.
"Then there's the Badger.... Who knows what the hell that crazy bustard is up to?" The thumb jerked toward the tavern door Curt had disappeared through half an hour earlier. My sense organs followed it. The bar's walls were throbbing to the punishing strings of an electric guitar.
Donnie trotted up beside us, breathing heavily, the half-devoured candy bar clutched in his pudgy palm.
"I ain't gonna ask what took you so long," Harry groused, glancing at his stomach. "You finally get enough to eat?"
The old receiver ignored the jibe. "We got a game!" he huffed breathlessly—seemingly oblivious that the stick of chocolate had begun to melt in his hand.
Through a full season of playing with him, I had seen Donnie this excited only once—the rapturous moment he'd leaped on me a few seconds after my nose crossed home plate the afternoon we'd finally broken the losing streak. I had no idea what had transported him this time, but I edged back up the sidewalk—remembering what it felt like when his gelatinous girth came down.
"You what?" Harry said, dumbfounded.
"I got us a game!.... This afternoon at three.... It's all set. I told 'em we'd play."
"What the Sam Hill?" Harry sputtered. "Told who we'd play? And who's 'we'?.... What the hell you gone and done?"
Donnie took a deep breath, about to explain—then suddenly lurched off the curb into the street as if I'd shoved him. The two women were approaching, just ahead of Bookie—all of them clearly curious to see what the excitement was about.
"That's *Allie!*" the catcher murmured incredulously. "And *Tina!.... Tina Egland!*"
He stumbled on to the other side—where he produced the kind of theatrics Harry and I had expected when Bookie had approached the

new arrivals a few minutes earlier. But this time neither of us paid much attention. We had a more pressing matter at hand.

"He's got us *'a game'*," I said, turning to face him.

"Them's the words you heard too?"

We stared at each other, shaking our heads.

"What do you think it means?" I went on, glancing again across the street, where Allie appeared to be showing the receiver some creative ways of flexing her biceps. I couldn't see Donnie's face. He stood knock-kneed, pitched slightly forward, like a child peering through a toy store window. It wasn't hard to remember him crouching behind the plate three decades earlier, decked out in his catcher's togs.

"May not mean nothin'," Harry mumbled unconvincingly. "He was the damndest fella I ever saw for always wantin' to be playin' somethin' with somebody, somewhere. Most likely he found himself a pinball machine in that rest'rant.... Way he's actin', must be one what don't register tilt."

"If it doesn't tilt for Donnie," I said, "they're giving away a hell of a lot of free games."

We watched as the reunion in the square continued—the catcher once again growing animated as the shock of the women's appearance dissipated. His toes tapped. The round body bobbed. The short arms flapped at his hips like the stubby wings of a penguin. When I saw Bookie's brow begin to wrinkle, I hooked Bail by the arm.

"We gotta get over there," I said. "I think he's telling them the same thing he just told us."

Bookie's hand brushed over the top of his head as we approached. His open mouth closed—then opened again without speaking. The syllables that did reach my ear came from Allie, and they drifted toward us like the beads of sweat trickling down my spine. *You've got to be kidding"* were some of them. So were *"At your age? You guys?... Right here?"*

Tina hung next to her, looking bored.

A queasiness was rising in my stomach by the time we reached them. Donnie was bouncing on his toes.

"—said it while I was sitting beside him," he jabbered. "This big ugly guy, eating liver and onions, swearing a blue streak at this little waitress.... I couldn't understand most of what he was saying, but I could tell he was a big fan. He kept bitchin' about how bad this team he likes has been playin'.... The 'Devils', I think it was."

"This is the bunch you want us to play?" Bookie groaned.

"No, no! They're just some high school team. That's what I was tellin' you—this guy's a big fan. He was just talkin' about the Devils because they lost to somebody who played so bad they couldn't of beat his old lady." The catcher suddenly caught himself—glanced quickly at the two women at his side. "That's how *he* put it, I mean.... I told you, he's this real ugly guy. Always cussin' and shoutin' and carryin' on.... You'll see."

"What do you mean, *'You'll see'?"*, I jumped in. "I don't plan to get near the guy.... Come on. Mare's coming. He's not going to stick around here forever. Let's shag Curt and Me out of the bar, try to rope in Stick and Pisser, and hit the road."

Allie had noticed Mare, who was still a block up the street, a half-second before I mentioned him. She took a quick step—as if about to go meet him—then turned back to Pierce.

"We *can't* go," he pleaded, turning to her for support. "You don't understand. They brought it up first. Called us a bunch of pussies. Looked out the window and said they hadn't ever seen such a crew of losers in their life.... I mean, we've got to!.... It's all set!"

There was desperation in the sweat-beaded face—a supplication that approached abjectness in the round, imploring eyes.

Bookie stepped nearer.

"Calm down a second," he said gently. "You're right. We don't understand. You need to back up a little—fill us in on most of all this you've been describing. Who you mean by 'we'. Who you want to play. Why it's so important to play them. That's a start, anyway. What others have I missed?" He looked at the rest of us, hoisting his brows.

"I'm not even sure *what* you want to play," I said. "I assume it's baseball."

"That's right!"

Profound relief flooded the catcher's face. He looked at me as if I'd just defused a bomb.

"Who'd be playin'?" Harry said, getting interested.

The catcher's eyes blinked so slowly it appeared he was trying to deconstruct the words. "Us," he finally said. "The team.... All of us guys that made the trip over here.... It'd be just like the old days."

"I hope not," Allie chipped in, moaning. "Some of us have suffered enough."

"And you was only there a couple years," Harry added, squinting at her. "'Magine what the hell it was like for me."

The sun had gotten so bright, so warm, that the sandy ground under our feet showed almost no sign of having been rained on. A baseball game was conceivable—at least with respect to the weather. But that was the only way I could conceive of it.

It was clear to me that—aside from Donnie—no one else in the crowd could imagine it either. Or maybe it was that we were *too* imaginative. Glancing at Allie, I sensed she was having the same apocalyptic vision I was—a diamond filled with wheezing, potbellied bodies lurching like bumper cars into various postures of cardiac arrest.

139

Bookie's dark orbs reflected even direr nightmares—no doubt visualizing how much ground he'd once had to cover playing between the line-hugging Jan Merchant and our resident Solomite. And that had been thirty years earlier, when both of them were still alive—although most games no one would have guessed it watching Big Stick. I took a second look at the centerfielder, trying to read him—wondered how it must feel to envision a baseball game in which he'd have to run down every ball that made it to the outfield grass.

None of it mattered to Donnie.

"Listen," he said, flapping his hands higher, "We can beat these guys— I'm tellin' ya. I've seen a couple of 'em.... We can beat these guys like a drum."

"*What* guys?" I yelped, suddenly out of patience. 'You still haven't told us who they *are*—these Devils or Saints or Angels you were lunatic enough to agree to play!"

He rolled his eyes.

"The Devils are some *high* school team.... I told you that. And I never said anything about any Angels or Saints."

Bookie cleared his throat. "I think Jeff's just being hypothetical. Spinning out possibilities.... Writers are like that."

"Shoeoff's a *writer*?" Allie said, smiling wickedly. "Who would have thought it? I *am* impressed."

"I'm not a writer," I said, blushing. "I went on the wagon a long time ago."

"He's a pote," Harry threw in. "Leastways, he used to be. Curt showed me one of them cards he wrote eight or ten year ago. I ain't no expert, but it looked to me like damn good po'try. I saved it and give it to Goodie when her next birthday come up."

"I'm even more impressed," Allie crooned. "By *both* of you.... Shoe's a published author. And you remembered the birthday of your wife."

The coach bit down on his cigar. "Damn lot of good it did me," he said. "Wadn't but a week later she had me sleepin' on a cot in the den."

"*What guys?*" I repeated to Donnie, ignoring them. "Who did you agree to play?"

"Well, I guess you'd.... I don't.... I can't exactly tell you who they are. I only talked to two of them. But the thing's on—I know that for sure. I set it all up with that real ugly guy—the one eatin' the liver and onions. He's their manager, their head honcho.... I think he might even try to play a little. Big pimply guy. Got a kind of raspy, croaky voice—like he's done more than his share of boozing. I'd be lyin' to you if I said I liked him.... But hey, who has to like 'em, right?.... How many of the Christians liked the lions?.... *We got a game!"*

'What's happenin'?"

The dulcet words floated like a puff of Acapulco Gold over my left shoulder. I didn't need to turn around. Mare had drifted in.

He shuffled past me, mumbling a quiet "Als" as he nodded almost imperceptibly at Allie—whose return nod was just as nonchalant. The two of them might have been next-door neighbors who saw each other every afternoon out weeding their flower gardens but didn't particularly get on.

Allie glanced at Tina before I could read anything more in her face. I looked away, a little woozy—turned back to Mare.

"I'll tell you what's happening," I grunted. "Donnie's got us a game.... Three o'clock this afternoon.... You'll be on the hill."

I waited expectantly. It was time to put an end to the whole screwball notion. The guy was wearing a two-thousand dollar suit, and the size of his paunch argued that the last rubber he'd stood on was somebody's welcome mat back in the days when he peddled his wares door to door.

"Gnarly," he said.

Even Donnie was stunned—a silence that lasted about three-quarters of a second.

"*See?*" the catcher shouted. "Lefty wants it! He's gotta have it! Got to get that old soupbone crankin'! Gonna go out there and start puttin' up those goose-eggs.... Sawin' those bats off.... Ridin' that K-brand back home to the barn!"

"Good God," Allie said, turning to Tina, who looked up briefly, then went back to filing her nails.

"You really want to *do* this?" I stammered to Mare.

The pitcher tongued his Gauloise into the corner of his mouth—blew a thin stream of smoke toward the horizon. "I can still bring it," he mumbled. "Let's get it on."

For the next five minutes, old Bees buzzed around the issue with a sense of urgency I hadn't witnessed since the Watergate hearings. Curt had finally returned from the bar, steering Me ahead of him—the latter's vocal cords in roughly the same wobbly condition as his appendages. Filtering out the blue notes, I managed to decipher enough to conclude that the old second-baseman was not only ready to play—he was willing to coldcock the first one of us who raised an objection. I began to rethink my own position. Saw a few things in Donnie's argument I had overlooked.

Curt hadn't signed on yet either—but neither had he declined. After registering his own speechless shock at our pair of leather-clad recent arrivals, he extended them a courtly welcome—then turned his attention to the matter under debate. The rest of us listened intently. We all knew it was his vote—the seal of the captain—that Donnie had to have if he was going to prevail.

"The idea does strike me as a bit quixotic," the lawman began, "and yet the world must surely still have a place for Quixotes.... Our Don here seems to have had something of a vision—reconstituting the old team to enter the lists again in quest of some of the old feats of arms."

His eyes moved from face to face. I followed them. What I didn't follow was what the hell he was talking about.

"And I do feel compelled to add," he went on, "without pointing any accusatory fingers—that over the last few hours, we've hardly covered ourselves with renown."

He stared up the street, toward the bony figure still crouched in the phone booth—then shook his head morosely and went on.

"Playing creditably at our age would be difficult, of course—that's a given. But I for one have always believed that difficulty is what makes a challenge worth accepting.... Donald's had a dream.... I don't think an impossible dream. And it might prove therapeutic for all of us to entertain it in the long run. But I come from Arizona....

"Desert country," he added—pausing as the rest of us looked at each other in bewilderment. "Perhaps it's made me more receptive to dreamers...visionaries...and more aware of how fragile even the noblest dreams can be."

When he ended, his eyes were fixed on the black man at my side.

Bookie stared back at him. He looked surprised—but not confused. Allie was faintly smiling. Donnie stood slack-jawed, peering at the rest of us, his round face moving back and forth trying to pick up a clue.

"Count me in," the centerfielder quietly said.

Curt slowly nodded—turned toward me.

"How about you, Jeffrey?.... Thumbs up? Or down?"

I was still staring at Bookie. I didn't react for some time.

"I'll take a shot at filling Jan's slot in left," I finally stammered. "Just don't ask me to stand in for Hotplate.... where the shots come back the other way."

"Harry?" Curt continued, patting me reassuringly on the arm.

Bail reacted as if a snake had bitten him.

"*Wha* — ? Me? What the hell you boys thinkin'? I'm too goddam old to—"

The captain cut him off—laid the reassuring paw on the old mentor's shoulder. "We don't expect you to *play,* Coach," he said. "Just handle what has to be done in the dugout.... The same way you used to. That will do fine."

The exhalation of relief from the leathery lungs might have fluttered the flag outside the barbershop.

"Hell yes," he barked. "You bustards crazy enough to go out there in your condition—I'll damn sure do whatever I can for you settin' on the goddammed bench."

"*Plus ça change,*" Allie said, winking.

"*Dommage,*" Tina chimed in.

"Fuckanay."

The last word was Mare's. Having contributed it, he shrugged his slouching shoulders and headed across the grass to the park bench, where he shed his resplendent coat and stretched out like a sated seal in the sun.

Curt studied him for a few seconds, then turned away. Clasping Donnie's hand, he put his official imprimatur on the decision.

"Fine," he said. "It's all set, then. We take the field this afternoon at three."

"That only gives us a half an hour," Harry announced, winding his watch.

"Good luck," I said, nodding to Curt. "I assume it's the captain's job to assemble the crew, and we're still short at least one body. Even that may be optimistic. If Pisser and Wick stay A.W.O.L., you'll have to come up with three."

"I don't get you," Donnie said.

"Figure it out. I'll try to muddle through in left, but even if we extract Blade from that phone booth and somehow manage to get Big Stick to put an amen on his devotionals, we still don't have a third baseman.... Who's going to fill in for Plate?"

"I hadn't thought of that," Donnie said, his hands plunging into his pants pockets. Dead silence engulfed everybody else.

Allie suddenly burst out laughing.

"As my old mentor here used to put it—listen at 'em, Sugar," she said, nudging Tina. "Did I hit it on the head—what I told you this morning? What we'd see if we managed to find them, out here in their native habitat?.... Take a look. Here they are in full display. Blinking their eyes. Scratching their crotches. Wracking their brains trying to figure out where they're going to come up with another baseball player.... It doesn't occur to a single one of them that you don't need a penis to stand around for two hours in the sun."

Nobody who could claim possession of the expendable organ responded. Mare lay on the bench snoring. The rest of us shuffled our feet in silence, waiting for her to go on.

She didn't.

"What exactly are you suggesting?" Curt finally risked.

"Call it a revolution, Sweetie.... Let's get some new blood in the old team."

Donnie glanced up the street as if he thought a young Devil were about to roll in on the next grain truck—then suddenly divined her meaning. He could have tripped over his tongue.

"*You* want to play for us?" he gasped.

He was a sitting duck—dead in the water.

To her credit, Allie kept her scarlet wraps over the heaviest guns. "*'For* you' isn't quite how I'd put it, sweetheart.... Try '*with'*."

"You want to play with us?" he repeated.

"Don't make it sound like an obscenity," she retorted. "And try to control yourself.... You'll wind up dreaming dreams wilder than the ones you've already got floating around in your brain."

Clouds formed in the open sky of the catcher's forehead. Harry staggered across the sidewalk behind him. "Lord have mercy," he croaked.

Bookie took a step toward her.

"Sounds fine to me," he said dryly. "I assume it's yourself you have in mind to play third.... Not Tina.... Correct me if that's another phallocentric stereotype."

"It is," she said. "But we have to start somewhere. As it happens, I am the one who's willing to anchor the left side of your infield."

"If there's one thing this bunch don't need, it's any more *anchorin'*," Bail Bond puffed—sufficiently recovered from the jolt to his synapses to risk bantering with her. "Put you over there in the Lobby with the rest of these lard buckets, I'm gonna need a new set of shocks."

He winked at her—then jerked a beetling eyebrow in my direction. "Couple of 'em gonna be damn lucky if they can bend over far enough to tie their shoelaces...let alone chase down a batted ball."

"If Mare's still got the stuff he seems to think he has," I countered, "Donnie's going to be the one doing most of the chasing. Anyway, Bookie will be out there with me. All I plan to do is stay out of his way."

"I'm not going to be out there with you unless somebody finds me a glove," the centerfielder responded. "That's something else we seem to have forgotten.... Whose equipment are we going to use?"

All of us turned toward Donnie, whose sweat-beaded brow grew even more overcast. "I don't know," he fumbled. "I thought.... I guess I just.... I don't know."

"'Quipment ain't a problem," Harry rescued him. "These other fellas got bats, ain't they? And balls. And gloves enough for ever' fieldin' position. That's most of it. Come the end of an inning, alls you do is toss your glove on the grass and leave it out there—the way we did it back when I was playin' the game.

"Only other thing you need is some catchin' gear—and if I recollect, I still got some of that stored away over in the Lobby. Got it tucked away back in the rear."

"*All right!*" Donnie whooped, taking three or four eager steps across the street.

The rest of us stayed put.

"What is this '*Lobby*' you keep talking about?" Allie asked.

"It's his van," I told her. "Bail's sanctuary. The place he spends most of his time when he and Goodie fall a tad shy of domestic accord."

She followed my gaze. The van's mud-splattered, crinkled sides resembled the skin of a doddering rhino. The radio antenna was a bent clothes-hanger wrapped with aluminum foil.

She turned back to me.

"They won't let him have his old cell in the jail?" she said.

Harry mumbled something incomprehensible, then shuffled off on the heels of Donnie. We watched as the two of them opened the rear door and began pawing through the pile of detritus behind the back seat.

The first thing to hit the ground was a duck decoy. It was followed by a tangled nest of tackle-box innards, a trio of rusted railroad spikes dangling in their wake. Next came a ripped pair of chest waders. Half a dozen corroded flashlight batteries. A heel-less cowboy boot smeared with camouflage paint.

Several unidentifiable items followed.

As the pile in the van gradually diminished, the one on the street rose steadily higher:

A Mason jar half-full of pickles. A withered orange. The broken arm of a lug wrench. Long underwear bottoms split in the seat.

The moving fingers dug on. The pile by Donnie's knees climbed toward his belt:

The shriveled residue of two more oranges. A cracked Louisville Slugger—black electrical tape sheathing its splintered handle. The petrified residue, even blacker, of what looked to be still another piece of fruit.

"Good God," Allie said, stepping closer. "I have measured out my life with orange peels."

"Only the ones that haven't stuck in the cuffs of his trousers," Bookie said. "Don't be surprised if he gets down to peach pits and oyster shells in a minute or two."

He did—just after he tossed out what was either a coonskin cap or the last remains of a roadkill.

Donnie stood quietly at his side, looking more and more dispirited. Finally the groping hand reappeared—clutching an elastic strap entangled in tattered green mesh.

Bail backed up a step, tugging at it. The handle of a fishing net gradually emerged from the carnage. He tugged some more, and the pile suddenly yielded—exposed an antique chest protector's corrugated ribs. Still more stretching of the moldy elastic produced a wire mask, its broken buckles dangling from stiff, sweat-cracked leather. It was so black he might have hauled it from the La Brea tar pit.

Pausing just long enough to catch his breath, the coach rummaged through the treasures that remained until he came out with one last artifact: a battered shin guard ancient enough it could have done time as one of Hector's greaves.

"Forget what I said earlier," Bookie nudged me. "I'll play without a glove if I have to—just to see the Fat Man climb into that gear."

Harry was already reloading, restocking the Lobby's depleted stores with the same care that had obviously gone into its provisioning. He waved an impatient paw at Donnie, who dropped his newly acquired armour on the sidewalk and staggered a dazed step forward to pitch in.

The job took less than a minute. When they had finished, Harry summoned the rest of us to his side.

"Time we got a goin'," he muttered as we reached him. "Gotta get over there and get loosened up."

"The hell you say," Me slurred, his red hair as spiky as wet hen hackle across his cranium. "I'm loose as a goddammed goose already.... Where are the fuckers? We're gonna kick their ass."

He tottered toward the driver's seat, fumbling in his pants for the keys.

"Now hold on, Robin!" Curt protested, stepping forward to restrain him—stopping only when Bail jingled the key-ring in his ear.

"Oh.... Very good," he sighed in relief. "Harry will be driving.... He's the only one of us," he added diplomatically, "who knows how to get to the field.

"But we're not quite prepared to go yet.... Some of our number still aren't here."

He turned toward the square.

"Arden!" he shouted. "We're boarding.... You'll want to warm up before the game begins."

Mare yawned, opened his eyes and stretched—draped the designer coat over his shoulders as he ambled toward us.

"How do you feel?" Donnie asked as he slouched by.

"I'm stoked," the pitcher mumbled, climbing through the open door.

Curt turned to Bookie. "Any headway with Wickliff?" His eyes rose toward the church spire, where a pair of pigeons drowsed in the sun.

"He seemed to want to spend a little more time with the Big Fella," the scholar murmured. "We can pick him up as we drive by."

He appeared abstracted—stood shaking his head as he peered through the van's mud-streaked rear window. "At least that's what I think he said," the centerfielder added. "I'm not as familiar with the King James Version as I once was."

The captain nodded, stepping off the curb. He plodded a few feet up the street in the direction of the phone booth.

"And then there's Oswald," he sighed, shaking his head.

It was as close to sarcasm as I'd ever heard the good man come.

"That's the Lizard up there?" Me bellowed, overhearing him. He staggered past us, squinting in the sun.

"I wondered where that little shit's been hidin'," he added. "What happened to him?.... He couldn't find a rock big enough to crawl under back where we dumped him on the road?"

"I suppose I'll have to try it once more," Curt murmured, ignoring him. "Perhaps he's cooled down a little.... But it's hard to be sanguine about the prospects. He was pretty exercised when I spoke to him before."

I stared at my feet.

It was a job I wouldn't have foisted on a stray dog. Yet I didn't have it in me to offer to relieve him. No one else moved either. Me shouted a crude negotiating strategy in his wake.

The lawman had taken half a dozen steps up the street—when Allie suddenly brushed past me.

"Wait," she piped. "I'll do it.... Give me a couple of minutes.... It shouldn't take more than that."

She was wrong. But not by much. She had the shortstop out of the booth, trudging gloomily toward the van, before Curt had managed to get our loaded second-sacker loaded. Pisser climbed past him into the rear without a word.

"How did you *do* that?" I whispered as she passed me on the way back to her motorcycle. "I don't believe wha—"

"Experience, Sugar," she crooned, fluttering her eyelashes. "Nobody's had more experience with men than I have."

I didn't doubt her, but it wasn't good enough.... It had to be alchemy. Nothing less could have gotten the job done.

Chapter 13

If Donnie had in fact had a dream, the field on the east edge of Jerome was as rough a diamond as he could have chosen to see it materialize.

"*Oot there?*" Pisser groaned as we splashed to a stop between a mudhole and a ramshackle row of wooden bleachers. "You got another think comin', ay. I'll sit this one oot."

"Ah, cut the whining!" Me shouted from the front. "It's the same damn field for them other assholes. What the hell difference does it make?"

For once I sided with my roommate. The place was the sorriest excuse for a baseball park I had ever seen.

My eyes were drawn first to the outfield, a hummocked expanse of virgin prairie that looked as if it still held wagon ruts from the Oregon Trail. It was ringed by the sagging remnants of what once must have been a snow fence—but served now as a baffle for tumbleweeds and windblown shreds of paper. A herd of Herefords grazed just beyond it, less than thirty yards from the pocky hillock where I had insanely agreed to man a post.

The infield was even less inviting. Its only grass sprouted in a marshy bog fish could have called home halfway between home plate and the pitcher's rubber. The higher patch of ground around second base was just the opposite—sun-baked as hard and unforgiving as the grassy fen was soggy and dark. The basepaths hadn't been dragged for a decade. I'd seen rock quarries with fewer stones.

Surveying it, even Me stayed put—as did all of the rest of us. We were still sitting in the van, gaping, when Allie's motorcycle pulled up by the driver's door.

Harry rolled down his window.

"I don't like the look o' this," he said to her. "You better forget about playin'.... This ain't no place for a woman to be out there foolin' around."

"I don't intend to be fooling," she countered. "If those guys can handle it," she nodded toward us, "so can I."

"But you ain't had no...no *'xperience*...'specially playin' on a field what's as bad as this one. Folks can get hurt playin' ball!"

Allie looked away—toward the cluster of cattle grazing outside the snow fence. The nearest had fed in so close its heavy jaws poked through a pair of broken slats, heavily munching. Its pink tongue stretched for a tuft of grass just beyond its reach.

Turning back, the biker slowly took off her helmet and handed it to her companion—then walked just as deliberately toward the third-base dugout. Tina stared at us frostily for a moment, then slipped off the Harley too. Cradling the helmet like a swaddled infant, she marched past the van and sat down in the front row of the rickety bleachers. Her own headgear remained strapped over her frosted hair.

"She's actually gonna do it," Donnie murmured incredulously. "A game of ball." Whether he was referring to Allie playing—or Tina watching—I wasn't sure. For most of us, the latter was probably harder to conceive.

We were climbing out to follow them when the pop of exhaust pipes and the clank of metal sounded from the street directly behind us. A van even older than Harry's bounced through the puddles past the gate—followed by a pair of rusting pickups. Engines coughing, all three screeched to a clattering halt behind the first-base dugout, their occupants filling the air with yawps and curses as they piled out. Through the dusty glass of the rear windows, the forks of a gun rack were barely visible behind a flag-draped thicket of rifle-clutching talons, beaks, and eagle wings.

Three fresh bumper stickers graced the rear end of the pickup nearest us.

One said *Better Dead Than Fed*. Another read *Where's Lee Harvey When We Need Him?* The last one had two inscriptions: *Set Back the Wetbacks* and *Nobody Had a Goddammed Green Card Inside the Alamo*.

As we stood gaping, a shaggy-haired pair of players scrambled over the tailgate and began tossing bats, balls, and other equipment onto the rutted field.

The whole crew were of wildly different shapes and ages, and were dressed in a grab-bag assortment of uniforms all of which looked to be of even older vintage than Donnie's antediluvian gear. Five or six had '*MANIACS*' stitched to their backs. A few others sported '*RAVENS*'. One, who looked to be the oldest, combined the two in a slightly less ragtag sweatshirt with '*RAVEN MANIACS*' emblazoned across his barrel chest. From the drill-sergeant volume of his yelps, I assumed he was the manager—the liver-and-onion man Donnie had somehow got hooked up with in the restaurant. But I wasn't sure. Donnie had described him as a *"real ugly guy"*—an epithet that could fairly have been applied to any of them. The most presentable—and I say this charitably—would have ranked among the most ill-favored human beings I had ever seen.

It was the kind of unnatural selection that leads you to conclude it could only have evolved from several generations of in-breeding—a collective cloning of slack jaws, sloping foreheads, flat, pimpled faces and crooked teeth. Long after their arrival, I stood planted with my teammates where we'd been standing when they rumbled in—the soles of our shoes rooted to the prairie. Our unbelieving eyes followed as the Raven Maniac, still cawing imperiously, led them onto the field.

"Jesus," Donnie said, crossing himself.
"You arranged for us to play *them?*" I gasped.
He stared at me dolefully, the dented wire mask dangling from his hand.
"I seen some bad lookin' Okies in my time," Harry mumbled, "but I ain't never seen nothin' what looks like that outfit. They'd make a pen full o' peccaries think it was time to go courtin'. And it ain't just that they're ugly...you can tell them bustards are *mean.*"

His anxious eyes moved toward Allie, who was standing on the dugout steps, studying them, the sun gleaming in bright shards off her hip-hugging red leather. A faint, ironic smile creased her face.

Donnie shrugged his shoulders—shuffled back to the van—returned a couple of minutes later with the rest of his equipment. "Strap me into this, will you," he said, handing me the chest protector. His voice had the enthusiasm of a schoolboy thanking a great-aunt for a large helping of squash.

Our bull-necked second-baseman excepted, the rest of my teammates didn't look much happier. They drifted resignedly toward the dugout and plopped down on its rotting timbers, peering intently out at the field.

I began buckling Donnie into his armor. Me stepped by and slapped me on the rear.

"Don't let anything get by you out there," he warned, waggling his finger toward the snowfence. "One or two of those ugly fuckers look like they've got good wheels."

I shot an irritated glance at him as he wobbled past me. He already had on his pre-game glare.

Donnie watched him pass, then sucked in his stomach as I pulled the protector's strap across his bloated back—tried to stretch it toward the crumpled buckle. The skin on his neck was the color of an overcooked beet. When I finally managed to snap the two pieces of rusted metal, the padding stretched across his chest like the pleats on the Michelin Man.

"You're gonna have to hit in that damn thing!" Me bellowed, glancing back over his shoulder. "You ever take it off, Fat Man, you'll never be able to get it back on again." He spat in the sand as he trotted on toward the bench. Donnie watched him, then bent—bent as far as he could bend—and began fumbling with the single guard Harry had found for his shins.

I stood for a moment, listening to him wheezing, then lifted the dented chunk of metal from his hand. "Let me give you some help with this too," I said. "Which leg do you want it on?"

"Left," he gasped.

"What are you going to do about the other one?" I said. "If somebody fouls a pitch off, you're going to be hobbling around moaning for a week."

"I'll kneel."

"You got a cup?" I added.

The receiver froze. I watched as he stared down at his loins—a part of his anatomy he seemed somehow to have forgotten. It was hard to believe. The chances of the old Don Pierce neglecting his privates were about as likely as learning he'd gone on a hunger strike.

"That does it," he croaked. "I can't play."

Mare, who still stood slouching against the van, took a slow, loose-limbed step in our direction. As Donnie struggled to unbuckle the shin guard, the pitcher turned back toward the open door.

"Chill out, man," he muttered. "I got somethin' you can use." Reaching in and sliding his suitcase off the seat, he snapped it open and turned nonchalantly back to the catcher. A pair of black lace panties hung from his hand.

Donnie gaped at them. I gaped at them. They had a wedge of stainless steel sewn into the crotch.

Mare tossed them to the receiver.

"Part of our ProsPerot line. We've started to sell a lot of 'em. They're hot as hell back in L. A."

He didn't explain. Neither of us asked him to. With Mare, there were always more possibilities than you wanted to consider.

Donnie glanced toward the field, blinking—then hastily stuffed the gift into his pocket and headed for a moldering outhouse just beyond the right-field fence.

I was halfway to the dugout, when the pitcher spoke up again.

"Got some other good shit here too," he drawled, digging deeper into his suitcase. "Had these made for you dudes a couple hours after I decided I was flyin' in."

He flipped me a baseball cap. It was white with a blue bill—the old Tabelard colors. On the crown, "THE SPIRIT OF '76" had been inscribed in red letters. Just above them, its stinger drooping, a dead honey bee lay belly-up in the sun.

Draping a set of t-shirts across his arm, the pitcher tossed one my way as he shuffled past, eight or ten of the logoed caps perched precariously above his bleached eyebrows. Reaching the dugout, he dropped them on the numbed pates of our other warriors, then ambled back handing out the shirts. He flipped the last one to Harry, who looked anesthetized. I glanced down to take a closer look at my own.

The cloth itself was standard issue stretchable cotton—the most sensible fabric he could have chosen for a team that would lug as many pounds out onto the diamond as we would. But the shirt's logo was as bizarre as the ones scrawled on the chests of our rivals. All it said—a funky, star-spangled inscription in tri-colored letters—was "_____ *SUCKS*."

I peered again at my teammates, who looked just as befuddled as I was. Hoping for an explanation, I headed for the dugout—arrived just after one of them had obviously asked our peripatetic clothier to explain:

".... so I started free associatin', man. Thinkin' about it. Everybody in the guppin' country thinks somebody sucks, right? Their boss. Dude they happen to be married to. Somebody with a different hairstyle, or way of dressin', or color of skin. Why not give all of 'em a chance to express it? Right there on their shirt front? Make their point as easy as fillin' in a blank with a pen.

"I mean, is this nectar, or is it nectar? Costs about a buck to make. One size fits all. Comes with a Magic Marker that's guaranteed washable ever' time you change it. You can get a fresh blank ever' time you clean the guppin' thing, if that's what turns you on."

He pulled one of the pens from his pocket—handed it to Bail.

"Different target every hour, if that's your kind of guava.... I mean, is this tubular shit, or what."

"You make big money oot of these things?" Pisser rasped, pressing up from the rear.

"Are you churnin' me, man? Christ, I stopped pushin' 'em for awhile—I was sellin' so many of 'em it was gettin' too guppin' easy. We were ridin' the nose on every wave that was breakin'.... Got so it wasn't any fun anymore."

"Tell me more aboot this, ay." The bony frame elbowed past me. "Who do you sell them to?"

Mare paused—peered at him—his eyes so hollow the beam of a flashlight might have penetrated to the back of his skull.

"Where the hell you been, man?" he said. "This is America. You could sell these fuckin' things back where we dumped you on the highway. I could prob'ly make one that said *'Ducks Suck'* and sell a couple of million of 'em to a bunch of geese."

Pisser looked as if he were about to try to lock up the franchise rights for wildlife refuges, when the pitcher went on.

"Only thing I can't figure is why *'SUCKS'* sells so good. I mean, you know... if you start to think about it... start considerin' all the possibilities—how many other things you can do with your bod. Don't get me wrong, I'm not knockin' our SuckCess line. I'm just sayin' it gets a little boring after awhile—doin' the same thing over and over. Lately, I been thinkin' about three or four whole new designs."

Either satisfied with the Suck-option, or simply unable to restrain himself any longer, Pisser abruptly terminated the marketing seminar. Snatching the pen out of Harry's pliant hand, the shortstop ferried his shirt to the far end of the dugout and got down to work. Mare stared at the wiry back for a few seconds, then reached into his pocket and pulled out more marking pens. Me grabbed one and headed for the bench. Curt and Bookie declined. Big Stick was still studying his cap—seemed confused by the moribund Bee on the logo. Allie took it from his hands and propped it gently on his forehead. "Go to the ant, thou slugger," she cajoled him. "Consider his ways, and give us R.B.I.'s."

I wandered off down the right-field foul line, toward where Donnie had just emerged from the teetering outhouse. Approaching me, he looked like the Queen Bee after her toilet—a portly dowager encased in corset ribs and shafts of bone.

"How's it feel?" I said.

He stopped, puffing heavily. Sweat glistened on his bald, hatless head.

"The cup, you mean?"

"All of it.... Looks a little tough to move around in to me."

He raised his arms as high as he could hoist them—tried a slow windmill—then attempted a deep knee bend that stopped several degrees short of a half-crouch. One thing was clear. He wasn't going to miss the lost shin guard. He'd have to catch the entire game on his knees.

"I'll be okay," he said. "I just need to get loosened up."

"You better pray Mare's still got the control he used to have," I said. "And that those guys we're playing are as stupid as they look.... If they start bunting on you, we'll have to find a fork-lift to haul you off the field."

He waddled on to the dugout. I turned toward the diamond, staring out at the team we were about to engage.

Some of them were clearly a lot younger than we were, but they didn't appear to be in much better shape—although it was a comparison akin to likening the size and speed of a mussel to a clam. Aside from Curt, Bookie, and Pisser, almost every player in the park had obviously spent a lot more time working out on ground beef than ground balls. The one advantage I was willing to concede us, after watching them for several minutes, was a slight superiority above the shoulders. Hard as it would have been to believe on the road a couple of hours earlier, we appeared to possess a little higher collective IQ.

I wasn't secure in the conclusion until I watched half of them charge fungoed grounders while the other half took batting practice—a drill that made a mad kind of sense only because they all would have looked better with fewer teeth.

Hoping to get a clearer idea of what we were up against, I edged up to the fence. Leaning against the chickenwire, I scrutinized each of them more closely. If you could overlook their dental condition, most looked like typical small-town beer-swillers who carried the circle brand of a tin of Red Man on their beefy butts.

My eyes drifted back to the one that stood out. Their player-manager. The Raven Maniac.

He was a goon so primevally ugly I wouldn't have been surprised to learn he'd crawled up on a mudflat an hour before.

I was watching him slash one-hoppers at his third baseman—turning the air blue with curses at every one the fielder booted—when another creaking vehicle braked to a stop alongside the bleachers a few feet away. I studied the liver-and-onion man a moment longer, then turned in time to see a stooped old man emerge from a truck so superannuated I thought for a second he'd stepped off the running board.

There was no question he too was a local. Yet unlike the others, he seemed neighborly enough, and it wasn't long before he sauntered over and struck up a conversation. What he had to say in the next few minutes didn't lessen any of my reservations about the road ahead.

Introducing himself as "P. E. DelNessa," he claimed he'd been caretaker of the ballpark as far back as he could remember—a fact that went a long way toward explaining the woeful state of the place. I won't attempt to describe him. Maybe it's enough to say that if he hadn't quite shuffled onto this mortal coil in time to help erect the fences in Eden, he might have been there when they came down. His bib overalls were so threadbare I was tempted to ask him if they'd been sewn by Betsy Ross.

But the old duffer was as informative as he was hoary. In five maundering minutes of creaky garrulousness, he gave me an oral history of the Raven Maniacs that included bonus coverage of the hamlet of Jerome.

The town's early chapters didn't sound much different from those played out in backwaters throughout America: Small farms. A rail line. New businesses that brought a few decades of mushrooming prosperity.

"We had us two banks here once," he boasted. "A drug store with an ice cream parlor. A couple of hardware stores."

All of it began to die in the fifties, he went on to inform me, when television brought "the outside world" to Garden County, and the combination of family cars and what he called "cut-rate prices" funneled the town's newly enlightened shoppers on to "the big city" to the west.

"Denver?" I asked, riding with him.

"Ogallala," he said.

Yet through all the changes, the old man assured me, there was one tradition that had altered only in the swelling numbers who had flocked in on Sunday afternoons to celebrate it. The town had remained a feverish hotbed of baseball—so much so that it had supported not one team, but two.

"Them was the glory days," he intoned elegiacally, his rheumy eyes rising toward a paint-parched grain silo on the horizon. "We had us a bunch of men here back then. Real ones. Men that knew what to do with a piece o' timber in their hands."

He proceeded to fill me in on the exploits of what I took to be a particularly gifted pair of the local worthies—one Walter "Mad Dog" Map, and his cousin, Theo "The Finger" Frastus. It took some gentle nudging to steer him back on the course I wanted him to navigate—the demise of the town's two teams.

According to P. E., one of them drew its diamond warriors mainly from the town itself—and they had marched into battle under the purple rubric "MANIACS." The other, comprised primarily of local farmers, had trotted onto his manicured greensward bearing "RAVENS" as their coat-of-arms. Both had survived "well into the eighties," as he put it (I'm fairly sure he was referring to the decade, not their ages), when so few teams remained in the county they'd ended up with no one but each other left to play. The internecine skirmishes had apparently grown so bloody the town fathers finally decided they had to put a stop to them. Or, in the words of the old groundskeeper—who told me this as he nodded out at a knot of the snaggle-toothed Jeromites elbowing one another in pursuit of a popup—"Got so them fellas was almost killin' each other ever' Sunday, 'spite the fact that they was most of 'em kin."

The last fact—their barnyard bloodlines—seemed to confirm my earlier surmises about their genetics, but *"kin"* struck my ear strangely—didn't quite square with any dialect I'd heard from a native Nebraskan before.

"Where are you from?" I interrupted him. *"DelNessa* doesn't sound local. And yet, from all this stuff you've been telling me, you must have lived in this country most of your life."

"Nope," he said cryptically. "But I lived here long enough."

I waited for him to elaborate.

He didn't.

"What's the story with that guy?" I finally moved on, trying to steer his attention back to the crew working out in front of us. I pointed to the barrel-chested liver-and-onion eater, who stood now in front of our dugout haranguing Harry, whose jabbing cigar was mounting its own counter-attack.

"That's what I was comin' to. Before you started astin' me all of them questions.... He's the head man. Does their pitchin'. But he ain't 'xactly what I'd call a friendly sort."

The last was obvious, but it still unsettled me. I risked one last query before trotting back to join my team.

"Why is his shirt different from everybody else's?" I said.

"'Cause he's the manager," the old man muttered. "Once he was just a Maniac, like all the rest. But when the town made the two teams join up together, they wouldn't let him stay that way if'n he was gonna be the head man for both of 'em. So now he's a Raven Maniac.... They only need one of 'em.... Ever'body else wanted to stay the way they was before."

I reached the dugout just as Bail plopped down on his customary perch at the near end of the bench, his grizzled face crimson with irritation. Everybody else had taken the field for our warmup—using the single ball and blighted assortment of mutilated gloves the liver-and-onion man had apparently agreed to yield.

"What's the deal?" I said to him.

He spat in the dirt.

"I seen my share of bad ones," he groused, "but that Sumbitch is the poorest excuse for a flesh 'n blood critter I ever run up against. If he don't kill us with his breath first, we're in for a hell of a rough ride out there this afternoon."

"What do you mean?" I quavered, not wanting to know.

"First he's not gonna let us use their gloves. Then it's their bats. He even put up a big stink about us takin' five or ten minutes of infield. All that was bad enough. But it wasn't nothin' compared to how he carried on when Allie walked out to third."

"Allie?.... He's got a problem with her playing?"

"I wouldn't call it a problem," the coach said, his voice suddenly turning reflective. "I'd call it the damndest dose of the red ass I ever run across—and I've by god been around a many of 'em in my lifetime.... He's a goddam maniac, is what he is."

I didn't have the heart to ask if he was also a raver. The words had already daunted me enough that all I could produce was a cowed, "What do you think he's going to do?"

The coach glanced at me—then turned his steely gaze back to the diamond, where Bookie was slapping practice grounders with a broken fungo Harry had dug from the rear of his van. The centerfielder chopped one through the bog to Allie, who knocked the ball down with her eye-riveting cleavage—then lobbed it in a high, looping arc across the field. The throw pulled Curt off the bag by ten feet.

Harry shook his head.

"She plays like that, he might not do nothin'. The Sumbitch wants to whip our rear-ends more than he wants anything else. Only way he'd let her on the field at all was when I told him we couldn't field a team without her—had to use her 'spite of the fact she ain't never set foot on a goddammed baseball diamond. It don't take a Ph.D. to know what he's thinkin'.... He's countin' on her err'rs 'n outs."

"But is it true?" I asked.

"Is what true?"

"That Allie ain't nev—...hasn't ever played before."

"How the hell do I know? You got better eyes than I do, and you been oglin' her ever since she pulled up on that mot'rcycle. What's your 'pinion? At least a little of your ganderin' must of been on the way she handles a glove."

"I'm not sure," I weaseled, reddening. "I guess if you want me to be honest—watching the way she's handled it so far—we could start calling her 'Allie Ooops.'

"But she's got a lot of heart," I added. "I wouldn't be surprised if she managed to stop just about anything they hit at her.... I'd say the biggest problem is she doesn't seem to have much of an arm."

"It's them damn weights they've started liftin'," the coach said mournfully. "Bulks 'em up so you can't hardly tell it's a goddam woman you're lookin' at anymore. Even Goodie's been raggin' me for one of them Not'less machines, if you can believe it. Ain't that the nuts? A woman her age. Workin' on her arms and thighs?"

We watched as Bookie hit a double-play ball to Me, who flipped it with a hard flick of the wrist to Pisser. For a pair on the shady side of fifty, they still moved with surprising panache. The shortstop snatched the crotch-high toss just short of second, toed the bag as he turned...then rifled a throw that wobbled like a shuttlecock and died in the dirt less than half-way to first. I looked back at the pivotman. His glove-hand moved faster getting to his shoulder than the ball had on its looping descent to Curt. Yowling in pain, he clutched it as if his arm had fallen off.

"We better pray they don't hit anything to our left side," I said—envisioning my own shot-put lobs from the outfield. "Allie's got a cannon compared to the Blademan. What the hell happened to his wing?"

"Got dislocated," my benchmate muttered. "I told you that. He's got an excuse."

Their warmup finished, our team came trotting off the field as Big Stick and I were trying to loosen up our own throbbing arms, tossing a waterlogged ball wrapped in black electrical tape that Donnie had found behind the outhouse. I dropped it and walked over to the patch of sand in front of the dugout. Our pre-game strategy session appeared about to begin.

"What's the batting order, Coach?" Curt asked.

Harry rolled the end of a fresh cigar between his lips. Struck a match across his thumbnail. Lit it with the slow, nervous attentiveness of a blizzard survivor nursing a wet fire. "Well, boys, the way I—"

"Not all of us are boys," Allie cut him off. "Thank God for that."

"Well...*team*, then," our mentor continued, sighing. He glanced warily at her face.

"Way I see it," he went on, "there's been 'nough goddam things what have changed the last thirty years we'd best not go tinkerin' too much with any of the rest of 'em.... Let's face it...we...we...."

"—managed to lose seventy-six games in a row doin' it the way you always used to do it," Pisser cut him off sourly. "Forget it. We need a new battin' order. One that's got some punch."

"Damned straight," Me added, appearing for a moment to agree with him. "Let's get the Lizard up in the clean-up slot. He'll give us some punch.... If we get lucky, the little dickhead might throw in some judy too."

Pisser fired a rejoinder; the second-baseman counter-attacked; and we spent the next five minutes picking our way through the rubble. Mare's t-shirts didn't help matters—sucking us in deeper—though both of our keystone combatants had outsmarted themselves overreaching for the Muse. Me—who three decades earlier had somehow managed to fail *Drawing I*, the biggest gut-course the college offered—had nonetheless chosen to fill his shirt's free space with what I assumed he intended to be a razor-headed reptile creeping under a toilet bowl. But it was hard to tell. The child-like squiggles were so crudely rendered they could have represented anything from a bratwurst to a zucchini.

Pisser had struck off in the opposite direction—going for verbal rather than pictorial overkill. It was clear he'd thought of so many organisms that sucked, he couldn't bring himself to narrow the list to a manageable handful. His shirt could have filled in for the Rosetta stone—its front covered with minute hieroglyphs illegible from more than a foot away.

Somehow, Curt managed to nudge us toward a temporary ceasefire, and the cold war over the batting order resumed.

Bookie would lead off. A given. His speed remained a threat no matter how low his average might have fallen as his age climbed toward half a century. Me was going to bat second—also a given—Me being Me. Harry plugged Curt in third, which roused another squeal from Pisser, who quieted only because Harry had arrived at the one spot in the order no one with even half a brain could have been curious about. The only person who said anything when the coach announced Big Stick as our clean-up hitter was the glowering Solomite himself.

"Men given to appetite," he declared stonily—his icy orbs trained on a clutch of Jeromites squabbling in their dugout over the last can of a depleted six-pack. "Poised to smite. The cudgel of the Lord."

I wasn't sure whether it was the earthly or the heavenly Big Hitter he had in mind as the cudgel-wielder—or even whether in his own mind there was much of a distinction. I was just glad he was staring across the diamond, now that he had his game face on.

The tension rose palpably as Bail moved on to the bottom half of the order.

I didn't care where I hit—would happily have batted ninth, on the assumption it offered the fewest opportunities for humiliation. But ninth belonged to Mare as enduringly as fourth belonged to Big Stick. In the words of the country poet, Mare couldn't have hit a bull in the butt with a banjo. The only question was where Harry had penciled the rest of us in.

What we all knew, of course, was what every player knows from the moment he's old enough to shoulder a Louisville Slugger. The lower your slot in the order, the less respect whoever is writing the card out has for your batting skills. It was gut-checkingly clear that to a couple of the combatants standing stiffly beside me, the coach's next few words were going to mean a great deal.

"We got a couple out of our old lineup missin'," he lurched on, clearing his throat, "so I'm afraid I'm gonna have to shake things up a little.... Just 'member it don't make no diff'rence where you're hittin'.... Goin' out there and gettin' the job done, that's the main thing. I seen times when—"

"Read the damn card!" Me bellowed. "If you can't do it, give me that fuckin' pencil. I'll make it out."

"That aboot cuts it!" Pisser squealed. "I'm not tak—"

"That's enough!"

Curt stepped between them, his new hat tumbling off his head—a harassed headmaster forced yet again to enter the fray as a peacemaker. He rubbed the back of his neck wearily—then nodded at Harry to go on.

The coach glanced up at the sky. Took a deep breath. Headed for the bench as the muted words trailed in the air behind him.

"*Donniesonnyozchoirboyandallie*," he mumbled as he slumped away.

We stood motionless, watching him. It took a few seconds for the fused syllables to register. When they parted into names, Allie stepped quickly toward the dugout and grabbed his arm.

"Just a minute," she said quietly. "You've got me hitting ninth?"

Harry coughed—turned slowly to acknowledge her. His shoulders were sagging. His eyes were Noah's on the thirty-ninth day of rain.

"Like I said," he said. "Ever' one of you's got to hit somewhere.... I put you last 'cause I ain't never seen you play before.... And 'cause ever'body else I'm puttin' out there is a man."

Allie sighed. Her response was so soft I could barely hear it. "Phallocratic bullshit," she said.

Harry stared at her. Numb.

With exaggerated care, she reached out and lifted the lineup card from his hand—removed it as tenderly as a pacifier being slipped from the mouth of a sleeping baby. Just as unhurriedly, using one of Mare's marking pens, she wrote in a change. Then she unfolded her t-shirt on the dugout roof, added an inscription, and slipped the jersey on.

Her biceps swelled beneath the fabric. She turned around and handed the card back to Bail.

The shirt read *Genitalism Sucks*. The card had her batting behind Wick.

I looked at Harry. His face was that of a man who had seen the four horses of the apocalypse on the near horizon, and none of the riders was male.

Allie had moved on—dropped on her leathered haunches near the end of the bench—began re-tying a pair of red sneakers she'd fetched from the saddlebags of her Harley. Bookie murmured something to Bail as he stepped by him, then sat down next to her. The rest of us followed, Pisser cursing as he stamped past me to a perch as close as he could come to the far end.

Out on the diamond, the Raven Maniac was taking his warm-up tosses to a receiver so well upholstered Donnie looked almost svelte by comparison. DelNessa crouched behind him, holding a whiskbroom. There was no other umpire on the field.

"Who is that old guy?" Donnie asked me. "Isn't he the one you were talking to when I was strapping on my gear?"

"He's the caretaker," I said. "He looks after this pleasure garden.... I guess he must do a little umpiring too."

Harry leaned closer—appeared to have recovered some of his old aplomb. "I hope to hell he can see the plate better than he 'pears to be lookin' after this ballyard," he mumbled. "Weren't for the dugouts, I'd of thought we was playin' in Mutt Manciple's potato patch."

"Will he be impartial?" Curt said. "Understand," he added quickly, "I'm not implying the old gentleman would consider acting otherwise.... I ask only because—" He trailed off, staring out at the pitcher's mound.

"Old gentleman, my ass," Me shouted from the steps, where he crouched swinging one of the two battle-scarred bats Harry had managed to cadge from the Jeromites. "That old fucker's gonna try to screw us. You can count on it. You got to get after him, Bail—be in his face the whole game."

"I ain't gonna be in nobody's face," the coach retorted. "At least I ain't if I understand what the hell you boys mean by that dumbass 'xpression.... You ever see any damn good come of it?—all that raggin' on people?.... Alls it does is commence to make 'em madder. Ridin' an umpire flat don't work."

"The hell it don't," Me countered. "It's the only way you can keep 'em honest.... You don't get in somebody's face, they screw you blind."

"I never seen all that yammerin' do nothin' but make a man even more willin' than he was before to grab you by the goddammed short hairs. If the man's fair, he's fair. If he ain't, there's only one thing you can do about it. A few bad calls don't mean diddly if you go out there and hit the hell out of the ball."

"I don't think we're going to have any trouble with him," I offered. "He may see bad, but he'll see bad both ways."

The old caretaker's voice drowned whatever additional wisdom Me was about to favor us with—as if to refute any doubts we might still have about the vigor of his organs.

"Play Ball!" he bawled.

Chapter 14

The game began.

The first pitch was a fastball—if that's the term to use for the lobbed dart thrown as hard as the potbellied Raven Maniac's juiceless wing could deliver it. The ball sailed into the catcher's mitt an inch under Bookie's chin.

"That Sumbitch!" Harry muttered. "He's head huntin' out there!"

Me, in the on-deck circle, spat on his bat and knocked dirt from the heels of his spikeless shoes.

Bookie waited, glaring—then swung from his heels at three roundhouse curveballs that missed the outer edge of the plate by a foot. The pitcher cackled derisively as the bloated receiver pegged the ball on the first leg of its celebratory loop around the horn.

The black man dropped the bat and turned back toward the dugout, shaking his head, his face a tight-lipped mask of fury. He sank down on the bench between Harry and me.

"That's the last time," he hissed, his voice cutting the dugout air like the too-taut draw of a bowstring. "Cracker got to me.... It's not going to happen again."

Harry put his hand on the centerfielder's knee.

"Just make him play your game," he mumbled. "Don't start playin' his."

The first pitch to Me was another fastball that floated a foot behind the second-baseman's back.

Bail shook his head. "That Sumbitch is as ign'rant as he is ugly," the coach said. "It takes a partic'lar kind of dumbass to come inside on the Badger.... I don't know what's gonna happen now—but I'm damned glad I ain't the one standin' out there on that hill."

What happened next was that the onion-man threw an outside curveball exactly like the second pitch he'd thrown to Bookie. Me swung at it. The bat flew from his hands—a scissoring boomerang launched dead-on at the pitcher's eyebrows. He barely managed to duck under it as the lumber pinwheeled on past second base.

"We gotta stop this right now," Harry said, lurching from the dugout. But in the few seconds it took him to hobble to home plate, the curses, threats, and finger-pointing had already risen to riot-squad levels. We were five pitches into the first inning, and the game was a flickering eyelash away from base-brawl.

That the flames were contained just short of a conflagration was due to the collective labors of Curt, Harry, and the old caretaker-umpire who threatened to call the game if the two principals didn't simmer down immediately. Both did—at least outwardly—though not without a parting shot from our bellicose barkeeper—who laid a bunt down the first-base line on the next offering the pitcher threw.

As the ball died in the sand, Me chugged hell-bent toward the bag—a cement truck bullyragging down two lanes of freeway. The shaken pitcher ventured only close enough to snatch the ball as if it were a chestnut from a fireplace, barely brush-tagging him on the toe as he barreled by.

The game's second out had been recorded—and a message sent. If the bunt had dropped a foot nearer the foul line, the pitcher might have ended his days as an outsized road kill in the back of Harry's van.

When Curt popped up to end the inning, I felt good about only one thing as I trotted faintheartedly out toward my patch of hardscrabble pasture: for the time being, the Herefords were a lot closer than home plate.

They couldn't have munched more than a few mouthfuls before the Raven Maniacs were threatening us again—although this time, momentarily at least, they were merely threatening to score.

Their first hitter tapped a slow roller between Curt's legs. The second hit one to Pisser, who fielded it cleanly but duplicated the throw Harry and I had watched him make in the warmup. When the third hitter bounced a grounder off Allie's arm, the Jeromites had loaded the bases without punching the ball out of the infield. I looked toward our dugout. The brim of Harry's *Spirit of '76* cap hung so low all I could see were his neck and ears.

I moved in a few steps to see how Mare was handling it.

Thirty years earlier, I wouldn't have worried. The pitcher could look as comatose after a dozen errors had been committed behind him as he did peering in for the game's first sign. But that had been a long time ago. If the events of the day had offered indisputable evidence that behind the sartorial gloss, he was still the Mare Gilding all of us remembered—it was just as apparent that he still carried his chameleon genes. I had no precedent for judging the current state of his emotions. As far as I knew, he was the first hurler who ever faced a bases-loaded, no-out jam wearing a Rolex watch and a pair of tasseled Gucci shoes.

Me trotted in from second to talk to him.

It appeared, from the contrasting body language, that the pitcher remained as unrattled as he'd been in his salad days. Only his glove twitched as he slouched on the hill above his fireball counselor. The second baseman's stubby arms, on the other hand, slashed the air like a worker in a slaughterhouse wielding a pair of cleavers over a pork loin.

Behind them, Pisser picked up a handful of dirt and threw it down disgustedly—shouted something I couldn't hear in the direction of our dugout. Ten seconds later, Me trotted back to his position, flashing his middle finger in the shortstop's face.

But whatever he had said, it helped. Mare bore down and struck out the next hitter—the clean-up man—who flung his bat away toward the backstop. He then induced the next batter to loft a towering pop foul that Donnie staggered under like a wobbling gyroscope but somehow collared between his chest protector and his mitt.

It looked as if we might wriggle out of it. Mare stared down now at the Raven Maniac, who waggled his bat menacingly but clearly remained mindful of the threats Me had hurled his way in the earlier half of the inning. He peered out at the pitcher face to face, belly to belly—his front foot so far in the bucket he looked like an over-the-hill gunslinger belatedly aware of the doom to which his mouth had led. Mare threw him two outside-corner curveballs that he flailed at impotently, missing each by a foot. He couldn't have hit either one if his bat had been the bottom of Harry's duck boat. His swing reminded me of an octogenarian stretching a pair of scissors toward a rose-bush swarming with bees.

We had him. Everybody on the field knew it—knew it as surely as we knew the mantra Harry had to be moaning at that moment in the dugout. *"Waste one. Waste a pitch and get him to chase it.... Whatever you do, don't th'ow that Sumbitch a strike!"*

I watched as Mare leaned forward—peered in—held the ball so long DelNessa might have fallen asleep before the languid leg moved skyward. When the fateful delivery reached the plate, it was a straight down-the-middle changeup that the hitter squibbed on a slow roll between second and third.

The ball barely eluded both Allie and Pisser, dying twenty yards in front of me. By the time I scuttled in and retrieved it, the third run had crossed the plate.

The hitter rumbled into second base, cackling like a goosed-up cock pheasant as the other Jeromites whooped and danced around the plate in a two-minute orgy of butt-slapping and high fives. Mare shook his head phlegmatically—stared out at the cows—then down at the mud-caked ball that had finally found its way back into his hand.

This time it was Pisser who trotted to the mound.

The pitcher's maned head nodded once, almost imperceptibly, as the shortstop's wiry body pressed so close only his pointed chin seemed to span the few inches between them. He whispered in the lefthander's ear for half a minute—then returned to his position in the field.

Mare stared into space, finally climbed the hill—stood stolidly an inch or two behind the rubber. When the onionman took a short lead off second, Pisser slipped in behind him and tagged him with his glove.

"*He's oot! He's oot!*" the shortstop screeched, holding the glove-hidden baseball toward the heavens. The rest of us looked anxiously toward the bewildered, still crouching umpire—who had yet to make his call. Pisser ran all the way to the plate, brandishing the horsehide in front of him. The old arbiter gaped at it—delayed his verdict so long I began to think he'd decided to sleep on the decision. But at last, his right arm rose shakily into the air.

The baserunner stood where he'd been tagged, his barrel body quaking like an aspen leaf. As Bookie loped past him toward our dugout, he trailed behind, charging the plate.

"*Dirt ball!*" he roared. "That weas'ly little bastard is playin' dirt ball on us!" He snatched the evidence from the umpire's hand and waved it under his hatbrim. "Look at it! How filthy it is!.... He put mud in his glove and rubbed it on when he snuck in to the mound and started whisperin' to that fairy. You gotta throw 'em out! *Both* of 'em! It ain't right—havin' to put up with that shit, plus a goddammed spook and that red-legged bitch they got on third too!"

The caretaker took the ball and studied it again, then dropped it into the pocket of his overalls, out of which he slowly extracted a marginally whiter one. He flipped it to the hurler. "The next hitter's stepping in here in sixty seconds," he said, eyeing his pocket watch. "If you plan to take any of your warmup pitches, you better get out there on that mound."

The atmosphere in our dugout wasn't a whole lot warmer as we stood watching, preparing ourselves to hit. Me railed at Mare for the strike he'd delivered—"that stupid moron pitch that cost us three runs," as he put it. Harry didn't say anything, but his clenched teeth left little doubt that he agreed with the charge. Pisser asked if I was pulling a plow getting to the ball—then went on to suggest that Allie could have turned it into the inning-ending force out if she were carrying fewer pounds on her posterior. Allie told him she'd logged more hours in the "gyneasium" than his sheared skull had spent registering active brain waves. She added that he would have seen the ball himself, in plenty of time to reach it, if his mouth hadn't sealed off his eyes.

The bickering ended only with Curt's quiet but pointed reminder that Big Stick was due up next. Our clean-up hitter hadn't said a word as he reached the bench, but he'd hoisted a bat and begun swinging it in the on-deck circle like a lumberjack brandishing an axe. He had also begun to mutter under his breath. I couldn't tell for certain what he was saying, but I know it included "seed of Beelzebub" and something about a "winnowing fan."

As we stood watching, Mare suddenly rose and wandered off toward the parking lot. Harry took a step after him, looking concerned—either out of contriteness for the silent treatment he'd given the pitcher or fear he was going to hijack his van.

"Somebody better go check on Choirboy," the coach murmured. "He ain't lookin' so good."

Nobody responded.

After a few seconds, I grudgingly decided it must be my turn.

When I reached him, the hurler was hunkered down by the Lobby's rear bumper—was dipping into a large bottle of Vaseline.

"Everything okay?" I asked.

He didn't say anything. I watched as he smeared a gob of goo under the bill of his cap—then reached for another load that found a home on the underside of his belt buckle. A couple of larger dollops ended up in more imaginative locations. When he'd finished, the bottle was empty. He smelled like a lab worker for a pharmaceutical plant.

"Got bent out there, Shoeman," he finally said. "Thought I had that fat fucker. But I'm gonna be in the tube for the rest of it. You can stamp it on your lemons.... Just get me four."

"What's the bustard doin'?" Harry asked anxiously when I got back to the bench.

"He's getting himself ready for the next inning," I said. "I think he plans to be a little more scientific out there."

Although I was due to hit fourth, I settled back to watch—more interested in the first pair who would step in against the onion-eater. We needed a power surge, and when I had last played with Big Stick, he'd been the league's most feared long-ball hitter. And having had a full inning to reflect on it, I'd come to see the aptness of Allie following him in the order—since she had been our dugout's most potent verbal force. None of us had ever seen her swing a bat, but if an eye-popping physique was a good omen, we had the right player hitting fifth.

The suspense didn't have long to build. When the still enraged hurler delivered the first pitch of the second inning, Big Stick launched a swinging-from-the-heels bullet that headed straight at his quivering gut. It was the kind of laser shot that can jerk a slumbering moundsman bolt upright a decade later, trembling with visions of doom. Unfortunately for our more immediate prospects, this one stuck in the pocket of his glove.

I don't know whether Wick's missile would best be described as a wicked liner or a liner at the wicked. All I know is that somehow, astoundingly, it found its way into the petrified fingers of the Jeromite's left hand. I watched from the dugout, no less paralyzed, as he staggered backward and fell tumbling off the rubber. His mouth slowly opened to the sky.

The ensuing howl sent a few of the cattle barn-ward, but it didn't bring any succor from his terrorized teammates. They gaped at their fallen leader for several seconds in slack-jawed stupefaction—then started to bay with such nervous laughter some of them too were soon rolling on the ground. The pitcher was left to pick himself up, gabbling incoherently, rubbing the reddening flesh of his palm.

The hitter hadn't moved in the batter's box. He stood where he'd stood, the bat in his hand, staring balefully out at the diamond. When the pitcher finally rose, he dropped his weapon behind him and strode back to the bench, his sepulchral eyes raised heavenward.

Allie picked up the lumber. Stroked it lovingly. Then spit on her hands and rubbed the handle as she stepped in where he'd stood. The shaken hurler glowered at her, his neck red as her leathers, his curled lips quivering with contempt.

"Be careful," Harry whispered beside me. "Just be careful. That's the main thing."

"*Allieallieallieallieallie!*" Tina cried from the bleachers, jumping up and down as if she'd smuggled a pogo stick into the park under her hairdo. "*Allieallieallieallieal!*.... Come on! You can do it! Bat a home run!"

The first pitch sailed ten feet above the umpire's head—bounced like a dead bird off the chickenwire. The second was slightly lower, but also beyond the catcher's reach—five or six feet outside. The last two were close enough for the receiver to get his mitt on, but only with headlong dives.

Allie flipped the bat behind her and trotted to first base as the nettled pitcher kicked the rubber and threw his glove halfway to second. I moved into the on-deck circle. Wheezing as he picked up the lumber, Donnie stepped in to hit.

The pitcher threw him two more balls, but the color was returning to his face, and I could see that he was finding the range again. I wasn't sure whether the fact made me feel better or worse. Waiting for the next offering, Donnie stood at the plate, squeezing the bat—still buckled into his pleated chest protector. In his knock-kneed crouch, he resembled a sea tortoise that had somehow managed to hoist itself onto its hind legs.

The third pitch was a thigh-high strike that he topped on a soft, lazy roll a few feet to the right of the shortstop. The ball was hit so slowly Allie was standing on second, brushing herself off after sliding, when the throw slapped into the first-baseman's glove. Unhappily, Donnie's resemblance to a tortoise didn't end with the way he had stood at the plate.

DelNessa turned and waved me into the box.

Suddenly, irrevocably, I found myself in the position I'd dreaded from the moment our catcher's crackpot dream had materialized: at bat, with two outs in a game we trailed, facing a head-hunting pitcher with a chance to knock home a run.... That the baserunner was Allie made the situation all the worse.

"Come on, Shoeoff. You can do it, babe!" she shouted, dancing off the base like a Rubens nymph clad in red leotards. "Bring me on home!"

Behind me I could hear Harry, his sandpaper growl as familiar as it had been thirty years before. "Watch that Sumbitch. Don't bite on that big roundhouse. Wait on it. All you got to do is *wait*."

I struck out on three pitches, the last a sweeping curveball in the dirt.

Chapter 15

But Mare was as good as his word. He was "in the tube"—or more accurately, in the jar—from the moment he took the mound after my rally-killing humiliation. What his Vaseline-aided arm produced over the next couple of innings was a virtuoso performance so inspired it rose to the loftiest heights of tragicomedy. Comic because every hitter who faced him came away looking like a schoolboy struggling to swat a mosquito out of the air with a tea strainer. Tragic because our own bats remained almost as impotent—and because no audience but the oblivious Tina was present to watch the pitcher work.

For those of us out on the diamond, it was a little like watching Heifetz have a career day warming up in his garage.

Mare's ball darted. It swooped. It sailed toward the plate eyebrow high—then dropped into Donnie's mitt like a marble egg bumped off a mantelpiece. Shackled in his protective armor, the catcher returned to the dugout after each half-inning's labors looking as if he'd just spent the night under a meteor barrage. But a smile that rivaled the width of his stomach creased his oval face.

"Did you *see* that?" he marveled. "I can't believe it! Did you *catch* that last one he threw?"

"Better than you did," Allie cackled, jumping shamelessly on the hanging verb.

The fat man carried on, undeterred.

"How the mighty have fallen, huh?" he crowed. "First one comes up there, standin' on his high horse, thinkin' it's all gonna be a piece of cake just like it was that first inning. And what happens? *Boom!* Mare sends him back to the bench.... Next one comes struttin' up there like he's the cock of the walk, grinnin' down at me and kicking dirt all over my pants leg. What happens? *Boom!* Mare throws him that scroogie and cuts him down like a stalk of corn. Third guy steps—"

"We get the picture," Harry short-circuited him. "Choirboy's got it goin' now. If the rest of you dildos can make a play or two behind him, we could get after 'em. 'Least we could if a couple of you could recollect why you was holdin' that goddam piece o' lumber in your hands. You got to start makin' a little noise up there. My old mama did more damage with her broom."

"She was swinging at you," Allie said, winking at me. "How could she miss?"

"Listen at her," Bail said. He was about to retaliate, when a salvo of grunts and squeals cut the air behind him. He spun on his heel, as we all did. A war that made our own recent skirmishes look like polite diplomacy had erupted on the opposition bench. For the next five minutes we watched, wide-eyed, as the finger-pointing flared into a flurry of punches that expired only in an even wilder spate of angry roars and bellows. Maniacs heckled Ravens. Ravens cawed at Maniacs. The onionman moved back and forth between them, raving at both. It finally required the even more leathery lung-power of DelNessa to effect a temporary cessation of hostilities. Who or what had triggered the explosion, none of us could fathom. But it was clear the exasperated umpire had seen it all before. Arthritic thumb waggling, he herded our rivals back onto the field.

We moved into our half of the fourth still trailing by three. Me led off with a first-pitch double, but the second-baseman tagged him out when he slid ten feet past the bag trying to knock the shortstop halfway to the left-field foul line. Sitting beside me, Harry stomped on his new cap and tore what remained of his hair.

Curt was up next. He swung late and hit a short, drifting fly that the right fielder snatched out of the air with a hot-dog flourish. He compounded the insult by miming an old-maid's shoulder motion as he flipped the ball back toward the mound.

It brought Big Stick to the plate in the worst possible situation—two out and nobody on.

"The Sumbitch is gonna walk him," Harry said gloomily. "Even he ain't dumb enough to pitch to the Preacher here."

We all knew he was right. The only suspense was whether the rattled hurler had recovered enough from his earlier brush with dismemberment to deliver four balls within catching distance of the hitter's glowering frame. It was the first intentional walk I'd ever seen where the catcher speared the quartet of lobs closer to his dugout than to home plate.

Stick reluctantly dropped his cudgel and trotted to first as Allie stepped in for the second time. It struck me that we still didn't have the slightest notion whether her faith in herself was justified. We'd had no batting practice. Her first time up she'd walked on four pitches. None of us had yet seen her take so much as a single practice swing.

I glanced at Harry. He didn't look as if he were ready to bet his parsonage on our prospects when she finally did.

What was clear was that the coach would be happiest if the lumber remained exactly where his new third-baseman was holding it. "Make him pitch to you!" he shouted. "Work the Sumbitch for another walk!"

Allie called time. She backed out of the box. She slowly turned and directed a tight-lipped glare at her cigar-chewing counselor. Then she stepped back in and belted the first pitch the Raven Maniac threw her into a patch of prairie hay last occupied by one of the crumple-horned cows.

The dugout went dead—stunned to momentary silence—then exploded with a noise I hadn't heard since I'd belly-flopped into the promised land three decades earlier. Stumbling off the bench, we poured onto the field like a troop of urchins descending on a Fourth of July picnic—baying, slapping backs, whooping in the springtime air. Big Stick rounded the bases and planted a ponderous sole on home plate—gave Curt the first high five an avenging angel has likely ever given. Allie crossed just behind him, mobbed, sunlight gleaming off her crimson pants.

The old caretaker bent to sweep off the suddenly un-virginal dish as we escorted her back to the bench.

"Did you *see* that?" Donnie kept shouting. "She got all of it! Took him deep! Airmailed that baby into the Mountain time zone! I can't believe it. She went downtown on him! Dialed 8 on that—"

"Ease off the throttle a second, Round Knees," our newfound redeemer interrupted him. "I'm here...the one with her hand on your shoulder. You sound like you're talking about some Amazon."

The rest of us reacted as if we weren't convinced he hadn't been.

"Ain't that somethin'," Harry said, chortling, his gaze still fixed on the hallowed turf where the ball had landed. "Ain't that the damndest thing you ever seen?.... I'd of give 'bout ever'thing I own to see one of you boys give that ugly Sumbitch even a tad o' proper schoolin', and it's a goddammed woman what steps up there and gets the job done."

"In due season, she too shall deliver," Big Stick expatiated. "The she ass, the ewe, and the woman in travail."

"Oot of the park!" Pisser squeaked, his voice rising an octave. "That's where she hit it. She knocked it—"

"Play *Ball!*"

The raspy command nearly lifted the dugout roof off. We turned to find DelNessa frowning at us from the top step. "Get somebody up there!" he barked, pocketing his timepiece. "It's gettin' on toward chore time. I've got cows to milk."

"The man's right," Harry mumbled, glancing at his own watch. "'Any case, now ain't the time for too much celebratin'. Last I checked, we was still down by a run."

The reminder was the more sobering when I remembered I was on deck—due to hit immediately after Donnie. If he got on, I'd come to the plate with two outs and another chance to drive somebody home—a second opportunity to fail.

But this time, it didn't happen—a fact that left me to face other private demons as I trotted out to my position for the bottom half of the inning. What had I truly felt when Donnie struck out, I asked myself. Disappointment at a dead rally? Or profound relief? *"Both,"* the silent voice murmured. Characteristically, I'd come down on the side of ambivalence. It was familiar ground.

I forced my attention back to the action in front of me—where Mare was introducing the Jeromites to some further creative uses of petrochemicals. We moved into the fifth inning still trailing by the single run. This time, I stepped to the plate determined not to bite again on the onionman's roundhouse curveball—then concentrated so hard on not letting it happen that his first two pitches sailed past me over the heart of the plate for strikes.

I called time and stepped out of the batter's box, making a show of tying my shoes, but in fact because my brain was reeling.

It was the same old dilemma. At least it had always been so for me—the most unbridgeable of the countless chasms that separated genuine athletes from the legions of us who were merely struggling pretenders. They *reacted*. We *thought*—tying our bodies into immobilized knots while our overprogrammed minds spun dizzily on toward paralysis. Or, conversely, when we simply reacted—let pure instinct run the shop, as I had done in my first plate appearance—the predictable result was a bat-flailing slapstick farce. But when they thought, they "got focused," or "locked in."

"*Come on, Shoe! You can do it, sugar.*"

Allie's voice burrowed through the self-recriminations to my burning ear.

I pulled up my socks. Cleaned my glasses. Suppressed the flickering thought that "*My hitting SUCKS*" is what I should have scribbled on the front of my shirt.

Her vote of confidence was another familiar marker of the abyss:

Words of encouragement—the roar of the crowd—somehow inspired true athletes to doughty feats of glory. They only added to the doubts the pretender felt tightening like bands of steel around his rubbery loins.

To think, or not to think.... To be...or sting like a Bee. A new Bee, like Allie. A Bee with an attitude.... A new Bee attitude....

The third pitch moved toward me like Hamlet's ghost and I swung with cerebral abandon. It bounced three feet in front of the plate—so far outside that the cursing receiver couldn't have caught it with a mitt the size of a washtub. He stumbled out of his crouch—lurched back toward the chickenwire backstop—as I dropped my head in shame.

"Run! Run, Shoe! Run!"

Her voice cut like an arrow through the chaos. Then dawned the old memory that a third strike had to be caught and this one hadn't been and I was still alive and had better haul my pathetic derrière toward first base like I had never hauled it. *Running. Running hard.* I chugged up the line as the pitcher churned toward first and the ball bounced off the screen—the first baseman now chasing it too—*everybody running and then all of us arriving at the bag together the pitcher and my foot and the throw.*

He lay on the ground, bellowing. I lay on the base, wallowing. The ball spun in the dirt between us as both dugouts emptied onto the field.

To my dying day, I'll say this for DelNessa. He was old and indecisive, but he was honest. It took another full minute before he rendered a verdict, but when the dust finally settled, I remained on the bag. The Raven Maniac was still bellowing as thunderously as he had when he'd rolled over me—but he did it now from the rocky patch of ground near second, where he'd been forced to retreat rubbing his bruised right arm.

Massaging my own throbbing shoulder, I tried to decipher the few words I could snatch from the stream of curses he directed at the umpire—an idiom that sounded like *"Questio juris"* but was probably a lot closer to "Kiss your ass." My body felt as if he were pounding it with a jackhammer. It didn't matter. I had gotten on.

The relief pitcher was the considerably younger Maniac whose place the onionman had taken at second. It quickly became clear that what he lacked of his surly skipper's vitriol he more than made up for in the juice that pulsed through his sidewinding right arm. For whatever remained of the contest, we were clearly going to be playing hardball in every sense of the word.

My momentary glow dimmed further when he proceeded to strike Pisser out on three pitches. It dissipated entirely when I realized that the whiff meant Mare was about to step into the (in his case, absurdly named) "batter's box." I peered toward the dugout to see how Harry was handling the situation—a private agony we'd all seen the coach suffer so often Allie had once likened it to the seven stages of the cross: Mare picks up the bat and stares at it sorrowfully; he hoists it wearily to his shoulder; he lugs it slouching toward the plate as if his cap were a crown of thorns.

Thirty years later, things proved to be no different. He simply had a lot more weight to carry back to the somber tomb our dugout had turned into when he was done.

I stood now where I had perched euphorically scant moments earlier, but April's promise had faded to the two-out pall of a chill November. Bookie stood now at the plate—a hitter who had burned scores of rivals with his swiftness, but almost none with his bat. Even if the outfielder did manage to scratch out a bingle, it was a virtual certainty the ball wouldn't travel far enough for me to score. He had almost no power; I had even less speed. Yet that—a fluke long-ball—

seemed the only conceivable way we were going to get the run home. The chances of us stringing two or more hits together against a pitcher who threw as hard as this younger Maniac were almost nil.

I decided at that instant to do something so outrageous my brain suddenly switched off—stopped functioning lest I pause for even a split-second to reconsider. I forgot abysses. Said to hell with princes of Denmark. Abandoned my roly-poly bones to an unthinkable absurdity. Cold feet warmed by the ghost of Hotplate, I was going to try to steal.

When it was over—and my shoeless foot lay on second base, where it had come to rest after knocking the waiting ball from the glove of the incensed Raven Maniac, the roar from our dugout swelled to a crescendo, then sealed off as suddenly as my mind had done seconds before. I'm fairly sure the tumult continued. I just didn't hear it—red-faced, reckless fool that I'd been.

But the recklessness had been the only reason it had worked. When I'd scuttled head-down off first, no one else in the park had believed it either. The odds on Harry giving me the steal sign were about the same as his spending the night with Goodie. By the time the startled catcher had recovered his bearings, I'd stolen the precious few steps I needed to make the theft attempt close—close enough that the onionman hadn't secured the ball in his glove when my foot hit his elbow. His squeals of outrage when the ball flew from the webbing were almost worth the withering assault of his breath in my face.

I stood now on second base. Scoring position. Peered in at the black man whose thin-handled bat might have been the weight of the world resting on his narrow shoulders. His jaws gleamed with perspiration. His burning eyes were riveted on the mound.

When he punched the pitcher's next pitch into short right field for a high-bouncing, seeing-eye single, I had just enough time to slide home with the run that tied the game.

Me mauled me before I could rise—hammered my back as I trotted to the dugout—where the reception was only slightly less restrained. Allie kissed me on the cheek. Donnie hugged me like a brother. Big Stick fell back on the bench with his arms in the air, no doubt thanking the Lord for fat kine.

"Did you *see* that?" Donnie shouted. "Shoe stole on him! The *Shoeoff!* Got the good lead. Got the jump. Got into their heads and started doin' all kinds of weird stuff with their psychos. The Shoe Man! The Slough Man! *Stole* that sucker blind!.... Next time I'm up there, I'm gonna take off all this crap and—"

"You ain't gonna let the idee get within hollerin' distance of whatever you got left for a brain!" Harry derailed him. He clapped me on the shoulder. "Sure, this knot-head here fooled 'em once. I said *once*! He's just fast enough he might could run a hunnert yards and finish sometime in the twentieth century. You couldn't. You'd be the first fella ever got tagged out by a catcher what just trotted down to second and never even had to th'ow the goddammed ball."

"I don't think you have much to worry about, Coach," Allie said, grinning. "He'd have to get on base first." She turned back toward the diamond, hollering at Me—urging him to lay off the flustered pitcher's next delivery. The touch of her lips still flamed on my face.

"*Speed kills!*" Donnie yelled, turning too toward the hurler—familiar enough with the alien turf to grasp what the rest of us also instinctively took for granted. Bookie danced off first as Donnie cranked it up a notch beside me: *"Hey rag-arm!"* he shouted. *"Yabba-dabba-dabba-dabba-dabba! Speed kills!"*

Me laid off a fastball as the runner stole second without sliding—the Raven Maniac slapping a hard, frustrated tag on his thigh a full second after he'd reached the bag. He stole third on the next pitch, though this time our second-baseman was swinging. Beside me, Donnie had gotten hyper as a caged monkey. The rest of us weren't far behind.

The count went to three and one as the rattled pitcher threw two balls a foot outside, uncertain who to concentrate on—the menacing hitter flipping him the finger after every pitch, or the fleet runner who danced down the line daring the catcher to try to pick him off.

A passed ball. A wild throw. Bookie's still amazing legs had given us a number of ways to score now. His set jaw carried such fierce resolve it occurred to me he might even try to steal home—a feat I think he actually might have attempted if he'd been staring down the barrel of any other bat. Bookie had always been brave, but he wasn't suicidal—which a baserunner would have to be to contemplate heading for home with Me Miller crouching there squeezing the lumber in his fists.

When the second-baseman swung mightily at the next pitch—and the next one—missing both to loud groans of disappointment—our rally died with Bookie still at third. Yet groans were all the strikeout generated. There was no second-guessing. None at least that I could hear. Even Pisser managed to keep his lips buttoned as he trotted out to his position. And from two or three others, including Bookie, the failed hitter got butt-slaps and verbal boosts as we followed the Blademan onto the field.

The fragile communion took deeper root as Mare proceeded to fan the first two rival batters, then got the third on a play—inconceivable a few innings earlier—that was one of the most original I had ever seen.

The Jeromite catcher chopped a ball deep in the hole between Pisser and Allie, a ball the bum-winged shortstop somehow reached, snatched out of the air, and flipped underhand to our startled third-basewoman—who had enough presence of mind to re-route it across the diamond toward Curt's outstretched glove. The sphere arced across the infield like a spent Roman candle. When it nipped the lead-footed runner by half a step, the three of them had turned a slow ground ball into a comic symphony of team resourcefulness transcending individual afflictions. Watching from left as the play unfolded, I was reminded of a bucket brigade passing a tub of water to stanch a fire.

Back in the dugout, born-again Bees buzzed as loudly as we had when our scarlet woman had launched her epic home run a few minutes earlier. But this time we'd been roused by the excruciating parabola of the relayed ball's flight.

"I seen it all now," Harry crowed. "Damned if I ain't. That play might could change the game of baseball forever. They'll call it the Pony Express. Ride one arm as far as it'll carry you—then get whatever the hell you can out of the next one. Old infielders with dead wings wouldn't have to retire 'till they started collectin' their Social Security checks."

"We're hearing you, Coach," Allie cackled. "And you're the one that's got the right to name it.... You were there when the Pony Express first rode through."

Chortling, Harry rose and headed toward home plate, where DelNessa was waving the two managers onto the diamond. He fired a parting volley as he hobbled away.

"I was there, all right," he barked, "and it's watchin' you over there at third made me recollect it. The way you been jerkin' your head out of the way of them grounders, you look like a quarter-horse spittin' the bit."

As he shuffled on toward the summit meeting, I glanced at our rivals' dugout, where the onionman had also paused on the top step to level a parting barrage at his sullen charges. We'd clearly gotten into his "psycho," as Donnie had so aptly put it. The recognition served only to jack the high spirits on our bench up another notch or two.

"We've got to set up a match race," Me shouted, elbowing Donnie in the chest protector. "That catcher of theirs against the lard ass wearin' all this shit here. World's Slowest Human.... I'll put my money on Fat."

"Beasts of burden," Big Stick added. "Men who toil."

"It'd be no contest," Donnie countered.

I wasn't sure whether he meant he'd finish first—or second. Or which place he'd consider to have won.

"I'd eat him for lunch," the catcher continued. "It'd be a piece of cake. You can take it to the bank."

"I don't know," Bookie chuckled, still shaking his head incredulously every time he looked at the receiver's strap-stretching armor. "It's a tough call. If pride goeth before the fall, you sound to me like a man that's ready to topple. Count me in with Me. I'm layin' my bones on your back."

"The hinder parts of the ass.... Ever heavy laden," Big Stick chipped in.

Donnie ignored him. "I don't get it," he said, his puzzled eyes still fixed on the scholar he'd roomed with the night before.

"Get what?" Bookie said.

"How you're going to put your bones on me.... You think I'd make that bet if I had to haul you around like some jockey on my tail?"

Bookie stared at him, then began to laugh softly. *"Bones,"* he said. "It's slang for money. At least it is where I come from.... Sorry. Once in awhile I forget."

"Forget what?"

"Forget it," the centerfielder said, turning away as Harry hobbled into the dugout and dropped down on the bench.

The coach wore an expression that combined irritation, relief, and a heavy dose of anxiety. Our chatter died.

"The old fart mad because we woke him up from his nap?" Pisser said, smirking.

Bail shook his head. "He told the both of us it's gettin' late. He's got his cows to 'tend to.... This is gonna be the last inning—no matter what the score is when it's over. The man needs to get on home."

"Then we've gotta go out there and *get* one!" Donnie yelped. "Gotta go out there and jump all over 'em! It's us that's got it rollin' now. We got the Big Mo in our corner. Let's take that puppy and run it right into the barn!"

"Damn straight," Me seconded him. "We're goin' out there and kick some ass!"

The furrows in the coach's brow deepened.

"It'd be nice to win this one, sure," he said. "And we might could do just that—we keep playin' the way we have the last couple of innings. But winnin' it ain't the main thing.... We got to be careful nobody gets hurt."

He stared out at second, where the liver-and-onion man was lumbering toward a practice grounder. When the ball bounced off his wrist, he slammed his glove savagely against his thigh and raked the bag with his spikes.

"That fella's a real bad one," the coach went on. "Bad as I ever seen—and I ain't just talkin' about the game of baseball. And he's gonna get worse, now things ain't goin' his way."

Curt paused on the dugout step, then picked up a bat and stepped into the on-deck circle. DelNessa bent over the plate and swept it clean. Moving behind the crouching catcher, he waved the captain in to hit.

The Maniac's pitch had too much steam for him to get around on, but he dumped it behind first base—just in front of the charging rightfielder. Harry's words still echoing in our brains, our cheers were muted. But they were enough to provoke the enraged onion-eater to another outburst. The veins in his neck bulged as Big Stick stepped in.

The pitcher had reacted to the fluke single almost as angrily—since it eliminated the possibility of another intentional walk to our cudgel-wielding clean-up man. He reached nervously for the rosin bag—dropped it from his trembling fingers—threw a fastball as hard as his sleeveless right arm could deliver it. Big Stick ripped it on a low line toward the shortstop—a mirror image of the shot that had somehow stuck in the onionman's glove a few innings earlier. But this time the ball caromed off the cowed fielder's wrist and bounced across the foul line fifty feet behind third.

Only the ball's velocity and the runners' stone feet prevented the go-ahead run from scoring. Still, we now had men on second and third with nobody out, and our Harley-riding home-run hitter was stepping into the batter's box. A ripple of anticipation coursed through the dugout. Me offered a crude paean to "our big knocker with the big knockers." Standing on second, Big Stick muttered something about days of judgment. Donnie rocked back and forth on the balls of his feet.

"Allieallieallieallieallie!" Tina screamed from the bleachers, pogoing higher and higher. "Do it again, sweetie! Do it once more!"

"Just walk her," Harry breathed tensely beside me. "First base is open. Do the smart thing.... Put her on." Leaning forward, he peered at the pitcher with such teeth-clenching intensity the cigar bobbed up and down above his chin.

The air suddenly went silent—dead still—as everyone in the park waited for the pitcher's next delivery. And then it began—just as unexpectedly—the swelling voice from the round-bodied receiver bouncing at my side. The words washed across the field and the sagging snowfence encircling it in a rapturous, full-throated cry:

"Go Big Red! Go Big Red! Go Big Red!"

Almost at once another voice joined in, then another—then two or three more in an intoxicated, insurgent drumming from our dugout:

"Go Big Red! Go Big Red! Go Big Red!"

I was shouting too now—chanting defiantly—my swimming eyes locked on the luminous woman at the plate.

Crouched near second, the Raven Maniac moved a few steps closer to the mound, picked up a handful of dirt and angrily hurled it skyward. The puff of dust blew toward the outfield like smoke from the barrel of a gun. "Stick it in her ear!" he shrieked. "The fat-assed bitch! Stick the goddammed thing in her fucking ear!"

Harry rose off the bench—a split second before the ball left the pitcher's hand.

He did exactly as he'd been told.

Chapter 16

Allie sprawled on her back, her legs twitching, as the field dissolved into a terrifying blur of sound and motion: Tina's keening wail—sickened groans—heaving bodies lunging heavily past me. Engines gunned. Tires squealed. Sprayed gravel pinged against metal and wood.

"Get a doctor!" half a dozen voices shrieked, swelling to a chorus near the dazed DelNessa. I wiped my eyes and looked briefly away from the stricken hitter, who lay motionless on the plate. The old caretaker was the only local who remained in the park.

"We don't *have* a doctor," he croaked. "We had one once, years ago, but they took away his license for taking kickbacks from the druggist. He was bleeding people out of every pen—"

"What difference does it make—you fool!" Pisser shouted. "Go get him, ay! What in God's name are you talking aboot!"

"I can't get him.... He's been dead for ten years."

"How about a policeman?" Curt said, gasping, struggling for breath after his exertion on the basepaths.

"We don't have one of them either. Couldn't get anybody to take the job when we could afford one.... Ain't enough money or people left in town now to try."

I felt a feathery body slam into my left shoulder—shove me aside and press on past me toward the fallen hitter. Sobbing, Tina knelt and cradled Allie's head in her lap, then suddenly began to scream. "Get away! All of you! *All of you!* You're nothing but a bunch of barbarians!.... All of you.... Please. Get away!"

Her voice broke as she bent again over the unseeing face, a weeping madonna in a motorcycle helmet. I pushed past Donnie to her side.

"We've got to get her to a hospital," I shouted, grabbing DelNessa's arm. "What's the nearest one?"

"St. Thomas. South Fork. Back the way you came."

"My God," someone said.

Curt knelt beside me, still panting, but repossessed of his lawman's self-control. He took her pulse. Lifted an eyelid and studied her pupils. Bent over her chest to check the sound of her heart and lungs. No one spoke as he ministered to her. The only sounds were Tina's sobbing and the quickened, collective gathering of our breath.

"This is heavy shit, man," Mare whispered. "Heavy shit."

Curt looked up. Turned to Harry.

"Her breathing and pulse are fairly regular, but she doesn't show any sign of regaining consciousness. We've got to get her back to South Fork. How fast will your van go?"

"I'll take care of that," Me broke in. "Don't worry about it. I'll crank the sonofabitch up and get her there."

The captain's face furrowed, but he went on. "It would help if we had somebody out front on that motorcycle. A lead vehicle. To warn any oncoming traffic.... I could do it, but I think I'd better stay with her inside." He glanced at Tina, whose tear-streaked gaze never wavered from the prostrate body beneath it, then quickly on to the rest of us ringing home plate.

"Anybody else know how to handle one?"

Mare had already taken a slouching step toward the parking lot. "No problemo," he said. "Let's hit the trail."

We were still easing Allie toward the van when the left-hander returned—carrying a bright neon scrap of cloth he'd apparently pulled from his bottomless suitcase. It dangled from his hand as he continued on past us, toward the bleachers, where he scooped up the red helmet that Tina had held for two hours in her lap. Shambling back the way he'd come, he sidled up to the big motorcycle's seat and rolled a straddling leg over the leather. Stretching the orange cloth across the helmet's crown, he buckled it over his saffron mane, the thin strands falling like gossamer down his spine.

We slid Allie onto the seat behind the driver, then climbed in too—Tina kneeling on the floor beside her. Curt leaned forward from the third seat, monitoring her pulse. The rest of us squeezed into whatever spaces we could.

Mare already had the Harley roaring—sat slouched on the motorcycle's seat waiting for the van to start rolling. The gaudy cloth I'd first taken to be a warning patch for deer hunters proved on closer inspection to be a pair of blaze orange woman's underpants. All that showed of Allie's helmet were two swatches of hard plastic that gleamed through the panties' stretched legholes like a pair of outsized ears.

Curt waited just long enough for Harry to haul himself up onto the front seat before signaling DelNessa to slide the door closed behind him. "Call the hospital," he commanded. "Tell them to have a doctor and a gurney waiting. Emergency priority. We're coming in." The caretaker nodded as Me jerked the van into reverse and spun it backward through the mudhole, clattering the door shut on its own.

We followed Mare out of town, down the narrow highway, his helmet glowing brighter as the late afternoon shadows lengthened—a neon beacon homed in on a hospital I barely remembered walking past the night before. No one said much. There wasn't anything to say, and the rumble of the speeding van swallowed all but our occasional shouted questions concerning the victim's condition. As to that, our eyes gave glum enough witness. It hadn't changed since the baseball bounced off her unprotected skull and spun crazily, sickeningly, toward our bench.

She lay unmoving—eerily peaceful—a faint smile on her lips as if she had simply fallen asleep.

The bridge loomed ahead. As we crested the rise above it, the river gleamed under the low-hanging western sun like a ribbon of gold unfurling across the prairie. Dropping into the valley, I peered anxiously through the windshield—prayed that whatever traffic we came upon would be flowing the same direction we were. But there was no traffic, only the startled flagwomen, who still stood like a pair of weary sentries at the bridgeheads as we approached. No sign of the workmen remained but their ponderous equipment. Mare blew by it all without slowing, the van trailing in his wake.

The sun hung lower in the sky, a crimson disc, as the road bent back toward the river a few miles outside of South Fork. Five minutes later, we sped down the street flanking the college and careened to a stop in front of the emergency room door.

Chapter 17

I'd often heard it remarked that a crisis brings out the best in people, but it was a truth I had never directly experienced. I did in those next few minutes, as the ten of us clustered anxiously in the waiting room while evening fell across the silver river a hundred yards away.

Curt offered quiet consolation. Tina wept softly—but her bitterness seemed to have dissipated. Big Stick asked if he could lead us in prayer—and then, in the face of tight-jawed skepticism—proceeded to deliver a supplication that was itself a little trinity of miracles: He managed to be brief, ecumenical, and clear.

"I *got* it," Donnie whispered to me when he finished. "That's the first time I ever understood anything he said."

And yet as we lingered on, uninformed about Allie's condition, the gloom in the room began to weigh heavier—the more so because the flaming sun had dipped behind a cloak of clouds. The rays flooding the room when we entered now seemed as irretrievable as the hard jangle of her laughter. The floor we sat staring at was a battleship gray.

Harry looked especially stricken, berating himself in head-shaking denunciations that even Curt's heartfelt counsel couldn't stem.

"Why didn't I make her wear that hamlet?" the coach mourned. "This would never of happened if she'd of had it on her head."

"But it's a *motorcycle* helmet," Donnie said, trying to be helpful.

"What the hell diff'rence does that make?.... A hamlet's a hamlet. It would of protected her head just as good as any other kind would of. I was about to stop the game to tell her to put it on—was startin' on my way out there—just as that bustard threw the pitch."

"Why didn't you do it sooner, ay?" Pisser asked.

The pained expression on the shortstop's face argued that he didn't intend to be cruel—accusatory. But Pisser was Pisser, and the words only rekindled the coach's self-abuse.

"Why didn't I?" he answered, one gnarled hand clenching the other. "Because there ain't no fool like an old fool—that's why.... I was like Donnie. I thought the damn thing would look ridic'lous. Just the same as I was thinkin' earlier she didn't have no bi'ness out on that field. That's the thing of it. You get hidebound—get so the only way you can think about some goddammed thing is the way you always thought about it. And there ain't no excuse for that. 'Specially when you spent the better part of your life coachin' a sport what flat can't be played right if you ain't able to handle all the bad hops and other damn su'prises the game's gonna throw your way.

"For fifty years," he went on, "I'm out there tellin' kids they can't try to force it. Got to develop soft hands. Got to learn there are times you back off on a ball same as there's others when you got to charge one.... I'm tellin' all this to other folks. And what am I doin' myself?.... Not a goddammed thing."

We were staring at our shoes when he concluded. Silence had descended on the room like a gravestone. There was no sound but the muffled swell of our breathing, torn every few seconds by one of Tina's soft, jagged sobs.

"We aren't kids anymore," Bookie finally murmured. "It wasn't your job to look after us.... Allie made a choice. We all did. You're not to blame."

The guilt-ridden old coach nodded, but his eyes had drifted toward the window—were fixed on the river. He didn't look convinced.

"He's right," Tina said.

They were the first words she had spoken to any of us since her anguished indictment. Every eye in the room turned toward the bench where she sat. Through the pane of glass behind her, the branches of a weeping willow tree swayed in the wind.

"I'm sorry about what I said back there," she continued. "Some of it wasn't fair.... I know you're not all barbarians."

I looked at my teammates, one or two of whom appeared relieved at the news.

"Sometimes I still get carried away," she resumed. "Things build up.... I haven't learned yet how to handle... handle all of my feelings about men."

Nine men stared again at their shoetops, waiting. I didn't know how eight of them felt about the prospect of her continuing. I wasn't sure how I felt myself.

"I can tell you think that I don't like you.... And I suppose maybe it's still true. I can't deny it once was true. True in ways none of you would be able to appreciate. But it's not personal. It's just, well...*men*.... None of you really have anything to do with it."

"I don't get it," Donnie said. "What do you mean? You don't like...*guys*?

"I mean...you know," he added quietly, "in general, I mean." He looked as if he'd just run into a human being who couldn't abide the thought of a chicken-fried steak.

"Don't get me wrong," he added. "I'm not saying all of us are God's gift to women. It's just, you know...*you know*?"

Curt came to his rescue—or tried to.

"Please forgive me if this is something I have no right to ask," he said to her. "But I've been wondering about your...your relationship with Allison." He cleared his throat in embarrassment, then lurched on. "Back in the sixties, I wasn't aware that you two were.... that you were...friends."

Tina stared at him, hard, but there was only nervousness and concern in the big man's face—not the slightest hint of innuendo. No one could have looked into it without feeling its benevolent good will.

"We weren't friends.... Back then," she said. "What you call '*our relationship*' hadn't begun."

We waited for her to go on. A door squeaked open down the corridor—yielded to the unseen clatter of a rolling gurney. A second door opened. Closed. Sealed off the soft clicking of footsteps in the hallway. The waiting room fell silent once more.

"I'm going to tell you a story," Tina said. "A story about a woman.... A woman who had learned to hate men."

Again we waited. Watched as she wiped her eyes free of tears, dropped the wadded tissue into a wastebasket under the window. The eyes were large. Clear. Gray as the cloud that drifted over the sloping lawn behind her. Her small mouth and straight nose accentuated the remarkable width of her forehead.

"The woman married well," she began. "Or thought she had. Lived for several years the life she had always dreamed of.... She had a providing husband. Plenty of money. Expensive jewelry and foreign vacations and country clubs and a cellar stocked with imported wines.

"But it was a life built on illusion. Desperation. A dependency that left her reeling when she looked back after all of it ended.... During these early years of her marriage, it would not be an exaggeration to say that she worshipped her husband—saw him in much the same way she thought of God."

Donnie glanced up at the crucifix above her head. His right hand fingered the smaller one dangling outside his shirt.

"In the third year of her marriage she bore a child—a son—and the woman was even more deliriously happy. Her one remaining wish had been granted. Her last need had been filled. She was complete now. Whole. Left with nothing to desire except the continuing of what already existed. She nursed the child with total devotion. Watched him gr—"

The narrator suddenly stopped—shook her head. "No," she said, "I'm sorry. '*Watched*' doesn't begin to describe the way she perceived him. Every gurgle and coo, every bubble at his tiny lips, she *revered*."

Fascinated, I looked around the room—studied the faces of my teammates leaning toward her. Most were as rapt as the doting mother she described.

"One morning when the baby was a year old, the woman left her beautiful home to attend a luncheon at the home of an old acquaintance. It was the first time she had left him, and she felt guilty, even though her husband had encouraged—no, had *insisted*—that she go. 'This can't go on,' he had argued. 'You need to get out—do something besides sit around this empty house idolizing the baby every moment. It's not good.'

"The woman had not thought of the house as empty. Had in fact never been anywhere that seemed as full—as rewarding—as it seemed to her. But reluctantly, she at last agreed to go.

"'She backed her sports car out of the garage, which itself caused her anxiety, since she'd hardly driven at all since the birth of her baby—then set off down the suburban street toward her friend's home less than a mile away. But it was a destination she never reached. She had driven only a few blocks, when she remembered she hadn't shown her husband where she kept the list of emergency telephone numbers. Turning around, she drove back up the leafy street and hurried through the door."

The narrator pulled another Kleenex from her purse—dabbed it angrily at her eyes, which were fixed on the door to the corridor Allie's gurney had been wheeled down a half-hour earlier. The pink tissue remained in her trembling fingers as she went on.

"Her husband hadn't heard her enter. Stood with his back to her. Was talking to another woman on the phone. By the time he noticed her, the dream had shattered. The wife stood in the kitchen, clutching her purse, knowing nothing in her life would ever be the same again.

"The child grew. The parents fought. The woman did everything in her power to keep the little boy away from his father. He was so tiny, so vulnerable—would become whatever he learned to be in these next crucial years of his growth.... And the woman loved him enough to die before she would let a monster take him under his wing.

"The husband protested, of course—but he didn't immediately retaliate—did nothing until he'd complained to his widowed mother. She was a harridan who had never liked the woman from the moment her son had chosen her as his wife. She pressed him to put his foot down—take control of the marriage. She even tried to convince him that the wife was unstable and ought to be put away.

"But the husband only got angrier—now threatened both of them—began to cheat openly on his wife and told her he'd been unfaithful almost from the beginning. She struck him. He struck her harder. Later he hit her harder still.

"Finally the woman left him.

"She waited until a winter morning when he had gone to work—then bundled up the child and fled all night through a raging storm all the way back to the home she'd grown up in. It was a miracle that she made it safely—reached her father's house—where she planned to stay only until she had gotten her life back together again.

"She had filed for divorce—was waiting for the court date—when God sent an angel of justice to take care of her needs."

"*What?*" Donnie blurted, crossing himself. His eyes were as round as a pair of golf balls.

"Vengeance is mine, saith the Lord," Big Stick intoned.

Tina paused only long enough to turn toward him slightly, and nod.

"Her husband died," she continued. "He was murdered—took his last breath as he sat alone at the dinner table. The authorities never discovered who killed him—said he had choked to death on a piece of fruit—but the woman knew it was a ministering angel who put poison in her mother-in-law's hand."

Me jumped off the bench, groaning.

"You're trying to tell us this dude's own mother offed him? Give me a friggin' break. Why would she do it?.... That's nuts!"

He dropped to his seat again, peeling half a pack of gum from the wrappers and jamming the sticks into his jaw.

"I said the *woman* was sure her mother-in-law had killed him," Tina responded. "She had reasons.... There were a lot of reasons a woman would think of killing such a man."

"I ain't following this anymore either," Harry said, looking helplessly across the room at Donnie. "It's gettin' too deep for me. What the hell is goin' on?"

"Let her finish," Curt said, raising a palm for silence as he turned solicitously back to the woman who sat motionless by the window. "I'm sure all of it will clear up in the end."

"You can't be sure of that," the storyteller corrected him. *"I'm* not sure of it.... In any case, none of you can *let* me do anything.... What I do now, I do on my own."

The captain blanched—had the mealy look of a parking-lot attendant who had opened the door for a lady and felt it slam on his fingers. A tinge of pity colored Tina's face.

"Don't take it personally, Curtis," she added. "Consider it a history lesson.... I had to learn it too."

"We don't have to ask who your teacher was, ay?" Pisser cackled. The words cut through the tension like a knife.

"It's true," Tina said softly. "I learned it from Allie. How not to forget.... And how to try to forgive."

We sat waiting, but she said nothing more.

"Go on with your story," Bookie said. "What happened to this woman after her husband died?"

"She survived. Learned how to live alone. Moved to the city and rented a small apartment. For the next several years, she devoted every waking hour to the responsibility of raising her son."

"Didn't she have to work?" Donnie said.

"Child-raising is work.... Harder work than you'll ever recognize."

"I'm sorry.... I just meant, you know.... Didn't she have a...didn't she—"

"She didn't have *employment,* no," Tina said. "Not at that point. Financially speaking, she would in fact never have needed to look for any. When her husband died, his will hadn't yet been changed, and his insurance paid a double indemnity. She had enough money to live comfortably for the rest of her life.

"But she was a widow, and she felt even more vulnerable—withdrew even further behind the walls of her apartment. She had doted on her child before.... Now she became obsessed with protecting him. Thought of little else but keeping him safe from the perils that lay just outside the door. He was her only reason now for living, and she smothered him—*worshipped* him. Wouldn't let him out of her sight. Or her mind.

"The little boy grew—had his fifth birthday—then his sixth. And still he had not spent a single moment outside the apartment except under the watchful eye of his mother. Eventually the authorities discovered this. They ordered her to enroll the child in a school.

"The widow was enraged—terrified—but finally she was forced either to agree or surrender custody. She moved into a new apartment. It was even closer to the danger—but it was only a block from a private school where she could send her son.

"Now the widow's life changed even more than it had when she'd left her husband. The child who for six years had not spent a heartbeat out of her protective direction now spent hours every day under the influence of countless strangers. And even though she walked the little boy to and from the classroom—tried to love him even more while he was home to make up for the missing hours—he began to change.... The school had begun to poison him."

"*Whaaaa?*" Donnie blurted, rocking back on his heels. "First her husband gets poisoned, and now her *kid* does too?.... Jeez, I'm with Me on this one. Schools don't poison kids."

"She don't mean it literal," Harry offered. "Leastways I don't guess she does." He turned to the storyteller for confirmation. The room fell silent as Tina sat staring out the window, then went on.

"The widow saw more and more signs of the poison's work—its corrupting power. Grew still more frantic trying to counteract its deadly influence. She resumed the home lessons she'd foolishly stopped when the little boy started school. She lengthened his bedtime stories. She bought him so many clothes and toys there soon wasn't room in his closet to hold them. But it was no use. The poison was too strong—too virulent—the daily dosage he received out in the evil city too much for even her passionate mothering to overcome. The little boy was lost.

"He was seven now—had grown quiet and sullen—then almost overnight became actively rebellious. The home lessons ended in crying fits. The bedtime stories brought only a hateful glare—not the flood of hugs and kisses he once couldn't get enough of. He demanded a lock on his door. An allowance. Freedom to buy his own food and make his own snacks and lunch.... Then came the morning when he clung to the staircase screaming that he wouldn't either go to school or return home if his mother continued to walk him there."

Dabbing her eyes, the speaker looked past us—across the room at the corridor door.

"Her son had made a friend.

"The two of them would walk the block to school together.... He didn't want his mother anywhere near.

"The horrified widow refused, of course. But the child screamed louder, threw himself down on the steps, began beating the carpet so wildly his tiny fists started bleeding. Finally she yielded—allowed him to leave her.... For the next seven hours, she sat petrified with fear until the door opened once again and the child stood safely in the hall.... This continued for several more days—her terror getting worse—the fears preying on her over-active imagination every time she peered out at the city streets. For there were things out there that she...things that...things she had learned."

No one responded, but the storyteller seemed to have hit a roadblock. She glanced at Bookie, then began to fumble in her purse.

"What kind of things?" the scholar said softly.

Tina continued to dig in her pocketbook. It was clear she was also fumbling for the right words to go on.

"The kid's friend was black.... And the school wasn't very far from the ghetto.... That's it, isn't it?" Bookie said.

The voice was hard, flat. But its edge was more weary than resentful.

"Tell whatever truth you have to tell...the straightest way you can tell it," he added. "If anything's ever going to change in this country, that's where it has to begin."

Tina wiped her eyes and went on.

"What you guessed is true.... The other boy was black. And older. And the ghetto was only a few blocks from where he and his mother lived. There were no limits now to the widow's terror. She had nurtured the child for seven years—and in less than a month, every strand she had woven to protect him had come unraveled. She couldn't deal with it. All she could see to do was to weave a stronger, more sheltering cocoon.

"Now she was the one who turned to poison.... tried to recapture her child's mind by filling it with doubts about his schoolmate. But these desperate attempts only increased his rebelliousness—intensified his loyalty—loyalty not only to the friend, but to everything he was beginning to learn about his life. The little boy began using Negro slang. Demanding soul food. Singing a song over and over that he'd learned from a pop gospel album on the radio.... The more the mother objected, the more her son insisted on singing it—was finally singing the song dozens of times every day.

"One afternoon, a picture of a young black woman suddenly appeared over her son's bed. It was the singer who had made the song popular. The little boy was now singing the words so often the mother thought she would lose her mind if she had to listen to them again."

"That's one place where I'm with you," Me muttered, adding another stick of gum to the wad swelling his jawline. "They drive you nuts with that damned rap shit. Me and my wife are goin' through the same thing with our kid right now."

Bookie turned back to Tina.

"This singer," he said. "Who was it?.... Aretha? I'll take another shot in the dark—guess that all of this happened sometime back in the late sixties or early seventies. Am I right about that too?"

"Yes," she answered hesitantly. "But I don't know who the singer was. I nev—.... The widow never discovered that. Or if she did, she forgot."

"Cooking all that soul food will do that to you," the black man said, smiling thinly. "Angries up the fluids in your brain."

"No kidding?" Donnie said. "I never knew that." He stared uneasily at the scholar, as if his next revelation might be that eating chocolate cake could leave you impotent.

"I think you're safe," Bookie reassured him. "You don't look like a man that's big on collards. And ham hocks are supposed to counteract anything else you put away."

"You're kiddin' me," the catcher said. "You had me a little worried for a second there, though. I'd hate to have to give up ribs and sweet potato pie."

Harry rolled his eyes. "So what the hell happened to this kid?" he said, turning back to Tina. "I'm like Pierce, I don't know a goddam thing about that soul food. And I never heard of no singer name of Urethra.... You're gettin' me int'rested in her, though."

Tina was still staring at Donnie. She took a moment to collect herself before going on.

"For a few more days, things continued the way I've described them. The child obsessed. Fanatical. His mother almost out of her mind with concern. And then it happened, one Friday afternoon, that the little boy didn't come home at all.

"She telephoned the school at once—was assured that the child had left promptly—had departed with his friend just as he had done the several days preceding. The widow waited an hour, weeping and praying in her apartment, then began roaming the city streets searching desperately for her son.

"Night fell. But she walked on—stopped everyone she met to ask if they had seen him or heard him. Finally she returned to her apartment and called the police.

"An officer came. Asked some questions. Slipped his notebook in his pocket as he closed the door. The widow was left alone once more—sat staring into the gathering darkness. Peering out at the nightmare that lay just outside the window of her room.

"The nightmare inside—inside her soul—continued to swell as the outer darkness deepened. She became hysterical—filled with fear and hate.

"Men passed by beneath her window, under the streetlights—the distant faces of a modern city. Negroes. Puerto Ricans. Others whose race she was unable to identify.... She hated them all. Hated the ways they talked. The way the walked. Even the things they were wearing. They were Satan's disciples—all of them—the ones responsible for what had happened to her child."

She stopped abruptly, and this time I thought she might not be able to continue. The pain of the memory and the ongoing uncertainty of Allie's condition had made a ruin of her previously immaculate face.

"It's okay," Bookie murmured. "You don't have to say anything more."

"Oh but I do.... I do. Allie would want— Allie *wants* me to. She wants me to go on."

The centerfielder nodded, but said nothing—leaned slightly forward in his chair.

Tina's eyes remained fixed on his face as she resumed.

"The widow had been wrong. Terribly wrong. Her son had simply gone with his friend to another schoolmate's place for a birthday party.... When the older boy discovered that the child had lied about getting his mother's permission, he called his own mother, who insisted that he return the boy at once to his home."

"Great kid," Donnie whispered. "You don't see too many around anymore willin' to take that kind of responsibility. I hope that widow woman gave him a decent reward."

"She gave him nothing."

Her eyes fell away from Bookie's as she said it.

"What she did.... It shames me to describe it. She screamed at him. Called him horrible names. Told him she never again wanted to see him anywhere near her apartment. She didn't punish her own child—had never punished him. The very thought was as dangerous to her as all she felt throbbing in the darkness just outside her door. And so the only thing she could see to do was keep the little boy home from school and continue to rage at...at all the...."

Tears welled in her eyes. Her pale lips were quivering.

"We understand," Curt stopped her, rising from his chair. He took a half-step toward her—then hesitated, clearly weighing the words to come. "Was it then that.... Was it Allison who came to see you then?"

"Yes," Tina whispered. "She came to m— She came to the widow's apartment a few days later, as if by a miracle. I can't say how she knew. Only the police had been notified when the child returned. As far as the widow was aware, the incident hadn't even appeared in the newspapers. Allison was just, suddenly...*there*."

"I'll be damned," Harry said.

"And it was Allie who took it on herself to bring about your—the widow's—could we call it a *healing?*" Bookie asked.

"Yes.... At least yes to the first question. It was Allison who was responsible for the woman's new way of seeing things.... I'm not sure how to describe it. It's still continuing. '*Transformation*' might be a more accurate word."

"Or *alchemy*," I said.

"There he goes again," Harry muttered. "He's got this cussed alk'ny on the brain."

Tina turned toward me, staring. "Yes," she said. "That fits."

Five minutes later the door suddenly swung open and a grim-faced nurse stepped into the room—her eyes sweeping it until they fell on our captain. She gestured to him to follow, then turned back down the corridor without uttering a word. The door closed behind her as Curt jumped to his feet.

"I'm comin' too," Harry growled, scrambling up beside him. His game leg slowed him a little, but the pitch of his body and jut of his cigar said no authority lower than the county jailer was going to keep him in the room.

Chapter 18

The sound of their footsteps faded to silence down the hallway, leaving the rest of us to our private thoughts and fears. I looked around the room at my companions—the aging crew of renegades, oddballs, and semi-respectable citizens thrown together for a few eventful hours in the futile pursuit of hare-brained dreams. They were strangers, really. But I was thinking how much I had come to know them again after thirty years. And how little I in fact knew them. How unknowable any of them—any of us—finally were.

It was the backwash of an exhausted brain. For the first time since the church bells had rung me awake before daybreak, it occurred to me how tired I felt—how utterly, mind-numbingly bone weary. I looked again at my companions, all of whom carried, as I did, half a century's settled weight. The marks of their own weariness were as indelible as the age lines creasing their skin.

I was standing beside Tina, staring out the window at the diminishing light, when the door again creaked open. She was halfway across the room before I'd turned to face the messenger.

It was Curt.

He raised a palm as several of the others lurched off their chairs—the restraining hand of one familiar with the sober protocol of hospital waiting rooms. The dread it evoked was harrowing, but it was also brief.

"I've just spoken with the doctor," he said quietly. "She may have some slight, permanent loss of hearing...but she's going to be all right."

"Oh God," Tina whispered. "Thank God." Her voice broke as Curt stepped closer and squeezed her hand.

"Praise the Lord," Big Stick murmured. "Amazing grace."

For some time no one said anything more. The room sounded only with the shuffle of feet—the quiet rustle of clothing. Someone coughed, cleared his throat. A gull floated mutely past the window—disappeared just as noiselessly from view.

It was Pisser who broke the silence.

"They could knock her oot, but they couldn't hurt her, ay?" he snickered. "Doesn't surprise me. She was always as hardheaded as they come."

"You could be right," Bookie retorted. "I'd have to think about it. Seems to me I've played with two or three other folks whose skulls are thicker.... One man's opinion, of course."

"Hell yes," Me added. "I have too."

I waited for Bail's inevitable riposte—felt the words scrape like sandpaper across my mind's ear: *"Allie caught one break out of all this, at least. For awhile she won't be able to hear you bustards"*—then suddenly realized that the coach hadn't rejoined us. Curt had reentered the room alone.

"What happened to Harry?" I said, glancing at the door.

"Coach?" Curt responded. "He's with Allison. Apparently she told the doctor that she wanted to see him. I'm not sure why."

"Maybe she's bugging him to get her a scholarship," Donnie said. "She'd still have four full years left of eligibility. If old T & A ever fields a team again, she could give 'em some real punch at third."

It was a testament to the inscrutability of the fat man's face that none of us knew whether he was kidding. No muscle twitched. The eyes didn't blink. The Zen-master expression remained seamless in the bald, round head.

"If Tabelard ever has another baseball team," Bookie finally said to him, "I'm going to tell them to try to lure you away from those Relief Pitchers to coach it.... I want to see what kind of running game you put in."

"We'd steal 'em blind," the catcher grinned. "'Specially if I could get Hotplate to come back and coach third for me." He paused, savoring the prospect. "Too bad it's prob'ly never gonna happen.... Depresses me to think the Bees rode for the last time today."

"Buzzed?" I said.

"What?"

He suddenly smiled. "Oh, I get it. The Bees *buzzed*.... That's pretty good. I'll have to remember it when I get back to the plant and tell everybody all the stuff that's happened. They're not gonna believe it.... I just wish I had a picture or two of the game."

He shook his head regretfully, his eyes glazed.

"God, it was great, though, wasn't it," he continued. "Strappin' it on again.... Feelin' all the old vibrations. It felt so...I don't know...so *natural*, you know what I mean?"

"You'll feel it even more in the morning," Bookie noted. "When you try to get out of bed."

"You figure he's gonna make it to bed?" Me grunted. "Don't forget, he's been talkin' about all the old vibrations. The Fat Man used to get most of his in the back seat of his car."

"That was back when he could still squeeze his butt in one, ay?" Pisser cackled.

"He can always ask Bail if he can use the Lobby," I joined in, unable to resist the temptation. "Then again, if it's vibrations he wants, all he has to do is ask for the room Blade and I had last night at the Red Rooster. My bed jumped like a corn popper all night long. Whenever it wasn't a freight train rolling by, it was my roomie cranking up the snores."

"You got that right," Bookie nodded. "My bed too. It's got to be the only hotel in America where you drop a quarter in a slot to make your mattress *not* move."

"*What?*" Donnie blurted. "You're kiddin' me.... And I was bouncin' around like crazy durin' all those trains."

Harry hobbled into a room that had erupted. Even Big Stick had loosed a clerical button, and Tina was hooting louder than anyone. The old coach watched us from just inside the doorway, a crooked grin seaming his face.

"What the hell's got into you dildos?" he muttered, patting his shirt pockets, searching for the day's umpteenth cigar. "You're actin' like you been munchin' loco weed."

"Could be. They grow it around here," Bookie responded. "*In loco parentis.* Spend an hour or two around Tabelard, doesn't seem to matter how old you are—you start acting like a sophomore again."

"What did he just say?" Donnie whispered, nudging me in the ribs. "I'm gettin' worried about that guy. He's startin' to sound like Big Stick."

Harry grimaced too—either out of a similar befuddlement or the fact he'd just noticed the room's *No Smoking* sign. Unable to catch his eye, I stepped to his side.

"How's she doing?" I murmured. "You weren't in there with her very long."

"Didn't need to be," he said with a cryptic smirk.

He looked different somehow—a change that went beyond the transformation of guilt and anxiety to the profound relief he obviously felt. There was something in his face I hadn't seen before. An expression that somehow made him look both older—or maybe it was just a little wiser—and at the same time, several years younger. I looked around the room—saw that the others had noticed it too. We waited for him to go on.

"She's doin' just fine," he continued. "It's gonna take a lot more than them ugly sumbitches to get the better of that gal. But they wouldn't let me stay no longer. The nurse says she's got to get some rest."

"We can't see her?" Donnie said plaintively. "Just for a minute? I really want to go buck her up." He started for the door.

"No you can't!" the coach stopped him. "You can all go in and see her in the mornin'. And don't go gettin' your daubers down, 'cause there's not no cause to. She damn sure don't need no buckin' up."

"Pardon me for pointing it out, Coach," Curt said, grinning. "But it doesn't appear that right now you need much of a boost either. Did she say something...do something...to..." The question trailed off, unfinished. But it was clear even Donnie understood what he meant.

Harry flushed—bought a few seconds of recovery time fiddling with the tip of the cigar wrapper. He rolled the stogie in his fingers as if he were studying the Dead Sea Scrolls, then extracted it and jammed it into his jaw.

"I suppose you might could say she did," he growled—"if you're one of them folks what notices it ever' time a man changes his britches.... Allie and I had a little talk. Let's put it that way. Now you'll pardon me while I go over yonder to that telephone and try to find somebody in Cranberry what can maybe get hold of my wife."

"Good luck, Coach" I said as he hobbled past me.

"I'll need it," he said, pausing, patting the fraying pockets of his pants. "Luck and a goddam twenty-five-cent piece.... You got one? That's another thing about this damn country I'll never understand—how the hell they've managed to screw up even the couple o' things what were workin' good—like the goddam telephone system. Ever'thing's goin' along fine—you can call somebody for a dime—then they jump it up to a quarter and you can't call nobody without a bunch o' sprintin' and bell ringin' and a whole crapload full of that ay-tee and teein'. It tees me off, is what it does. It's like what the sumbitches have gone and done to the game of baseball. There's some changes even that gal layin' in on that bed ain't gonna get me to take to, and not bein' able to read my goddam phone bill is one."

I flipped him a quarter. It bounced off his hands and clinked on the floor.

"Don't say nothin', you bustards," he snorted, straining to pick it up. "I know my mitts ain't what they used to be. But judgin' from what I saw out on that field today, mine look like Willie Mays' compared to yours."

We stood watching as he reached the phone, inserted the coin, and fumbled to dial the number. When the potato face turned pugnaciously back to face us, Curt took a discreet step toward the door.

"I think he might appreciate some privacy," the captain said. "Maybe it would be best for us to wait for him out in the van."

The others followed him obediently toward the exit. I remained where I stood, a few feet behind them—looking through the small window that revealed all I could see of the hospital corridor. A young nurse stood reading a chart just inside the door.

"You go on ahead," I mumbled. "I...I think I'll walk back.... It's not far, and my back has started to stiffen up on me. A little hike will do me good.... I'll see you back at the hotel."

The big patrolman was clearly taken aback—skeptical. "Are you sure that's a good idea?" he frowned.

"Absolutely. I'll take the path along the river. I won't be long."

Standing at his side, Bookie nodded—flashed me a discreet thumbs-up sign as he followed the others through the doorway. Curt fell in behind him, then hesitated, looking back.

"We'll meet you at the Weathered Nut for dinner," he said, winking. He glanced at the inside window. "I'm not sure you can pull off that kamikaze maneuver twice in one afternoon," he added, "but if you manage to steal another one, give her a kiss for me."

The door closed behind him.

I looked again at Harry, whose head was bent as earnestly into the telephone as his fingers were busy diddling with the coin return. I couldn't see his face, but he was nodding. The receiver was pressed against his ear.

The nurse remained where she stood a few feet behind the glass. Swallowing, I swung the door open and stepped in.

She looked up, startled. Her uniform was immaculate, freshly laundered—so white it almost made me blink as I approached her. A plastic nameplate on her chest read "Ceci Lee., R. N."

"I'm sorry, Sir," she said. "But you're not allowed here. This is—"

"I know about the restrictions," I interrupted. "This won't take long, I promise you. But I have to ask you something before I go."

"Yes?"

"The woman who came out of the emergency room a little while ago. Allison Bathgate. Is there any possibility I could see her—say a couple of words to her—just for a minute? I know she's not supposed to have any more visitors—needs to get some rest—but she's well enough to have seen two of my friends already. I wouldn't press it, but this is...this is pretty important to me."

She had the reddest hair I had ever seen. And the bluest eyes.

"I'm afraid not," she said firmly. "She really does need to get some rest now. I don't have the authority to—"

"I know that," I stopped her. "And I respect it—respect you for being so responsible. All you'll have to do is tell me a second time to leave, and I'll walk back through that door without harassing you any further.... It's not life or death. But it means a lot to me.... Thanks for listening, either way."

She glanced down at the chart she was holding—then shook her head slowly and looked toward an open door farther down the hallway. But she didn't speak.

"If it's impossible," I stumbled on, "would you just tell her that Shoeoff did the best he could to see her?.... Just say he tried to slip one past the infield, but couldn't get past first base."

She smiled.

"I can't let you stay for more than a minute," she said, demurely raising an admonitory finger. "I mean that literally. I'm sorry, but sixty seconds of charity is all I can give."

"You're an angel. Sixty seconds is an eternity. Ask any old football coach."

She shook her head, beckoning me to follow her down the corridor—which led to another—then to still another that seemed to lie even deeper in the old hospital's catacombs. But when we emerged, it was on a floor with windows. And when we finally reached the room, I could see the slate-colored ripples of the river through an open door.

"Remember," the nurse whispered as she left me, "*Five* minutes. I'll be back to show you out."

"Thanks," I mumbled in gratitude. "You really are an angel. If I could afford one, there'd be a star in your crown."

Allie lay propped up in the bed when I entered—wide awake—a large bandage stretched across her left ear.

"Can you hear me?" I asked solicitously.

The syllables assaulted my own ears—bounced around the tiny room like echoes reverberating from a loudspeaker. I blushed as the patient cringed and covered her face, feigning shell shock. The jangle of her laughter echoed louder than my words.

"I can always hear you, Sugar," she said, winking. "I even heard your footsteps—way back down the corridor.... I hoped it was you."

"I don't believe it," I said, flushing even deeper, "but I like hearing it anyway.... I tried to sound as much like your dream lover as I could."

She smiled, but said nothing. Below the bandage, the bruise had already started to darken on her cheek.

"It's going to burn me for a long time—what that guy did to you," I went on, looking away from her. "Not the pitcher, but that big ugly devil that provoked him. Me spent the first ten minutes out in the lobby after we got you here trying to rouse a vigilante party to go back and do something about it. For once, Pisser seemed to agree with him."

"For God's sake," she said. "I like that. Here I am in a hospital room—for all they know, lying on my deathbed—and those idiots are out there in that wreck of a van thinking about nothing but revenge."

I stared at her, momentarily confused—before the misconception registered.

"Not the *Lobby*. What I meant was that we were all out in the waiting room.... Don't be too hard on them. Getting that guy jailed is about the only way they know how to show you they care."

"I appreciate the sentiment. But tell them to forget him. Bail's right—the guy is 'a real ugly Sumbitch', but eventually the world will be rid of him. Until then, he has to live in Jerome. That's punishment enough. What a hell of a place to die."

"You're probably right.... I'm sure you're right.... It just doesn't feel like enough right now."

She nodded almost imperceptibly—slowly smoothed the sheet over her chest.

"People can change," she said softly. "Oh, I know he won't. He's too far gone. But some of the others might.... Look at Harry.... That was Harry who was in here a few minutes ago, wasn't it?.... Or, for that matter...look at me."

Her eyes drifted past me, out the window—at the running river and the open prairie that lay beyond it. For half a minute neither of us said anything. When she finally spoke again, I had to lean forward to hear her voice.

"It's beautiful here," she murmured. "It must always have been beautiful.... It's incredible, isn't it? The things you can't see when you're half-blind."

I was staring into her eyes. Somewhere off in the distance, a dog barked. The wild cry of a goose sounded over the Platte.

I turned away.

"Hey, listen," I mumbled. "I've only got a few more seconds. I just wanted to tell you how much I.... how glad I am that you're okay.... And that I think it's amazing what you've done for Harry. I don't know how you pulled it off, but he looks like a new man."

"He just needed a little attitude adjusting...like all of you do."

I looked back at her as she said it. A smile creased her lips, but the words weren't as flippant as they might appear. I wanted to say something more—or hear something more—but footsteps were clicking down the hall.

Impulsively, I bent to take her hand.

"I have to go. They're coming for me. They tell me the bowels of this place are full of visitors who overstayed their welcome...."

"I'll be back with the others tomorrow."

"You'd better be."

She pulled me closer—gave me a long kiss on the lips as the swirl of red hair and white cloth materialized in the doorway. Whispered something the nurse's words obscured in my ear.

"Time's up—and none too soon, it would appear, for our patient."

The nurse eyed me with mock severity. Then, turning to Allie, she added, "I bent the rules to the breaking point to let this guy see you.... He's one of those persistent types. Hope it's okay."

"Shoeoff? *Persistent?*.... My God, we *are* talking change."

My ear still flamed with whatever it was she had said to me. Her own face seemed to glow above the bed.

"What's got into him?" she added. "I feel flattered—and unworthy. I mean, he could have had me tomorrow morning, fresh and beautiful. But he chose to see me like *this*!"

She ran a finger around the bandage as she said it—looked down at the drab hospital gown in a goofy parody of debutantish chagrin.

"Sounds to me like I can't lose," I said. "She looks great to me now. And she's promising to be even more stunning tomorrow."

"Shoeoff," she cackled. "You don't know from stunning. Just wait till I get out of this bed. I just bought a new set of red leathers. You ain't seen nothin' yet."

I was a step from the door when I stopped and turned.

"*Now* what?" the nurse said.

"I just want to ask her one last question," I wheedled, looking back at Allie's face.

"Yes?"

Her eyes shone below the bandage as she said it. They disconcerted me, and I had to clear my throat before going on.

"Tina's little boy.... The kid that was so overprotected. What finally happened to him?"

She stared at me for a long moment, reflecting, her gaze piercing my heart.

"He's a man now. Or at least—an adult. He's doing okay.... Not the greatest. But okay."

The seductive slit between her teeth reappeared as a thin smile flickered over her lips. I felt the nurse's hand tighten on my arm.

"It's like most of the things that really matter, Sugar. You can't rush it.... But from what I can see, down the road ahead of us, things are looking awfully good right now."

Harry was gone when I passed back through the waiting room. The space was empty where Me had parked the van. I walked on through the parking lot, across the freshly mowed lawn, down to the bike path that wound along the river. The gray spires of Tabelard rose above the willows a half mile downstream—loomed over a landscape that might have been painted from the stern of a wagon bound for Oregon a hundred and fifty years before. To the west, the direction I was headed, I could hear the unhurried murmur of traffic in downtown South Fork. The wind that had stiffened an hour earlier was now no more than a quiet breath through the trees.

I stopped by a gnarled cottonwood, gazing out at the water. A large flock of waterfowl had congregated near a weed-cloaked sand bar—resting before resuming their migration north. There were dozens of birds—hundreds—and they formed a patchwork quilt of sound and wildly disparate shapes and sizes. Snow-white gulls drifted above a raft of mallards, whose dark silhouettes bobbed placidly near a pair of redheads. A heron beat its wings and lifted off the sand bar. A flock of bluebills cupped their wings and splashed down in a ring of spray.

I walked on, toward the western horizon, where the setting sun suddenly broke free of the cloud cover. In the last few moments of the day, it had dropped below the wafered sky—fired the willows and turned the leaden water crimson. Behind me, the birds seemed to gabble louder. The silky rustle of wings whispered over the trees.

I stopped again and looked back, beyond them. Turned and raised my eyes above the dappled shimmer of the river. I thought I could make out Allie's room in the light.

The Author

Kent Cowgill is a medievalist and fiction writer whose previous publications include scholarly articles in some of America's most respected academic journals, short stories in various university quarterlies and literary reviews, and a range of stories and essays, chiefly on fly fishing, in such outdoor publications as *Gray's Sporting Journal*, *Fly Rod & Reel*, and *Field & Stream*. His collection of comic fiction on life in the north woods, *Raising Hackles on the Hattie's Fork*, was published by the Atlantic Monthly Press in 1990.

Cowgill received his Ph.D. in English Literature at the University of Nebraska-Lincoln in 1970, and currently teaches at Winona State University in Minnesota. In the 1960's, as an undergraduate at a small college in Nebraska, he was a four-year starter on the varsity baseball team.

The Artist

Dennis Johnson is a painter and photographer who lives in Winona, Minnesota. In 1964, while earning his bachelor's degree from the University of Minnesota, he pitched on the N.C.A.A. national championship baseball team. He later took a master's degree from Winona State University and has been a teacher of art in the Winona Public School system for thirty-one years.